Sexual ASSAULT

The Medical-Legal Examination

Sharon R. Crowley, RN, MN, PHN
Forensic Clinical Nurse Specialist
Sexual Assault Nurse Examiner
Pediatric SART Examiner
Santa Cruz, California

APPLETON & LANGE
Stamford, CT

www.appletonlange.com

99 00 01 02 / 10 9 8 7 6 5 4 3 2 1

Prentice Hall International (UK) Limited, *London*
Prentice Hall of Australia Pty. Limited, *Sydney*
Prentice Hall Canada, Inc., *Toronto*
Prentice Hall Hispanoamericana, S.A., *Mexico*
Prentice Hall of India Private Limited, *New Delhi*
Prentice Hall of Japan, Inc., *Tokyo*
Simon & Schuster Asia Pte. Ltd., *Singapore*
Editora Prentice Hall do Brasil Ltda., *Rio de Janeiro*
Prentice Hall, *Upper Saddle River, New Jersey*

Library of Congress Cataloging-in-Publication Data
Crowley, Sharon R.
    Sexual assault : the medical-legal examination / Sharon R. Crowley.
        p. cm.
    Includes bibliographical references and index.
    ISBN (invalid) 0-8385-8533-0 (case : alk. paper)
    1. Rape victims—Medical examinations.   2. Forensic nursing.
  I. Title.
    [DNLM: 1. Sex Offenses.   2. Forensic Medicine—methods.
  3. Genitalia—anatomy & histology.   4. Rape.   W 795C953s 1998]
  RA1141.C76   1999
  614'.1—dc21
  for Library of Congress   98-37949

Acquisitions Editor: Nancy Anselment
Associate Editor: Elisabeth Church Garofalo
Production Editor: Angela Dion
Designer: Aimee Nordin

ISBN 0-8385-8533-7 NB2I

90000

9 788385 853374

PRINTED IN THE UNITED STATES OF AMERICA

This book is dedicated to Cops, everywhere.

CONTENTS

REVIEWERS

Jorge Grimes, RN, EdD
Chair of Graduate Nursing Program
SUNY Health Science Center Syracuse
Syracuse, New York

Ginny Wacker Guido, JD, MSN, RN
Professor and Chair
Department of Nursing
Eastern New Mexico University
Portales, New Mexico

Colleen O'Brien, RN, MS
Clinical Director of the YWCA/SANE
    Program
Meriter Hospital
Madison, Wisconsin

Nancy M. Valentage, RPA, C, MS
Clinical Coordinator, RIT Physician
    Assistant Program
Rochester Institute of Technology
Rochester, New York

Beatrice A. Yorker, JD, MS, RN, FAAN
Associate Provost for Faculty Relations
Associate Professor of Nursing
Georgia State University
Atlanta, Georgia

Elizabeth Devine
Los Angeles County Sheriff's Department
Scientific Services Bureau
Los Angeles, California

Michael Prodan
Special Agent
South Carolina Law Enforcement Division
Behavioral Science Unit
Columbia, South Carolina

Robert Barsley, DDS, DABFO
Louisiana State University
School of Dentistry
New Orleans, Louisiana

PREFACE

The focus of clinical practice for the last decade of my nursing career has been the sexual assault victim. When a case proceeds to trial, the role of expert witness invariably comes into play and questions arise about the credibility of a nurse's testimony in such areas of expertise. As in other specialized areas of nursing, sexual assault examiners have come into our own. All clinical forensic examiners must continue to explore new territory and further define roles and expectations. Because we have chosen the responsibility for the care and evaluation of these victims, we must find within our own ranks, specialists who epitomize the qualities we revere, and who exhibit standards of practice that we admire and adopt. I felt we needed a reference text that would cover the myriad things one needs to know to properly do these exams. Nurses have always been great at putting the pieces together and tying up the loose ends, or looking at the whole person. As we stand at the border of a new frontier, on the verge of a new millennium, we have an exciting future and a very proud past.

The book strives to reflect a universal approach to the victim, rather than to advocate the model of a particular state. Recommendations for clinical practice are based on current research and contributions from other disciplines. Not all practitioners and programs will have access to all the individual and technological resources described. Adaptations and modifications can be made to fit local needs and capabilities, but the clinical forensic examiner can at least be cognizant of current trends.

Chapter 1 introduces the roles of the professionals encountered by victims as they emerge from the situation that brings us all together. Pioneer multidisciplinary programs for the treatment of the sexual assault victim, such as Sexual Assault Treatment Unit (SATU), in Ireland, and sites throughout the United Sates, are noted for their outstanding early achievements. Forensic nursing is presented as a growing specialty area of practice. Specific skills and expertise required by Sexual Assault Nurse Examiners are described, and are applicable to all health care providers who take on this role, be they registered nurses, physicians, physician's assistants, or nurse practitioners.

Chapter 2 attempts to describe some of the many variables that exist in rape. Each rape victim is unique; so is their experience. Some of the issues are well-known and widely discussed. Other, like female genital mutilation, and lesbian rape-related issues, have had little mention, but great impact. The individual(s) who suffers this experience is referred as a "victim," for that is their predicament within the context of the medical-legal exam. It is that state which draws us all together for symbiotic goals. As medical care givers, we are present as part of a victim-oriented service. While it is true that our efforts must proceed with the goal of their eventual emergence as a survivor, we must validate their experience and all they have gone through to get to us. Rape trauma syndrome and post-traumatic stress disorder are proffered as components of the psychological aftermath of rape. Variations on the theme of sexual assault, such as incest, acquaintance rape, and stranger assault are defined. Salient issues for adolescent victims, male victims, pregnant, and elderly victims are presented.

Chapter 3 is designed to summarize for the clinical forensic examiner the salient aspects of genital anatomy necessary to perform a complete exam, understand injury, and appreciate physiological responses to consensual sexual encounters. Physiological changes in the body that occur during normal aging are discussed relevant to concomitant impact on sexual response in women of reproductive age and beyond. A discourse on anal intercourse is based on poignant interviews with gay men, in the hope of elucidating for us some of the dynamics of consensual anal sexual behavior.

Chapter 4 and 5 are interdependent and complementary. Chapter 4 explores the medical-legal exam from start to finish, from the planning stage, through exam techniques, equipment, and technology. Integral components of this chapter are the victim interview and the principles and techniques for the general physical exam, genital and speculum exam, and anal and rectal exam. Collection of evidence from the victim's clothing and body is described. Research pertinent to the types and nature of injuries seen in sexual assault victims is discussed, including adolescent and postmenopausal victims. The use of technology encompasses the utilization of photographic equipment, colposcopy, the Wood's lamp, and alternate light source. The eval-

uation of bitemarks serves as the model for assessment of other nongenital trauma, and incorporates protocols developed and implemented by forensic odontologists.

Chapter 5 strives to provide the scientific basis for the collection and analysis of evidence gathered during the medical-legal exam. This includes clothing, swabs, and evidentiary samples from the victim's body. All components of the sexual assault evidence kit are depicted. Analysis of blood and urine for typing drugs and alcohol is included. Special focus is placed on the correct packaging, preservation, and storage of evidence. The application of DNA to sexual assault cases is set forth. The prevalence of rape drugs, such as Rohypnol and GHB, have required new protocols and training needs for recognition and testing.

Chapter 6 takes us on a darker journey, albeit one that ultimately serves the victim. The goal is to shed some light on behaviors that we come to hear of as we are involved with victims, case after case, and year after year. Research promulgated by the FBI and the process of Criminal Investigative Analysis elucidates the crime from the rapist's perspective. While not a savory view, it does help clarify offender behavior that is targeted toward the victim. Understanding these ideas can alert the examiner to subtle cues in the history and physical exam of the victim that may assist law enforcement with the identification and apprehension of the offender. It can also further enlighten us as to the horror of the experience suffered by the victim; we must never lose sight of this in the midst of all our technological advancements.

A four-color insert within Chapter 4 provides an important visual aid for the examination of patients who report having been a victim of sexual assault. The photographs include a collection of the normal genital, perianal, and oral anatomy of adolescent and adult females and males. Other photographs are of findings present in sexual assault. These are magnified via colposcopy at 7.5 to 15×, to include the external genitalia, vagina, external anus, anoscopic views, and skin variations of the pre-pubertal, adolescent and adult female.

The **Glossary** and all the **Appendices** are simply to serve as additional sources of information and as a handy reference. Some of the content of the appendices have received mention within the chapters. The appendix on STDs is designed to provide the clinical forensic examiner with a reference for practice. Sexual assault is perceived as a public health issue and information within this appendix comes primarily from resources within the public health arena. The disposition of physical evidence is a crucial facet of the medical-legal exam. Technology and scientific knowledge in this area is complex and often progresses at a breakneck pace, making it a major task for the clinician to keep pace. It is hoped that this and the other appendices will be pragmatic tools for medical practitioners, as well as other members of the investigative team.

The goal of *Sexual Assault: The Medical-Legal Examination* is to provide a conceptual framework of information to perform a thorough assessment of the adult and adolescent sexual assault victim. Evaluation of the victim encompasses much more than a physical examination and collection of swabs. Incorporation of a multidisciplinary approach requires insight and knowledge into the various disciplines which impinge on a victim. None of us can work within a vacuum. Medical professionals must collaborate with other specialists and glean as much knowledge as possible. All of the professionals mentioned within this book are essential to the process: the nurses and other medical practitioners, cops, criminalists, advocates, forensic pathologists, forensic odontologists, and lawyers. We have so much to learn and report on, from each other, and from those who matter most, the victims. It is hoped that this book will be a start.

Sharon R. Crowley

ACKNOWLEDGMENTS

Those who inspired me: Michael, Bridget, and Patrick Crowley: I miss you, yet am still heartened by you.

My children, for putting up with me: Michael, Maggie, and Bridget (my greatest blessings).

For those who embody the spirit of nursing, I honor: Edith Cavell, Nurse (1865–1915), Brussels, Belgium, WW I. You went beyond the job of caring for wounded allied soldiers; you helped them escape. For that, you lost your life: executed October 12, 1915.

Helen Marcinko, RN: The first nurse I knew.

Anne Stagnaro, Marion Stoops, and Rose B: In your 70s and 80s and still giving direct patient care.

The Santa Cruz Beach and Boardwalk First Aid nurses and Norene Baily RN, PHN.

Thank you for your prayers and encouragement: Fr. Jim Henry (for listening), Nancy Crowley James (and for all the Sunday calls), Fr. Tom Foster, Orla Ryder, David Shackelford, DC, Peggy, Roger, Tom, Mike Crowley, and Patti Morelli.

For those who so generously assisted me: Nancy Kellogg, MD (for colposcopic photos and support); Robert Barsley, DDS, JD; Elizabeth Devine (Criminalist Extraordinaire); Detective Trinka Porrata, LAPD; John Miller, Leisegang Medical, Inc.; Christine Phillips; Janet Barber-Duval, MS, RN, CEN.

The lads from SLO: Gabbie, Bubba, and Tommie.

For fabulous editors: Elisabeth Church Garofalo, Angela Dion, and Lauren Keller.

Police: Arroyo Grande Police Department (especially Vanessa), Los Angeles County Sheriff's Department, San Luis Obispo Police Department, Los Angeles Police Department, San Luis Obispo County Sheriff's Department, California Sexual Assault Investigators Association (CSAIA), California Commission on Peace Officers Standards & Training (POST), and many more . . .

The U.S. Navy

But most of all: To God (thanks, I owe you big time).

1 Introduction

The last decade has seen revolutionary changes in the medical care of the sexual assault victim. Forensic nurses, specially trained in the arena of sexual assault, are being recognized for their contribution to the entire process, both from the criminal justice standpoint and the holistic perspective of patient (victim/survivor) care. Concomitant with this approach has been the movement toward getting the care of the rape victim out of the emergency room. Specifically designed rooms provide this service in a compassionate, private setting which simultaneously allows for the full use of current technology to augment the examination process.

The "traditional" approach to the rape victim examination within the emergency room setting has been a cursory medical interview, general physical exam, and a pelvic exam, utilizing gross visual inspection for both nongenital and genital trauma. A sexual assault evidence kit, provided either by law enforcement or housed at the hospital, can be as cryptic and mysterious as a cookbook written in a foreign language to practitioners not completely familiar with its contents or purpose. Although this traditional model of intervention gave victims access to pregnancy and sexually transmitted disease testing and prophylaxis, they were required to wait until life-threatening emergencies were handled, possibly causing biological evidence to degrade during the interim. Despite the best efforts by concerned staff, the emergency room is a difficult place for victims who have just endured a crime which by its very nature is a violation of their privacy and sense of control. The victim needs reassurance that she or he is now safe and protected, and can once again begin to regain some semblance of control over life.

According to Lenehan (1991), even when emergency department staff want to help rape victims, services can be inconsistent and problematic. Some departments may not see enough victims to allow all staff the opportunity to become skilled examiners. This results in victims in crisis being cared for by staff in crisis.

INCIDENCE DATA

Crimes that come to the attention of law enforcement form the basis for statistics defined in the Federal Bureau of Investigation *Uniform Crime Report.* This is prepared by the FBI, in conjunction with the U.S. Department of Justice, and depicts crimes committed in the United States within a given year. The National Crime Victimization Survey (NCVS) is conducted by the Bureau of Justice, in conjunction with the U.S. Census Bureau. This survey provides information on crime statistics nationwide, as well as those not reported to law enforcement. The following statistics on sexual assault for 1995 are from publications of the U.S. Department of Justice Statistics, *An Analysis of Data on Rape and Sexual Assault* (February 1997) and *The Executive Summary: An Analysis of Data on Rape and Sexual Assault. Sex Offenses and Offenders,* (1997) summarized in Table 1–1.

As defined by the NCVS, *rape* is defined as forced sexual intercourse; the victim may be male or female. The offender may be of the same or opposite sex. Included within this definition are victims 12 years of age and older. Also included are threats and attempts to commit rape. *Sexual assault* includes a wide range of victimizations that include acts of unwanted sexual contact between offender and victim, as well as threats and attempts to commit sexual assault. As defined in the Unified Crime Report (UCR) *forcible rape* is the carnal knowledge of a female forcibly and against her will; this includes assaults or attempts to commit rape by force or threat of force. Statutory rape (without force), and other sex offenses are not included in the UCR definition (Greenfeld, 1997).

INTERNATIONAL ASSOCIATION OF FORENSIC NURSES (IAFN)

In August 1992, 74 nurses, primarily sexual assault nurse examiners (SANEs), met in Minneapolis, Minnesota, to form the *International Association of Forensic Nurses.* The goal was to establish an organization that would encompass all of the diverse areas of nursing practice within the medical–legal arena. Areas of specialization defined within the scope of forensic nursing practice by the IAFN are death investigators, correctional nurses, forensic psychiatric nurses, legal nurse consultants and nurse attorneys, forensic gerontology nurses, forensic clinical nurse specialists, SANEs, pediatric nurses specializing in child abuse and neglect, nurse educators and researchers, trauma and critical care nurses, and any nurse specializing in clinical or community-based practice involving victims of crime or catastrophic accidents (IAFN, 1997).

The first scientific assembly of the IAFN was held in Sacramento, California in 1993. Forensic nursing was formally recognized by the American Nurses Association Congress of Nursing Practice Act in 1995. Standards of practice for SANEs were approved in 1997 (McHugh, J. & Leake, D., 1997).

THE TEAM APPROACH TO SEXUAL TRAUMA

International Endeavors

The promulgation of a multidisciplinary approach to the investigation of sexual assault has led to the birth of *SARTs,* or Sexual Assault Response Teams, for both compassionate and effective treatment of victims within a given community. The team approach of SARTs enables the victim to be treated with priority, and triaged according to a specific protocol designed to meet the needs of both the victim and the criminal justice system. On-call coverage and prompt response to sexual assault cases is usually on a 24-hour basis, 365 days a year. The three *core* members that comprise the team are: *medical, law enforcement,* and *victim advocacy* services. Although local policy may predicate some variance in

► **TABLE 1–1.** AN ANALYSIS OF DATA ON RAPE AND SEXUAL ASSAULT FOR 1995

Estimated attempted or completed rapes ≥ 12 y.o.	260,300
+ Threatened or completed sexual assaults, other than rape	+ 95,000
Total estimated no. of rapes, sexual assault victimizations ≥ 12 y.o.	355,300
Minus those reported to law enforcement	– 113,000
= Estimated unreported rapes, sexual assault	242,300
Reported forcible rapes	97,460
Rate of reporting	32% (1994, 1995); no racial differences
Forcible rapes cleared by an arrest	50% (regardless of jurisdiction size)
Month with highest incidence of rapes	August
Month with lowest incidence of rapes	December
% Female victims	91%
% Male offenders (single victim cases)	99%
Victims < 18 y.o.	44%
Victims with highest incidence	16–19 y.o.; low income, urban resident
% Single offender cases	90%
Prior relationship (ie, family member, intimate acquaintance) with rapist	75%
Prior relationship, 18–29 y.o.	67%
Stranger	
single assailant rapes	20%
multiple assailant rapes	76%
Location of assault:	
in home of victim, friend, relative, or neighbor	60%
within 1 mile of victim's home	>50%
Time of day: between 6 PM to 6 AM	67%
Reported, forcible rapes determined to be unfounded	8%
Weapon use:	12%
gun	5%
knife	7%
Collateral injury	40%
major physical injury: (severe lacerations, fractures, internal injuries, unconsciousness)	5%
Rapes by spouses, ex-spouses, strangers	>50% result in victim injury
Rapes by parent of child resulting in major injury	25%
Victim age with greatest incidence injury	≥30 y.o. (and where suspect used a knife)

Adapted from Greenfeld, L. (1997, February). An analysis of data on rape and sexual assault. Sex Offenses and Offenders (NCJ-163932). Bureau of Justice Statistics. U.S. Department of Justice. Washington, DC.

specific team roles and responsibilities, the basic morphology is usually fairly constant. For example, in some geographic areas, victims may receive a medical examination without initial referral by a law enforcement agency to the SART program, whereas other SART programs are designed in such a manner that the exam itself is set in motion by a call-out from a police agency. Additional agencies that play a major role in the investigation of sexual assault, and that should be considered vital members of the team, are the crime laboratory and the district, or prosecuting attorney's staff.

In Dublin, Ireland, the Sexual Assault Treatment Unit (SATU), at the Rotunda Hospital, was the first of its kind in Europe. The Rape Crisis Centre was established in 1979, and SATU was officially opened by the Minister for Health in 1985. The disparity between the number of cases reported to the Rape Crisis Centre and the gardai (police) led to SATU's formation. Formerly, the police doctor would examine the victim, in cases reported to the gardai. The female SATU physician not only collects forensic evidence, but addresses the other short-term psychological and physical aspects of the sexual trauma, including sexually transmitted diseases. These individuals have 24-hour availability to a theatre, ie, examination rooms, and provide annual training to physicians, nurses, and police.

Advantages of a Team Approach

To summarize, the primary advantages of a team approach to sexual assault include the following:

- *Comprehensive.* This approach should encompass most of the victim's needs that arise from the crisis situation incurred by the rape.
- *Efficient.* More data (ie, medical, forensic, crisis) related to the sexual assault can be gleaned by merging and pooling efforts and talents. Communication is facilitated among all members of the team and fosters sharing of necessary information and ideas.
- *Compassionate.* Because key members should have a good working relationship with one another, they can help decrease the stressors on the victim by filling in the gaps of care and facilitating the criminal justice system experience.

Members of the Multidisciplinary Team

Law Enforcement

The agency with jurisdiction over the case is usually responsible for instigating the SART process and requesting the medical examination. Goals of law enforcement are protection of the victim, apprehension of the offender, and successful prosecution of the case.

A *few* of the initial responsibilities of the responding officer are to determine that a crime has been committed, ensure safety of

the victim(s), preserve the crime scene, identify, and apprehend the suspect(s).

Law enforcement is responsible for all physical (forensic) evidence related to the case, though they need not be present during the collection of evidence from the person of the victim during the medical exam. The primary responsibility for investigation of the crime includes the investigative interview of the victim(s), suspect(s), and any witnesses related to the sexual assault. If the victim is a minor, law enforcement will cross-report to other child protective agencies. Ongoing case management includes documentation via reports for their own agency.

The initial responder to a sexual assault is generally a uniformed officer or deputy. The case is usually then transferred to the investigations division, where a detective will complete the investigative process. This is often after the medical exam and evidence collection. In some agencies, the detective is the initial responder.

Victim Advocate

The advocate's role is unique and vital, not only to a successful prosecutorial outcome, but for the long-term well being, recovery, and healing of the victim. The advocate is present to support the victim and to ensure that information about all steps of the process is communicated and/or clarified. This support of the victim often begins at the time of the initial report of the crime. Indeed, many more cases are reported to rape crisis centers than to the criminal justice system. It is often the victim advocate who enables the rape survivor to cope with the many necessary, albeit intrusive events that occur subsequent to that first call for help. The advocate helps the victim feel comfortable with the team process.

The victim advocate offers to accompany and provide support to the victim during all phases of the criminal justice system proceedings, often starting with the medical examination. They provide short-term crisis intervention, or referrals and information to community resources for follow-up counseling. The advocate is most likely to best apprise other members of the team of salient victim needs or concerns which may impact the progress of the case. Ongoing collaboration with the advocacy center should include participation in education and training of other team members, ie, nurses, law enforcement, prosecutors, and judges on issues of victim dynamics.

Criminalist

A criminalist is a forensic scientist who uses scientific methods to collect, analyze, and interpret physical evidence. A criminalist differs from a criminologist. The latter studies the sociological and psychological aspects of criminal behavior.

Criminalists receive and analyze all physical evidence related to the sexual assault. They communicate these findings to appropriate members of the criminal justice system and provide courtroom testimony as expert witnesses. They can provide training to other team members on local crime lab protocols for the collection, preservation, and storage of evidence. Criminalists are invaluable consultants to the medical team for policies and procedures related to physical evidence.

District Attorney (DA)

The district, or prosecuting attorney's staff serves as a resource to all members of the investigative team. They are responsible for the prefiling investigation, filing decision, eventual prosecution of the case, and the myriad steps in between. They play a significant role in the education and training of other team members. This includes keeping team members informed of new sexual assault legislation and associated implications for clinical practice. The sexual assault response team can consult the DA on local medical–legal protocols and seek advice on issues pertaining to expert testimony.

SART Director/Program Coordinator

Some program duties of the SART director, such as protocol development, monitoring, and continuous quality improvement (CQI), are often dictated by the specific job description of the hiring agency. Other director-related responsibilities include liaison and resource to other members of the criminal justice system and the community at large. The director may be the custodian of the medical–legal records. Although the hospital medical records department may also serve as such, SART records are ideally stored separately from other hospital medical records to ensure very limited access. The director is responsible for recruitment, training, and ongoing supervision of clinical competency of the medical team members. If the director of the sexual assault response team is first and foremost a highly skilled and experienced forensic examiner, other team members have a valuable and accessible clinical resource.

Forensic Examiner

The forensic examiner is a licensed health practitioner, such as registered nurse, nurse practitioner, physician's assistant, or physician. There are two basic ways the medical team member comes into contact with the victim:

- The victim may self-report to the emergency department for care, without first calling the police. (In jurisdictions where it is required by law that authorities be notified of all cases of alleged sexual assault, the forensic examiner ensures that this has been done.)
- The alleged assault has already been reported to law enforcement; law enforcement calls the designated communications department, which then contacts the on-call SART examiner.

After all necessary consents for the medical–legal examination, treatment, photos, and evidence collection have been obtained, the physical exam proceeds. The examiner conducts a history of the sexual assault, and other relevant medical history. This may be done independently or conjointly with the investigative interview by law enforcement.

The clinician performs the medical exam for evidence of sexual assault; this includes collection, packaging, documentation, and transfer or appropriate storage of all physical evidence obtained during the exam. *Chain of custody* is maintained throughout. This means that every person who handles a particular piece of evidence assumes accountability by signing off at each point in the transfer process from initial collection to final storage in the crime lab.

Other appropriate tests for pregnancy, and testing or prophylaxis for sexually transmitted diseases are performed, as indicated and per local protocol. Any associated physical injuries are treated or referred. Injuries, bitemarks, and nongenital and genital trauma are photographed. The entire exam is recorded by thorough documentation on appropriate medical–legal forms. In cases of acute genital trauma, a follow-up medical examination is recommended for further assessment to document resolution of injury. If the case goes to trial, the forensic examiner provides expert witness testimony.

SEXUAL ASSAULT NURSE EXAMINERS (SANEs)

Specially trained forensic nurses, known as Sexual Assault Nurse Examiners, or SANEs, often form the medical component of the sexual assault response team. Over time, nurse examiners have become accepted, appreciated, and sought after for their unique contribution to the forensic team. They enthusiastically combine a unique type of warm, compassionate caring with specialized clinical skill and expertise. The role of the SANE is multifaceted and includes:

- Providing a comprehensive, objective physical examination, with collection of all appropriate physical evidence and reference standards.
- Thoroughly and succinctly documenting any physical findings on the medical–legal form.
- Ensuring that the victim receives adequate follow-up medical care and referrals to local resources for counseling.
- Possessing the necessary skills and knowledge to provide expert testimony in court, if called upon as a witness in the case.

Some existing nurse-based programs have their origins in the 1970s crisis movement when rape crisis was burgeoning. Among these are:

- The Memphis Sexual Assault Resource Center, established in 1975 as the first comprehensive Rape Crisis Program; initially it was part of the Police Services Division of the city of Memphis, Tennessee.
- The Sexual Assault Resource Service (SARS) program, formed in 1977, in Minneapolis, Minnesota, by nurse clinicians.
- A SANE program in Amarillo, Texas, established in 1979 at Northwest Texas hospitals; nurses received credentials through the hospital medical staff, with allied health privileges as SANEs after extensive didactic and clinical course objectives were completed (Antognoli-Toland, 1985).
- The Suspected Abuse Response Team (SART), formed in San Luis Obispo, California, in 1978, prompted by the endeavors of two emergency room nurses who sought to achieve more compassionate and efficient care for victims of sexual assault. In 1987, the program began using nurse examiners, along with physicians to examine patients.

In these and many other fine programs, the SANE's role requires and entitles the practice of skills beyond those of traditional nursing and independent of a physician. Inherent in this expanded role is the establishment of the SANE as an expert in a particular area of expertise. This is crucial for the development and implementation of practice standards and guidelines, as well as for the nurse's testimony to be valid in court as an expert witness.

Peer review, based on standards utilized in other areas of the scientific community, is the basis for evaluation of care. Precise, accurate, and thorough documentation of the physical findings and any trauma are analyzed and evaluated. The process of peer review also serves as an excellent preparation for court testimony.

Quality assurance, or continuous quality improvement (CQI), serves as a tool for overall program evaluation and can pinpoint areas of needed growth. For hospital-based programs, a SART program helps the hospital to comply with the Joint Commission on Accreditation of Healthcare Organizations (JCAHO) as these requirements pertain to the management and treatment of victims of abuse.

The foundation and theory for this relatively new field of clinical nursing expertise parallels that of clinical forensic medicine. Living forensics is concerned with survivors of violent crimes or liability-related trauma. It has been part of the medical–legal and public health care systems in other parts of the world for 200 years in the United Kingdom, South America, East Asia, and Russia. Forensic nursing is the application of the nursing process to public or legal proceedings; thus it is the application of forensic aspects of health care to the scientific investigation of trauma (Lynch, 1995). Areas of response include victims of rape, child abuse and neglect, elder abuse, and other forms of domestic violence. Drug and alcohol addiction also falls under the umbrella of clinical forensic medicine, as do motor vehicle accidents, attempted suicides, occupation-related injuries, medical malpractice, food and drug tampering, and tissue and organ donation (anatomic gifts).

Requisite Skills and Knowledge

Specific training requirements may vary, depending on the individual qualifications and

level of expertise of a particular examiner. The format of SART training institutes typically includes an initial period of didactic instruction for a minimum of 40 hours. Candidates then complete an individual clinical preceptorship in order to receive SART certification, which is usually granted by the individual SART training institute. The didactic curriculum should include all specialized areas of expertise upon which the medical–legal examination is based:

- The team process and roles of all team members
- Victim advocacy and victim dynamics
- The medical–legal exam, including victim interview, physical and gynecological exam, STD and pregnancy testing/prophylaxis, use of adjunctive equipment, evidence collection, medical and legal terminology, normal anogenital anatomy, common gynecological conditions, mechanisms and patterns of injury, and drug and alcohol testing
- Physical evidence collection, packaging, processing, and preservation of chain of custody
- Offender issues and dynamics
- Sexual assault laws, local and state protocols related to adult and adolescent sexual assault victims
- The criminal justice process and expert testimony
- Investigator wellness

Each section of the curriculum should be taught by a specialist in the particular area of content. Thus, criminalists should instruct all sections pertaining to physical evidence collection. In addition to providing appropriate theory, they can identify the need for any local preferences for procedures related to state protocols.

An adequate clinical preceptorship generally demands a minimum of 40 hours, and should include all of the core areas. The practicum can be tailored to meet the individual practitioner's requirements. Participation in the clinical preceptorship initiates the examiner into all phases of the team process.

Time spent with the local advocacy program and representatives from victim witness assistance programs will familiarize the examiner with the referral process and personnel involved in the advocacy system, follow-up counseling, and state victim crime programs. A ride-along with a patrol officer from one of the local law enforcement agencies is invaluable for the clinician who has never before worked closely with police. It gives the examiner a better sense of the responsibilities an officer may have when being a first responder at a crime scene.

Working with a local emergency room staff familiarizes the examiner with personnel, procedures, and routines. The pelvic exam lab should be thorough enough for the examiner to attain proficiency in the speculum exam, perform STD tests, and discern variations in normal anatomy and benign gynecological conditions. Techniques such as colposcopy, and other equipment used during the medical exam may be practiced in this portion of the preceptorship or during a practicum in the SART exam room. The examiner should observe or assist with a few actual SART examinations to assimilate the flow of the entire process. Observation of a sexual assault trial or participation in a "mock" trial gives the examiner knowledge of the courtroom process. A block of time spent in the crime lab with the criminalist allows the examiner to see actual processing of a sexual assault evidence kit. Just as a picture is worth a thousand words, the opportunity to witness the unwrapping of a real, completed kit can make a permanent impression on a nurse who will soon be responsible for the collection of the sexual assault evidence.

Orientation to the SART examination rooms, equipment, paperwork, medical–legal forms, ancillary lab testing, and other routine procedures can make the examiner comfortable in the SART environs. This in turn, will enable the examiner to foster a hospitable setting in which to conduct a stressful exam. Finally, completion of a requisite number of supervised examinations is suggested to ensure clinical competency prior to working independently.

The forensic examiner of sexual assault victims should strive to receive ongoing education related to this specialty, and should participate in regular peer review of cases. When individual members know and perform their roles and responsibilities adequately, the process becomes synergistic. Functioning as a team with similar goals, each member is able to achieve more as a team than as an individual. Undeniably, there will be cases where the judicial outcome is either contrary or less than what everyone, especially the victim, had envisioned. However, it is important to concede that a positive outcome can still be realized, even if an offender has not been prosecuted to the full extent of the law.

REFERENCES

Antognoli-Toland, P. (May/June 1985). Comprehensive program for examination of sexual assault victims by nurses: A hospital-based project in Texas. *Journal of Emergency Nursing, 11*(3): 132–135.

Di Nitto, D., Yancey Martin, P., Blum Norton, D. & Maxwell, S. (1986, May). After rape: Who should examine rape survivors? *AJN.* 538–540.

Greenfeld, L. (1997, February). An analysis of data on rape and sexual assault. *Sex Offenses and Offenders* (NCJ-163392). Bureau of Justice Statistics, U.S. Department of Justice. Washington, DC.

Greenfeld, L. (1997). Executive summary: An analysis of data on rape and sexual assault. *Sex Offenses and Offenders* (NCJ-163931). Bureau of Justice Statistics, U.S. Department of Justice. Washington, DC.

International Association of Forensic Nurses (IAFN) (September 1997). Meeting Program *Fifth Annual Scientific Assembly,* Irvine, CA.

Lenehan, G.P. (February 1991). [Editorial]. Sexual assault nurse examiners: A SANE way to care for rape victims. *Journal of Emergency Nursing, 17*(1):1–2.

Lynch, V. (1995). Clinical forensic nursing: A new perspective in the management of crime victims from trauma to trial. *Critical Care Nursing Clinics of North America, 7:*489–507.

McHugh, J. & Leake, D. (Eds.). (1997). *Scope and Standards of Forensic Nursing Practice.* International Association of Forensic Nurses (IAFN). Washington, DC: American Nurses Publishing.

Training Curriculum for the Examination of Sexual Assault and Child Sexual Abuse Victims. (1991). Sacramento, CA: Office of Criminal Justice Planning.

SUGGESTED READINGS

ACOG Educational Bulletin, No. 242. (1997, November). Sexual assault. Washington, DC: The American College of Obstetricians and Gynecologists, pp. 1–7.

Ledray, L. (1992). The sexual assault examination: Overview and lessons learned in one program. *Journal of Emergency Nursing, 18*(3): 223–232.

Ledray, L. (1993). Sexual assault nurse clinician: An emerging area of nursing expertise. *AWHONN'S Clinical Issues, 4*(2):180–190.

Lynch, V. (1991). Forensic nursing in the emergency department: A new role for the 1990s. *Critical Care Nursing Quarterly, 14:*69–86.

Lynch, V. (1993). [Editorial]. Forensic aspects of health care: New roles, new responsibilities. *Journal of Psychosocial Nursing, 31:*5–6.

Lynch, V. (1993). Forensic nursing, diversity in education and practice. *Journal of Psychosocial Nursing, 31:*7–14.

Roye, C. & Coonan, P. (1997). Adolescent rape. *AJN, 97*(4):45.

U.S. Department of Justice, Bureau of Justice web page. [statistics]. Address: http://www.ojp.usdoj.gov/bjs/

2 The Psychological Aftermath of Sexual Trauma

Dinah, Jacob's daughter, went out to visit the women of the region. Shechem, the son of Hamor, ruler of the region, saw her, carried her off and raped her, and so dishonored her. Captivated by Dinah, he fell in love and told Hamor, his father: "Get me this young girl, I want to marry her." Dinah's brothers were in the countryside with the livestock. On hearing the news, they were outraged; this was an offense that could not be overlooked. Shechem pleaded with Dinah's father and brothers: "If only I can win your favor, I will give you whatever you ask. Demand from me a huge bridal price and gifts; I will give you as much as you ask. Only let me marry the young girl."

The answer Jacob's sons gave was a crafty one, for Shechem had dishonored Dinah. "We cannot do such a thing. To give our sister to an uncircumcised man would be a disgrace for us. We can agree only on one condition: that you become like us by circumcising all your males." The young man did not hesitate about doing this, for he was deeply in love with Jacob's daughter. Moreover, he was the most important person in his father's household. All the citizens of the town agreed to the proposal made by Hamor and his son Shechem, and so all the males were circumcised.

On the third day, when the Shechemites were still in pain, Dinah's brothers took their swords and marched into the town unsuspected; they killed all the males, including Shechem and his father. After Dinah was rescued, Jacob was afraid of retribution, but his sons simply retorted, "Is our sister to be treated like a whore?"

Genesis: 34; 1–31

OVERVIEW

Few medical situations that present to the health professional are as emotionally charged as rape. Major catastrophic events such as war, motor vehicle accidents, and natural disasters can bring tremendous personal suffering and wide-scale destruction. Yet, the terrible anguish of the rape victim, while not always so visible, is ravaging and pervasive, as it permeates so many threads of the victim's life. The rape victim may sit silently for hours in the melee of the emergency room, with little or no obvious marks of the ordeal. Likewise, for myriad reasons, a person may not even identify her- or himself as a victim, attempting to go on with daily routines in an effort to put the horror of the rape behind them.

Rape and other forms of sexual trauma are wounds as real as any other; they not only afflict the body, but pierce the soul. Each professional involved with the victim must acknowledge his or her own vulnerability, and the vulnerability of those they love. Sexual assault is not a malady people particularly care to dwell on or foresee; you cannot take out an insurance policy "in case" the dreaded event occurs. Despite prevalent statistics, there is more peace of mind in preparing a will than exploring this dire possibility. The disaster happens; the victim wonders why. They know they didn't die, as feared. Afterward, life becomes turned around, and there is a new time line: before the rape, and after the rape. New roles emerge: that of victim, patient, witness, to name a few. During the immediate aftermath, the victim's body does not even seem to belong to them. It is now a *crime scene,* with clues that must be searched for if biological evidence is to be gathered.

While the *person* who was raped is given the role of victim, their chosen roles and expectations continue: that of mother, daughter, son, wife, husband, father, sister, brother, friend. Somehow they must meet the demands, cope with the necessary interventions, confront the horrors, and finally, climb out of the dark chasm that seems to envelop them.

By incorporating what we have learned about the experiences of the victim of sexual trauma, we can more compassionately and effectively utilize our own skills and expertise. To provide good medical and forensic services, we must be cognizant of the many ways that these crimes impact the victim. How each victim meets his or her own rape-related demons will influence how they respond to the interview, the medical exam, follow-up exam, testimony in court, and eventual emergence as a survivor.

DEFINING THE PROBLEM

The legal definition of rape varies from state to state. This distinction also exists in the literature, in the discussion of terms such as rape and sexual assault. The variance in interpretation can result in differences in the reported frequencies of the crimes in different sample populations. The word *rape* derives from the Latin, *rapere: to seize; to force; to have sexual intercourse.* The concept of seizure and taking by force is ageless. History abounds with the sagas of pain and angst that humankind has suffered as a consequence.

As defined by the National Crime Victimization Survey (NCVS), *rape* is forced sexual intercourse. The victim may be either male or female. The assailant may be either the same or different sex as the victim. *Sexual assault* includes a wider range of unwanted sexual activities, and includes threats and attempts to commit sexual assault. In this text, victims are 12 years of age or older, and the terms *rape* and *sexual assault* may be interchanged. *Penetration* includes the oral, vaginal, and anal openings.

Other defining aspects of sexual trauma follow.

Incest

This term refers to sexual activity between close blood relatives. In cases of incest, issues of family loyalty often become paramount. Family members may feel compelled to take sides, while the essential facts of the crime become obscured by a conflicting web of emotional responses to the disclosure of the incestuous acts. The adolescent male or female victim of incest may present for a medical–legal examination in various ways. The molestation/abuse may have been *chronic,* or ongoing for some time. If the most recent occurrence was *acute* (within 72 hours), these individuals may be referred for an evidentiary exam. The protocol in many regional centers is to perform the medical–legal examination on a scheduled basis, during regular clinic hours, if the most recent incident occurred more than 3 days previously (72 + hours). After 72 hours, the collection of biological evidence will not be warranted. Of equal importance will be the testing for sexually transmitted diseases and pregnancy and referrals for counseling. Another major factor may be the involvement of Child Protective Services, if the offender is an immediate family member, or another assailant who resides in the home. If the victim is a juvenile he/she may be removed from the home and placed in protective custody. Issues of betrayal of normal family boundaries further compound the trauma sustained by the adolescent. Adequate follow-up and supervision by competent and compassionate guardians is crucial to the young victim coping with this crisis. Although it is beyond the scope of short-term intervention to fully assess the psychological state of the juvenile, the forensic examiner must be astute to observe for any obvious signs or symptoms of acute distress, and ensure that any such concerns are relayed to members of the agency responsible for the welfare of the juvenile.

An adolescent may also fall prey to sexual molestation in an *extrafamilial* setting, where the assailant is known to the victim. This situation may also be chronic, of recent onset, or have elements of both. It may involve situations of *pressured sex,* if the assailant has a position of power over the victim. This power imbalance may arise because of age differences, position, authority, or other factors between the victim and assailant. These factors may include age, intelligence, maturity, developmental stage, or social skills, and result in a situation where the victim is duped or coerced into compliance.

Acquaintance Rape

The assailant is someone known to the victim in the vast majority of rapes (75–85%). In two-thirds of the rapes of 18- to 29-year-old women, the victim had some type of prior relationship with the assailant (Greenfeld, 1997). The rapist is someone who the victim had no reason to fear prior to the rape. Acquaintance rape usually occurs in the context of a relationship that originated in a socially acceptable way. It may even begin as a consensual encounter. This type of rape is far less reported than stranger rape. Abarbanel (1990) states that if a victim chooses to report at all, they are more likely to make delayed reports. Some of these victims succumb to "frozen fright," which may manifest itself via nonresistance. This state of panic and fear causes immobilization. Trapped by a state of psychological paralysis, the victim may not even try to escape. This behavior may be misconstrued to be consent on the part of the victim (Abarbanel & Richman, 1990).

Stranger Rape

The assailant is unknown to the victim at the time of the assault. This type of rapist accounts for approximately 25 percent of reported rapes (Greenfeld, 1997).

RAPE TRAUMA SYNDROME

Ann Wolbert Burgess and Lynda Holmstrom designed and conducted landmark research in the early 1970s to study and report the immediate and long-term effects of rape. At that time, very little was known or published on this topic. During a one-year period, Burgess and Holmstrom were called by emergency room nurses at Boston City College every time a rape victim was admitted. The sample size was 146 and included 109 women, 34 female children, and 3 male children. The results were published in 1974 in the *American Journal of Psychiatry*. The U.S. Department of Justice Crime Statistics for 1970 contained 37,000 cases of rape for the year (Burgess & Holmstrom, 1974). After the silence was broken, women began to come forward with their stories on this previously taboo subject. The emergence of rape crisis centers, rape reform legislation, and the development of medical protocols followed. Between 1970 and 1980, the rape reporting rate increased by 100 percent across the United States (Abarbanel & Richman, 1990).

Burgess and Holmstrom's original evaluations gave rise to 25 articles and chapters and two books. From their study of victim interviews the authors devised the following typology of sexual trauma, based on issues of consent:

1. *Rape trauma:* No consent; the acts are clearly against the victim's will and are potentially life-threatening.
2. *Pressured sex:* Inability to deny consent. The victim is pressured into sexual activity by an individual who holds a position of power over them through age, authority, or some other factor.
3. *Sex-stress:* Consent followed by significant distress (Burgess & Holmstrom, 1986; Burgess & Hartman, 1997).

Rape trauma syndrome is both the acute phase and a long-term reorganization process that results from either a forcible or attempted forcible rape. (Burgess & Holmstrom, 1974). The term and its definition were derived from the analysis of symptoms of adult females in the original study population. "Rape trauma syndrome is a clinical nursing term and describes a clustering of bio-psycho-social and cognitive symptoms exhibited by the victim following a rape" (cited in Burgess & Hartman, 1997, p. 426). The syndrome consists of two phases: acute and reorganization. Some characteristics and symptoms that the victim may exhibit during each phase are summarized in Table 2–1.

▶ **TABLE 2–1.** RAPE TRAUMA SYNDROME: PHASES

Acute Phase	Reorganization Phase
Initial period; lasts from a few days to several weeks	*Longer* phase; begins when victim attempts to reorganize her or his disrupted lifestyle and return to precrisis status
Indicators and Manifestations	
Skeletal muscle tension (headaches, fatigue)	Increased motor activity; may change telephone number or place of residence
Gastrointestinal irritability	Increased need for family and social support network (may not give reason)
Genitourinary disturbance	Fears and phobic reactions to circumstances of the assault
Marked disruption in eating and sleeping patterns	Daytime anxiety
Wide range of emotions; may be shock and disbelief	Nightmares

Data from Burgess, A. & Holmstrom, L. (1974). Rape trauma syndrome. Am J Psychiatry, 131(9):981–986; and Burgess, A. & Hartman, C. (1997). In: Burgess, A. (Ed.) Victims of sexual assault, Psychiatric Nursing. Stamford, CT: Appleton & Lange.

The emotional demeanor exhibited by victims experiencing rape trauma syndrome has traditionally been delineated into two emotional styles: *expressed* and *controlled.* Burgess and Holmstrom (1974) noted about a 50/50 distribution of each. Table 2–2 describes some of these behaviors.

Other phobic reactions to the trauma, include virtually any situation that the victim associates with the rape, eg, fear of the outdoors or indoors, of being alone (or conversely, in a crowd), fear of people walking behind them, and fears related to sexual intimacy (Burgess & Holmstrom, 1974).

Psychological coping mechanisms help the victim cope with the trauma at three points relative to the attack: during early awareness of danger, during the attack itself, and the period following the attack. How the victim reacts at these points on the continuum play a major role in subsequent adjustment (Burgess & Holmstrom, 1976; Burgess & Hartman, 1997).

Although one might presume that a victim's first choice after escape would be to run for help and immediately report the traumatic event, that may not be the case at all. The very act of disclosure itself is another great stressor on a person already in crisis. Will she or he be believed? What will people think? How will (family, police, doctors, nurses, friends) respond? The crisis of rape is one of self-preservation, best managed with a model of crisis intervention.

▶ **TABLE 2–2.** RAPE TRAUMA SYNDROME: EMOTIONAL STYLES

Expressed Demeanor	Controlled Demeanor
Crying	Calm, quiet
Anger	Seemingly emotionless
Extreme agitation	affect

Data from Burgess, A. & Holmstrom, L. (1974). Rape trauma syndrome. Am J Psychiatry, 131 (9):981–986; and Burgess, A. & Hartman, C. (1997). In Burgess, A. (Ed.) Victims of sexual assault, Psychiatric Nursing. Stamford, CT: Appleton & Lange.

POSTTRAUMATIC STRESS DISORDER

Posttraumatic stress disorder (PTSD) is "an anxiety disorder in which exposure to an exceptional mental or physical stressor is followed, sometimes immediately, and sometimes not until 3 months or more after the stress, by persistent re-experiencing of the event, avoidance of stimuli associated with the trauma or numbing of general responsiveness, and manifestations of increased arousal" (Edgerton, 1994). Persons with PTSD often have intrusive thoughts, memories, and flashbacks. They may feel emotionally detached and startle easily, and have difficulty with sleeping and concentration. PTSD can be further delineated by its duration. Acute PTSD usually lasts less than 3 months, while chronic PTSD can last 3 months or longer. The onset may also be delayed. Rape and incest can be linked in their symptomatology, to a wide variety of other traumatic events such as war, terrorism, and natural disasters. From a psychobiological perspective, patients with PTSD have an increased autonomic or sensory nervous system arousal when they are reminded of the trauma. Several neurological processes which involve the locus coeruleus, hypothalamus, and hippocampus, have shown abnormal responses in patients with PTSD (Burgess & Burgess, 1997).

Rape victims suffering from PTSD may have difficulty with interpersonal relationships as they attempt to avoid situations that they associate with the memory of the sexual trauma. A complete personality change, impulsive behavior, and suicide are also possible PTSD outcomes (Burgess & Burgess, 1997). Kilpatrick et al (1992) reported that almost one-third of all rape victims in their survey had developed PTSD at some time, and these victims were six times more likely to develop PTSD than females who had never been victims of a crime (31% vs. 5%). Thirty percent of rape victims had experienced at least one major depressive episode. They were four times more likely to have considered suicide, and 13 times more likely to have actually attempted it (Kilpatrick et al, 1992). Although there was greater use of drugs and alcohol among the rape victims as compared with noncrime victims, the age at the time of rape was generally younger than the age of *first* use of drugs or intoxication. When compared with noncrime victims, rape victims with PTSD were 13 times more likely to have two or more major alcohol problems and 26 times more likely to have two or more major drug abuse problems. These problems were defined as trouble with school or work, difficulties with family, friends or the police, health problems, and home and auto accidents (Kilpatrick et al, 1992).

A New Zealand study, which randomly surveyed women in the community, yielded higher scores on tests designed to measure psychopathology in women who gave a history of sexual abuse. Reported symptoms included depression, anxiety, and phobic reactions (Mullen et al, 1988). For women who presented to a primary care practice, McCauley and others found that 50 percent of women who suffered childhood abuse (physical or sexual) also experienced adult abuse of some type. Even if they did not endure abuse as an adult, they were more prone to psychological distress, substance abuse, suicide attempts, or ideation, findings similar to other studies (McCauley, 1997).

Tragic examples of widespread, catastrophic rape trauma came from survivors of "ethnic cleansing" during the war in Bosnia. First person testimonies of mass rape point to some of the most sadistic violence to occur in Europe since Hitler's reign of terror. Estimates of victims range from 30,000 to 50,000 women. Violations by neighbors and strangers alike, repeated rapes of girls as young as 6 and 7 years old, and rape of young girls in front of family members were common horrors. Brutal gang rapes often left the victim dead. In "rape camps," victims were routinely abused and murdered (Post et al, 1993).

PAST HISTORY OF ABUSE: SOMATIC COMPLAINTS

Chronic pelvic pain is defined as noncyclic pelvic pain of greater than 6 months' duration. It is a common gynecologic complaint and accounts for 10% of outpatient gynecologic consultations. This condition results in as many as 25% of the diagnostic laparoscopies and 10 to 19% of the hysterectomies performed in the United States (the third most common reason for this surgery). Data from two groups of women with chronic pelvic pain, those with probable somatic etiology (eg, endometriosis) and those without identifiable somatic abnormality, suggest that the psychosocial profile of women with nonsomatic chronic pelvic pain is different. Prior sexual trauma appears to be a predisposing risk for somatization and nonsomatic chronic pelvic pain (Reiter et al, 1991).

In a referral-based gastroenterology practice, Drossman found sexual and physical abuse a common component of female patient's past medical history. In this study, the patients' own physicians were aware of this history for only 17% of the abused women. About one-third of the women had never discussed their abuse with *anyone*. When compared to patients who had diagnoses of organic diseases, patients with functional bowel disorders reported significantly greater experiences of sexual abuse and frequently, physical abuse (Drossman et al, 1990).

ADOLESCENT EXAMINATION ISSUES: MALE AND FEMALE

A minor child as young as 12 years old may, in many jurisdictions, consent to the medical–legal examination and associated evidence collection. Throughout the United States, these adolescents may receive testing and treatment for STDs and pregnancy, without parental consent. The clinician must be cognizant of local laws. Parental notification may be required, but left to the discretion of authorities if that notification would jeopardize the child's welfare. It is appropriate to identify these situations and clarify responsibilities to ensure the protection of the juvenile victim.

The ideal support for any victim of sexual trauma comes from a caring, nurturing family. Although the victim's needs are first and foremost, those needs may best be met by viewing those who accompany the victim as a family unit, endeavoring to provide them with sufficient information and support to help answer questions, correct misconceptions, and cope with the immediate crisis. It is vital to recognize that parents, as well as the victim, are in crisis. This requires a gentle, tactful, comprehensive approach. It is impossible for the forensic examiner to singularly fulfill all of these needs. Herein lies the great value of having a rape crisis advocate present to ensure that these needs are met for both the victim and their loved ones.

If one or both parents are present, explain your role and briefly describe what will be happening for the next few hours. At this point, what the parents need is not lengthy details, but calm assurance that their child will be compassionately and competently taken care of. Let the parents know that you realize they have many questions and concerns; you need to proceed with your exam, but will get back to them. Then, of course, be sure to do so. For a young adolescent, it may be necessary to elicit some of the past medical history and other cursory health information from a parent, before moving on to the forensic interview. After necessary, basic information and consents are obtained, it is best to conduct the forensic interview out of the presence of parents. If parents are resistant to this, the law enforcement officer can lend a position of authority over the investigation of the crime, and be most helpful in explaining to the parents that it is in their child's best interest to be interviewed alone. The examiner can arrange privately with the officer beforehand to suggest this, so that the process moves smoothly and does not seem intrusive, or make the parents feel defensive. Later, during the physical examination, the teen may want a parent present. Suggest that the parent(s) get a cup of coffee or take a brief walk while the interview proceeds; the diversion may reduce some of their anxiety. Despite a close relationship between parent and child, the interview which takes place after a sexual assault is never a good time for a parent to discover aspects of their child's life of which they were unaware, such as consensual sexual activity or alcohol or drug use. This is not to say that nothing is ever as it seems to be, but it is not worth the risk; the teenager is uncomfortable enough without placing any extra burdens on either the victim or parents. These issues may have a bearing on the case and it is optimal to garner this information up front.

The advocate can ensure that the victim and family are provided with referrals needed for counseling. Parents need to understand that they can best support their children through this crisis if they themselves have healthy outlets for their own pain and anger. Teenagers often do well in a counseling group with other teens. It is not at all unusual for victims in this age group to be recalcitrant about counseling, especially when they may feel more comfortable talking it over with close friends, if at all. The door can be opened for them, so that they know if they refuse immediate support, they can always contact the Rape Crisis Center later. Most advocates ask the victim at the time of the medical exam if they may call or contact them in a day or so, just to see how they are doing. Arrangements can be made at the medical–legal examination, if the teen does not want to be called at home. Sometimes a caring teacher or other trusted adult friend can serve as a conduit for information, messages, and arrangements between the teen and support services, including a follow-up medical exam.

Depending on local protocol, prophylaxis against pregnancy and sexually transmitted diseases are provided, or cultures are taken after forensic evidence collection. The teen may have concerns, fears, or misconceptions related to all of these areas. Many adolescent females have their first pelvic exam in conjunction with a rape. The young male victim may be acutely embarrassed at having his penis and scrotum examined, especially if he experiences an erection during the exam. A calm, matter-of-fact approach by the examiner can help alleviate his anxiety. Reassurance, explanations, and calm efficiency will soothe and help relax the patient, facilitating the procedure. Pay attention to cues: some teens (and adults) do not want copious, detailed explanations for everything. They may want neither a lesson in anatomy nor a lengthy description for every procedure. Do not assume! Where a simple explanation seems desired, do not offer too much information.

Since many young people will be reluctant to voice concerns during the examination, it may be helpful to give them some choices:

- They can call you in a few days, when things have settled down a bit.
- They can ask the advocate or another trusted person to call you.
- They can write their issues down and bring them to the follow-up exam, at which time you will discuss them personally.

In any event, assure your young patients that their concerns are valid and important to you.

Keep in mind that teenagers may in all likelihood not seem too enthused by lengthy "lectures" by any adult, regardless how well intended. Do not try to be the adolescent's buddy. They have enough peers. What they need in this crisis are caring, competent adults who will gently guide them, while allowing them to make choices and be responsible for their own well being. Attune yourself to the teen's attention span and interest level. Teenagers appreciate frank honesty and are more likely to follow through if they respect the practitioner. Some teens will find a welcome relief from appropriate interjections of humor. Indeed, many will giggle or laugh at the oddest times during an interview or exam. Perhaps a giggle expresses where words are inadequate. Above all, appreciate them and accept their valiant attempts at coping with a very painful experience. Acknowledge their courage and the successful completion of the medical exam when it is finally over.

The Adolescent Male Victim of Assault

The young male victim of sexual assault presents with all of the concerns and growing pains that accompany youth. Sexual assault of young males is even less frequently reported than that of females, which is generally considered to be about 10% of actual reported cases. Finkelhor (1980) estimated that for every two female victims of sexual abuse there is one male victim. Most of these incidents go unreported.

Facets of the abuse of adolescents which may make their experience different from younger child victims are:

- Increased force.
- Increased potential for the abuse to occur outside the home. Adolescents have more mobility and independence. An increased risk exists for males in public places or during solitary outdoor activities (Deisher & Bidwell, 1987).

Deisher and Bidwell (1987) reported less frequency of sexual abuse at home *beginning* in adolescence. Among youths that are especially vulnerable for onset of abuse at this age are street youths. Even in these groups, with involvement in prostitution, there exists a lack of emotional and physical maturity and often as much lack of insight into issues of their sexuality as their nonstreet peers (Deisher & Bidwell, 1987).

In a study of 284 university men by Collings (1995), male child abuse involving contact forms of sexual abuse was associated with later difficulties with psychological development. Dysfunctional family relations posed a greater risk for abuse.

Many variables must be considered in the evaluation of family functioning. In this framework, child sexual abuse is one more negative variable within the broader negative experience that increases the child's vulnerability to mental disorders (Kinzl & Mangweth, 1996).

Recognition of Abuse in Adolescent Males

As with his older counterpart, the adolescent male victim may present to an emergency room or outpatient clinic for medical care for assault-related conditions, such as nongenital trauma, sexually transmitted diseases, or even psychiatric conditions such as depression, *without* initially reporting a chief complaint of sexual assault. In these situations, tactful and insightful discernment by the health care provider may bring the abuse to the forefront.

Conditions that warrant further consideration for the possibility of abuse include:

- Otherwise unexplained signs of anxiety, depression, or psychological problems
- Unexplained decrease in appetite or recent weight change
- Insomnia
- Anhedonia (lack of pleasurable feelings from activities that normally induce them)
- Suicidal ideation
- Self-harmful behavior
- Withdrawal from friends and family
- Decreased school performance (Deisher & Bidwell, 1987; Kinzl & Mangweth, 1996)

Some *somatic* complaints which *may* be associated with abuse include:

- Abdominal pain ("stomach hurts"), nausea, gastrointestinal distress
- Genital pain
- Headache
- Fatigue, listlessness
- Substance abuse

Upon review of some of the effects of early sexual abuse and ensuing long-term consequences, Kinzl and Mangweth (1996) purport that sexual abuse usually coexists with many problems, often physical and emotional in nature.

In a study of 66 adolescents between 12 and 17 years old, who were exploited via adult sex rings and pornography, most were subjected to sexual abuse and subsequently displayed patterns of negative social and psychological adjustment. Boys were the sexual preference of the adult male ringleaders. These adolescents exhibited sexual anxiety, gender confusion, avoidant, acting-out, and antisocial behaviors, and drug and alcohol abuse (Burgess et al, 1984).

Finkelhor has described the negative effect of sexual abuse on the child's sexuality as "traumatic sexualization." This term describes both the dysfunction of the interpersonal relationship and the inappropriate sexual behavior (Deisher & Bidwell, 1987:52).

Concern and confusion over issues of sexuality and sexual identity go part and parcel with adolescence. For the victim of sexual abuse, this is magnified. Misinformation may be great enough to result in subsequent interpersonal and sexual problems as an adult. Male survivors may be unable to recognize their symptoms, identify their feelings, or comfortably trust their own responses. Sexual responses may become confused with themes of anger, power, shame, or trust and affect their sense of trust and security (Bolton et al, 1989).

Whether the assault of the young man is self-reported or comes to the attention of the criminal justice system via another party, certain questions require special sensitivity, eg, inquiries into resistance behaviors by the victim and suspect behavior such as use of threats, force, weapons, or other acts of overt physical aggression. The young male may feel less masculine if he attributes assailant behavior to his own inability to fight back and protect himself. It may be easier to acknowledge anger than fear. These perceptions may persist even if he was obviously overpowered, or there were multiple assailants and physical brutality. The young man's own ideas of how he handled the situation are strongly influenced by his pre-assault concept and ideals of manhood and maleness.

While it is important to avoid stereotyping any sexual assault victim, regardless of age or gender, it is equally important to consider that all assailants may not fit the general picture of an "assailant". Due to changing penal codes, age-old scenarios such as sexual intimacies between an older woman and an adolescent male come to the forefront, but now as a crime. Such is the case in California, where a female can now be charged with rape. In Hickson's large study of gay males, out of the 27% who reported a history of sexual assault, 4% of the assailants in first-time assaults were women (Hickson et al, 1994). The clinician must be prepared for these scenarios. Though atypical, actual precedent has occurred wherein the medical–legal examination of the suspect in an alleged sexual assault was an adult female, while the victim was a juvenile male (Crowley, 1995). Conventional lore has held that such interactions were not only far from being a crime, but rather a seduction and bit of good luck on the part of the young man. This only served as double jeopardy to young boys who were violated. Most studies do indeed describe the typical sex offender as a male, and in the majority of situations, this is the case. Finkelhor and Russel (1984) concluded that female offenders were responsible for 24% of the sexual abuse of all male victims

and 13% of all female victims. The females acted alone or with a male partner (Gonsiorek, 1994). Some researchers postulate that female assailants may engage in less overtly sexual activities with young victims, eg, exposure, fondling, bathing, or dressing. This factor may partially explain some of the reluctance to report, especially in the adolescent, who is trying to establish his own sexual identity.

THE MALE VICTIM OF SEXUAL ASSAULT

While rape is an ancient violation, our scientific understanding is relatively new. Much of this information has emerged since the 1970s. Reports of male sexual assault in settings other than correctional institutions were rare until the 1980s. In a review of U.S. Department of Justice statistics for 1972, Kaufman (1987) found no identified cases of male sexual assaults out of 1100 reported rapes. In his review of the 90 articles on rape listed in the *Index Medicus* from 1975 to 1978, no articles appeared which were primarily concerned with the male rape victim, with the exception of children. Recognition and publicity of the problem of female rape gradually led to increased reporting. This burgeoning of interest and subsequent research into the problem of female rape victims finally began to include male victims as well.

Groth and Burgess (1980) list the following factors as barriers against the reporting of male sexual assault:

- Societal beliefs that a man is expected to defend himself against sexual assault.
- The victim may fear that his sexual orientation becomes suspect.
- The very act of reporting is distressing in itself.

If male victims do present for care, it is more likely to be for physical and emotional trauma, often without initially reporting the sexual component of the assault (Kaufman, 1987). While Burgess and Holmstrom approximated a 50/50 distribution pattern for controlled vs. expressed styles of behavior in females due to rape trauma syndrome, Kaufman reported an 80% prevalence for the controlled style in male victims. This was for a sample size of 15 males, with an age range between 15 and 49 years old; the mean age being 27 years. Kaufman contrasted his findings for the males with a control group of 100 female rape victims evaluated during the same 3-year period and revealed:

- The male population had a 60% incidence of multiple assailants, vs. 23% for the female group.
- There was increased brutality for the male group, as evidenced by an 80% incidence of nongenital trauma (27% stab wounds and 53% other physical injuries). This contrasts with a 36% incidence of such trauma for the female group.
- Male anogenital trauma was 53% (all sodomized); vs. female genital trauma: 28%.

Although the sample size was small, it is interesting to compare the nongenital trauma and genital trauma prevalence in Kaufman's groups with those of other studies. The 28% genital trauma in the female group is consistent with other studies published during that period, which report a frequency of genital injury ranging from 10 to 16% up to about 28% (Cartwright et al, 1987; Tintinalli & Hoelzer, 1985). Later studies using toluidine blue dye and colposcopic magnification at 15× yielded higher rates of genital trauma (Lauber & Souma, 1982; McCauley, 1986; Slaughter, Brown, Crowley & Peck, 1997). The finding of 53% anogenital trauma in the males, who were all sodomized, is possibly of greater significance, because it relied on gross visualization alone, and is still consistent with later colposcopic findings of anal trauma at 56% in females. The later study, incorporating colposcopic magnification, also showed an associ-

ation between increased brutality, as reflected by nongenital trauma, and a prevalence of anal sex acts (Slaughter, Brown, Crowley & Peck, 1997)

Haskett et al (1996) reviewed 126 articles published between 1989 and 1994, and concluded that adult males were grossly underrepresented in the research. Males were included in less than half of the articles reviewed. Only three studies focused exclusively on males. While the focus was on physical abuse, the authors felt that prevailing family situations involved in the histories of those who reported abuse may also be associated with other types of abuse and neglect, eg, emotional abuse and sexual abuse.

Surveys of nonclinical, adult male populations found prevalence rates of previous child sexual abuse from 3 to 29% (Finkelhor, 1994, in Kinzl & Mangweth, 1996). In reviews of the literature, Kinzl & Mangweth (1996) reported that adult males who were childhood victims of sexual abuse are more likely to have disturbed sexual functioning.

THE PREGNANT VICTIM OF ASSAULT

Pregnancy has been postulated as being an especially vulnerable time for physical and sexual abuse. A prevalence of 17%, or one in six pregnant women, reported physical or sexual abuse in a study by McFarlane et al (1992) in Maryland and Texas. Sixty percent of the females in this study reported two or more episodes of abuse during their pregnancy. The head was the most frequent location of injury. Abused women were twice as likely to begin their prenatal care in the third trimester as nonabused women. The assailant was almost always someone known intimately by the victim. Pregnant teenagers had a greater incidence of multiple assailants, usually boyfriend and parent(s). Women were interviewed during each trimester. Thus, those who initially reported no abuse in early pregnancy, but did fall victim in subsequent trimesters, were accounted for in the study (McFarlane et al, 1992).

The pregnant victim of sexual assault should receive the same medical forensic examination as the nonpregnant patient, with special attention to accommodate her gravid status. If the patient is known to be pregnant at the time of the exam, the forensic examiner must carefully evaluate her physical condition. Some protocols propose the standard exam routine until the 20th week of gestation, after initial medical screening rules out any obvious complications. After 20 weeks, monitoring is usually recommended to ensure stability of the fetus before proceeding with the forensic exam. Medical consultation with an obstetrician should be available, in the event of complications. If necessary, the evidentiary exam can be done conjointly with that of the attending obstetrician/gynecologist to minimize manipulation and instrumentation.

The increased vaginal lactobacilli and decreased vaginal anaerobes, with subsequent decreased vaginal pH, do not appear to alter the rate of recovery of motile sperm in pregnant sexual assault victims. In a large Dallas study of both pregnant and nonpregnant sexual assault victims, Satin et al (1991) noted that extragenital trauma was greater in the nonpregnant group. For both groups, the most common sites of injury were the head, face, neck, and extremities. Sites of penetration (vulvar, oral, anal) were also similar for both groups. It is postulated that the pregnant victim may be more likely to report due to fear of fetal injury (Satin et al, 1991). One-third of the assaults occurred after the 20th week of gestation, a time when the gravid condition should be obvious to any assailant. There was little fetal demise, despite escalation of low birth weight (24%) and preterm delivery (16%). The pregnant victim warrants special consideration and close follow-up for evaluation of medical status and referrals for counseling.

Pregnancy is one time in a woman's life when it is normal to have frequent, regular contact with a health care provider. Hence, this might be a prudent time for the routine screening for hallmarks of abuse, both past and concurrent. Prenatal detection of previously unreported and untreated physical, emotional, and psychological abuse could help put an end to this cycle and ensure both a healthy pregnancy outcome and a safe environment for the newborn.

RAPE OF THE OLDER WOMAN

Sexual assault is one form of elder abuse to which the older female may fall prey. Estimates for elder abuse in general run as high as one in 20 persons over 65 years of age. The prevalence tends to increase with age, with those who are most frail and dependent having the greatest prevalence. Ramin et al (1992) reported a sexual assault frequency of 2% in women 50 years of age and older, while Cartwright and Moore (1989) found a 3% incidence in women ages 60 to 90 years old. Weapon use was identified in 43% of these cases (Cartwright & Moore, 1989). Guns, knives, and blunt objects were the identified weapons. Ramin et al (1992) noted a difference in patterns of sex acts between postmenopausal and younger age female victims. The older women had a lower frequency of oral and multiple sites of penetration during the assault. Anal, combined with vulval penetration, was the most common pattern of sexual acts in older women, whereas in the younger group, oral and vulvar sex acts were reported more often. Postmenopausal victims who do report rape may come in earlier for medical treatment than younger victims, possibly because there tends to be more genital and nongenital trauma in the older victim. Drug and alcohol use by the victim was less in the older women (Satin, 1991). In a study by Hicks and Moon (1987), a much greater percentage (88%) of older women were assaulted by strangers; multiple assailants were involved for 21% of these victims.

Although the feelings and emotional consequences of the assault may parallel those of the younger victim, the older woman may suffer certain aspects in a uniquely distressful way. Depending on her past experiences with consensual sexual acts, she may be especially disturbed, even horrified, by certain sexual acts which occurred during the rape, such as fellatio and anal intercourse. If the older woman lives alone and the assault occurred in her home the psychological symptoms of fear may be especially intense. Though the younger victim may exhibit tendencies to mobilize and change residences or phone numbers, these same options may be especially traumatic, if not impossible, for the elderly. Financial limitations may preclude a move, or the woman may have resided in her home for many years with the same phone number. The older woman may be legitimately distraught at the prospect of losing these elements of her identity, concomitant with the sexual violation of her body.

Simply because of her age and possible frailty, and the greater likelihood of physical limitations, the elderly woman is at increased risk, even if she does not engage in obvious risk-taking behaviors. The very factors which are part of the natural aging process may make her more prone to victim selection because of greater vulnerability. The elderly victim may have greater dependency needs and be less resilient to the impact of the assault. Confronting this vulnerability may leave the victim feeling helpless and less able to protect herself.

Family members are bound to feel anguish with the assault of their elders. As with younger victims, recovery is dependent upon the nurturing and sensitive, appropriate interventions of significant others. It may be difficult for the older woman to discuss intensely personal feelings. The fact that the assault involves her sexuality makes it especially difficult, if not impossible. Like the younger victim, the older woman may have difficulty resuming normal, loving sexual intimacies. She may be less accustomed to expressing her needs and fears. Her family may react by constant surveillance, in effect "smothering" the woman. Feelings of independence and self-reliance are valuable vestiges of one's youth; their loss, whether real or perceived, can have profound effects.

Follow-up medical examinations are an opportunity to evaluate how the older woman seems to be coping with her physical and emotional trauma. All possible efforts should be made to have counseling with someone cognizant of special issues and needs of older victims. The forensic examiner can ask the police to come by her residence, while she is at home, to check for security measures. Simple suggestions and reassurances by a caring officer may go far in alleviating at least a few of the older woman's fears. Police may be able to suggest certain safety precautions she can implement or request of her landlord if she lives in a rental unit. Encourage the woman to call the police department if she has concerns about safety and security. Reassure her that she is not "putting people out." Older members of the community are often reluctant to call police with concerns, as they worry that they are "bothering" the officers (Carrasco, 1997).

Each victim, no matter what their age, brings to this tragedy all of their resources and strengths, as well as their vulnerabilities. Being cognizant of special needs or concerns at different times in a person's life can facilitate the delivery of compassionate care. The aggregation of insults resulting from sexual trauma at any point along life's continuum is a public health issue with broad implications for recognition, intervention, and ultimately prevention.

GAY AND LESBIAN VICTIMS OF SEXUAL TRAUMA

The Gay Male Victim of a Gay Male Assailant

In a 6-year longitudinal study of 930 gay males in England and Wales, Hickson et al

(1994) made a strong case in their appeal to victim service agencies and the community at large, that recognition be given to the subject of rape of gay men by other gay men. Because their findings and interpretations differ from the conventional literature and mainstream theory, their study warrants discussion. Of the 930 men who responded, 28% reported a history of prior sexual assault at some time in their lives. In reviewing first-time assaults, the authors acknowledged over-representation of incidents from childhood and adolescent events. However, in almost one-third of the sexual assaults, some sort of consensual sexual activity had already taken place between the victim and assailant, identifying them as homosexually active males (adult or young adult ages) (Hickson et al, 1994). Their final sample size consisted of 212, after exclusion of those who did not elaborate, did not remember, had no actual physical contact, or had female assailants (4%). In this study, strangers were the assailants 16% of the time, while 11% of assaults involved multiple assailants.

Hickson et al challenge the widespread assumptions that:

- Male rape is usually committed by heterosexual men as an expression of power, control, and domination.
- Sexual assault on males, as on females, is not sexually motivated; that the act is sexualized is a means to an end, not the motivation. On the contrary, Hickson et al maintain that the assaults *were* sexually motivated; the assailant disregarded the victim and forced a particular sexual act (usually anal intercourse), in three-fourths of the cases.

Hickson et al suggest that defining characteristics of sexual assault are indeed dependent upon the study population. Gay men may place less faith in the criminal justice system. Therefore, if assault arises out of a previously consensual relationship, there is even less likelihood of reporting. This enigma is strikingly similar to the early disposition of spousal rape

cases in heterosexual relationships. Fears surrounding the acknowledgment of the exploitation and assault of gay men by gay men revolve around perceived damage to the gay community at large.

A particularly poignant discussion in this study is the significance of forced sodomy for a gay male. Anal intercourse is full of interpersonal meaning for gay men. The epidemic of HIV and AIDS has propelled this sexual act to foremost consideration. The decision to engage in consensual anal intercourse is, for a gay male, a significant decision of great import. To have the choice obviated can cause even more trauma to the gay male victim when compounded with these issues than in the past.

Lesbian Rape

The lesbian who most often reports a sexual assault to authorities is the victim of a heterosexual male. She may be a random victim, or one who has been targeted by the assailant because of her sexual orientation. When a lesbian is raped by another lesbian, stigmas surrounding the crime, the victim, and the assailant, make it very difficult for her to disclose and report. Inherent and preconceived fear and distrust of police make gay and lesbian victims even more unlikely to come forward. Some lesbian victims may feel that in reporting a case of lesbian/lesbian rape, they are being disloyal to the lesbian community at large, and perhaps to a close circle of friends in particular. Many of these assaults occur in relationships already plagued by domestic violence. The assaults include violent and coerced sexual acts, without the consent of the victim. Most of the time, the assailant does not view her own actions as rape. The victim not only has to deal with her violation, but a concomitant vulnerability within the very community where she previously felt safe. She may keep the assault a secret, fearing rejection and disbelief, both by her peers, and the criminal justice system. Because lesbians in general are less likely than gay men to seek out casual sex partners, the lesbian is more often raped by a girlfriend (Lowers, 1995). Stories do prevail within the lesbian community of gang-rape and date-rape sexual assaults by other women. The lesbian victim of rape by a woman may experience great difficulty in finding counselors and advocates with special training on the dynamics of this type of rape. Lesbian therapists in the community may be experienced only with heterosexual rape.

If this victim does report, she should be provided with equal services, including a medical examination, contact with a rape crisis advocate, and referrals for follow-up. Efforts should be made to ensure that the victim has adequate support throughout all phases of the criminal justice proceedings. Although responding victim advocates may not have particular training or experience with this special situation, they are trained to be skilled listeners and maintain a nonjudgmental approach. They are also highly motivated to help the victim find additional resources for follow up.

The examiner should strive to make the medical–legal examination as safe a setting as possible for any victim. This becomes paramount for the gay and lesbian person. The painful crisis of a sexual assault can be worsened by insensitive words or gestures. These individuals may need subtle assurance that you are a *safe* person before they can feel comfortable disclosing intricate details of the assault during the interview. Simple signals, such as asking if they would like to have a "partner" (rather than spouse or boyfriend) notified, can cue them to your own respect for their dignity.

Collaboration between members of the gay and lesbian community who are knowledgeable about these issues, and those of us in the forensic community who provide medical services to victims, is clearly invaluable. Regardless of the gender, sexual orientation, or cultural influences of any victim, the forensic examiner should strive to understand as much as possible about related issues, dynamics, and physical injuries in order to enhance the delivery of compassionate and competent medical care and forensic evaluation.

SPECIAL CIRCUMSTANCES: FEMALE GENITAL MUTILATION

Political turmoil and economic problems in many countries of Africa, the Middle East, and portions of Malaysia and Indonesia, have brought a large flux of both students and refugees from these areas to North America and Europe. Many of the women who emigrate from these parts of the world have undergone female genital mutilation, commonly referred to as female circumcision. Worldwide, 80 to 110 million women are estimated to have been subjected to this practice. Female genital mutilation is the medically unnecessary modification of the female genitalia. It is usually performed when a girl is approximately 7 years of age or younger, and is typically done as part of a ritual introduction into adult life, albeit one that can result in long- and short-term severe medical complications. Anesthesia is not usually employed, except for the 12% of these procedures performed by physicians, usually for upper-class African and Middle Eastern families. For the remaining 88% of female children, the surgical "tools" are generally razors, knives, scissors, glass, and even the teeth of the individual performing the ritual.

The two categories of female genital mutilation are *clitoridectomy* and *infibulation.* Toubia (1994) has further classified each category into two types, based on the degree of excision performed. Based on this format, a *type 1 clitoridectomy* is the removal of all or part of the clitoris, and is also called a *sunna excision.* A *type 2 clitoridectomy* is the removal of the clitoris and all or part of the labia minora. A total infibulation is a *type 4, or pharaonic circumcision,* in which the clitoris, labia minora, and most of the labia majora are removed. Afterward, the vulva is approximated together with silk, catgut, or thorns. A small posterior opening is created, often using a matchstick, to allow drainage of urine and menstrual blood. A *type 3, or modified infibulation,* removes the anterior two-thirds of the labia majora and leaves a larger posterior opening.

Following these procedures, the child's legs are bound from hips to ankles for up to 40 days to allow scar formation (*JAMA,* Council Report, 1995). Women who have been tightly infibulated may need to have the scar opened (deinfibulation) prior to first coitus or first vaginal exam. Sometimes the scar is opened by the husband. Not surprising, these women may experience anxiety, frigidity, and fear of pain with coitus. Medical complications may be extensive and life-threatening and include sepsis, tetanus, hemorrhage, severe dysuria, and dysmenorrhea, to name but a few. Obstetric care requires skilled intervention to open the scar during delivery and to avoid severe complications including obstruction of the baby's head, perineal tears, fetal demise, and necrosis of the septum between the vagina and the bladder (Toubia, 1994).

The American Medical Association has joined the World Health Organization and World Medical Organization in opposition to all forms of medically unnecessary surgical modification of the female genitalia. The Foundation for Women's Health Research and Development (FORWARD) of the United Kingdom considers genital mutilation another form of child abuse and a human rights violation, similar to the now obsolete, but once traditional practices as the Victorian chastity belt and Chinese foot binding.

Practitioners of Western medicine are now learning to care for the unique medical and obstetric needs of the woman who has undergone female genital mutilation. Those of us in the field of sexual assault should be cognizant of this cultural practice in which the woman has a very unique gynecologic presentation. Some insight can prevent acute embarrassment for both the examiner and the victim if this woman does present as the victim of a rape.

A few considerations to bear in mind include:

- The woman comes from a culture in which privacy and modesty are paramount; careful draping is important.
- The woman may very well need permission from her husband or another male family member in order to be examined. He may insist on being present and will invariably insist that a female perform the exam.
- The culture may promote tolerance of pain, however severe, despite encouragement by the clinician to acknowledge it or treat it.
- The pelvic exam will probably be painful. This will depend on the extent of the mutilation, but pain should be anticipated. Comfort measures, like using a pediatric speculum and warming it first, can be helpful.

According to Toubia (1994), many infibulated women experience chronic anxiety and depression as a result of their preoccupation with genital problems. Further disfigurement may ensue from the formation of keloids and dermoid cysts. The woman may have a fear of infertility and suffer chronic dysmenorrhea. Reports of the sexual and psychological effects of genital mutilation is often *anecdotal.* It may be erroneous and speculative for health care providers to make gross assumptions about female genital mutilation and its sequelae, as these issues may be subtle, merged with denial, and reflect an acquiescence to cultural norms.

It is reasonable to assume that because of the genital modification, rape of the woman who has undergone genital mutilation will result in greater genital injury than what is seen in other sexual assault victims. Clearly, compassionate intervention is necessary. If, and when, these women come forward, it is necessary to be especially knowledgeable about their situation and sensitive to their special needs.

SUMMARY

It has been recorded from Biblical times on, how lives of victims have been devastated by sexual assault. Sexual assault encompasses victims of all ages and assumes myriad forms, from incest, extrafamilial abuse, or stranger assault in childhood, to acquaintance or stranger rape of the adolescent, adult, or the elderly. The summation of consequences are described by rape trauma syndrome and posttraumatic stress disorder. Untreated issues can manifest as somatic complaints related to almost any body system, and have been especially identified in those women suffering chronic pelvic pain and gastrointestinal problems.

Special populations of victims present with special needs, such as the elderly victim, the pregnant victim, or adolescent victims of either sex. While we surmise that only a fraction of all rapes are reported, we know it is even less so for male victims. As demographic factors change, so do the variety of clinical presentations and emotional circumstances that the clinician is faced with, exemplified by the woman or girl who has undergone female genital mutilation. Finally, the loneliness and isolation encountered by gay and lesbian victims of rape challenges all of us to broaden our perspectives and open our hearts as well as our minds to ensure that our theories, practice, and models are designed to include all victims.

REFERENCES

Abarbanel, G. & Richman, G. (1990). The rape victim. In: Parad, J. & Barrad, L.G. (Eds.). *Crisis Intervention Book 2: The Practitioner's Sourcebook for Brief Therapy*. Milwaukee: Family Service America.

Bolton, F., Morris, L. & MacEachron, A. (1989). Building a new life: The paths to recovery. *Chap. 4*. In: *Males at Risk: The Other Side of Child Sexual Abuse*. Newbury Park, CA: Sage Publications, pp. 94–133.

Burgess, A.W. & Burgess, L.M. (1997). Anxiety disorders. In: Burgess, A. (Ed.) *Psychiatric Nursing*. Stamford, CT: Appleton & Lange, pp. 201–221.

Burgess, A.W. & Hartman, C. (1997). Victims of sexual assault. In: Burgess, A. (Ed.) *Psychiatric Nursing*. Stamford, CT: Appleton & Lange, pp. 425–437.

Burgess, A.W., Hartman, C., McCausland, M. & Powers, P. (1984). Response patterns in children and adolescents exploited through sex rings and pornography. *Am J Psychiatry, 141*:656–662.

Burgess, A.W. & Holmstrom, L. (1974). Rape trauma syndrome. *Am J Psychiatry, 131*(9): 981–986.

Burgess, A.W. & Holmstrom, L. (1976). Coping behavior of the rape victim. *Am J Psychiatry, 133*(4):413–417.

Burgess, A.W. & Holmstrom, L. (1986). *Rape: Crisis and Recovery*. West Newton, MA: Awab, Inc.

Carrasco, Lt. B. (1997). San Luis Obispo Police Department, San Luis Obispo, CA., Personal communication.

Cartwright, P. & Moore, R. (1989). The elderly victim of rape. *Southern Med J, 82*(8):988–989.

Cartwright, P. & the Sexual Assault Study Group. (1987). Factors that correlate with injury sustained by survivors of sexual assault. *Obstet & Gynecol, 70*(1):44–46.

Collings, S. (1995). The long-term effects of contact and noncontact forms of child sexual abuse in a sample of university men. *Child Abuse & Neglect, 19*(1):1–6.

Council Report. (1995). Female genital mutilation. *JAMA, 274*(21): 1714–1716.

Crowley, S. (1995) San Luis Obispo, CA.

Deisher, R. & Bidwell, R. (1987). Sexual abuse of male adolescents. *Sem Adolesc Med, 3*(1): 47–54.

Drossman, D., Leserman, J., Nachman, G., et al. (1990). Sexual and physical abuse in women with functional or organic gastrointestinal disorders. *Ann Int Med, 113*(11):828–833.

Edgerton, J. (Ed). (1994). *American Psychiatric Glossary, 7th ed.* Washington, DC: American Psychiatric Press Inc.

Finkelhor, D. (1980). Risk factors in the sexual victimization of children. *Child Abuse & Neglect, 4*:265–273.

Finkelhor, D. & Russel, D. (1984). Cited in Gonsiorek, J., Bera, W. & Letourneau, D. (1994). Male victims of sexual abuse. In: *Male Victims of*

Sexual Abuse: A Trilogy of Intervention Strategies. Newbury Park, CA: Sage Publications.

Gonsiorek, J., Bera, W. & Letourneau, D. (1994). *Male Victims of Sexual Abuse: A Trilogy of Intervention Strategies.* Newbury Park, CA: Sage Publications.

Greenfeld, L. (1997). Executive summary: An analysis of data on rape and sexual assault. *Sex Offenses and Offenders* (NCJ-163392). Bureau of Justice. U.S. Department of Justice. Washington, DC.

Greenfeld, L. (1997, February). An analysis of data on rape and sexual assault. *Sex Offenses and Offenders* (NCJ-163392). Bureau of Justice Statistics. U.S. Department of Justice. Washington, DC.

Groth, N. & Burgess, A.W. (1980). Male rape: Offender and victims. *Am J Psychiatry, 137:* 806–810.

Haskett, M., Marziano, B. & Dover, E. (1996). Absence of males in maltreatment research: A survey of recent literature. *Child Abuse & Neglect, 20*(12):1175–1182.

Hicks, D. & Moon, D. (1987). Sexual assault of the older woman. In: *California Medical Protocol for Examination of Sexual Assault Victims: Informational Guide.* Sacramento, CA: Office of Criminal Justice Planning.

Hickson, F., Davies, P., Hunt, A., et al. (1994). Gay men as victims of nonconsensual sex. *Arch Sex Behav 23*(3): 281–294.

Kaufman, A. (1987). Rape of men in the community. In: *California Medical Protocol for Examination of Sexual Assault Victims: Informational Guide.* Sacramento, CA: Office of Criminal Justice Planning.

Kilpatrick, D., Edmunds, C. & Seymour, A. (1992, April). *Rape in America: A Report to the Nation.* The National Women's Study Crime Victim's Research and Treatment Center Charleston, SC and Arlington, VA: National Victim Center.

Kinzl, J. & Mangweth, B. (1996). Sexual dysfunction in males: Significance of adverse childhood experiences. *Child Abuse & Neglect, 20*(8): 759–766.

Lauber, A. & Souma, M. (1982). Use of toluidine blue for documentation of traumatic intercourse. *Obstet & Gynecol, 60*(5): 644–648.

Lowers, J. (1997, September/October). Rape: When the assailant is one of our own. *Deneuve.*

McCauley, J., Kern, D., Kolodner, K., et al. (1997). Clinical characteristics of women with a history of childhood abuse: Unhealed wounds. *JAMA, 277*(17):1362–1368.

McFarlane, J., Parker, B., Soeken, K. & Bullock, L. (1992). Assessing for abuse during pregnancy: Severity and frequency of injuries and associated entry into prenatal care. *JAMA, 267*(23): 3176–3178.

McCauley, J., Guzinski, G., Welch, R., Gorman, R. & Osmers, F. (1987). Toluidine blue in the corroboration of rape in the adult victim. *Amer J Emerg Med 5*(2):105–108.

Mullen, P., Romans-Clarkson, S., Walton, V. & Herbison, G.P. (1988). Impact of sexual and physical abuse on women's mental health. *Lancet,* 841–844.

Post, T., Stiglmayer, A., Lane, C., et al. (1993, January 4). A pattern of rape: War crimes in Bosnia. *Newsweek,* pp. 32–37.

Ramin, S., Satin, A., Stone, I. & Wendel, G. (1992). Sexual assault in postmenopausal women. *Obstet & Gynecol, 80*(5):860–864.

Reiter, R., Shakerin, L., Gambone, J. & Milburn, A. (1991). Correlation between sexual abuse and somatization in women with somatic and nonsomatic chronic pelvic pain. *Am J Obstet Gynecol, 165*(1):104–109.

Satin, A., Hemsell, D., Stone, I., Theriot, S. & Wendel, G. (1991). Sexual assault in pregnancy. *Obstet & Gynecol, 77*(5):710–714.

Slaughter, L., Brown, C., Crowley, S. & Peck, R. (1997). Patterns of genital injury in female sexual assault victims. *Am J Obstet Gynecol, 176*(3):609–616.

Tintinalli, J. & Hoelzer, M. (1985). Clinical findings and legal resolution in sexual assault. *Ann Emerg Med, 14*(5):113–119.

Toubia, N. (1994). Female circumcision as a public health issue. *N Engl J Med, 331*(11): 712–716.

SUGGESTED READINGS

Abarbanel, G. (1979). The sexual assault patient. In: R. Green (Ed.). *Human Sexuality: A Health Practitioner's Text.* Baltimore: Williams & Wilkins Co.

ACOG Technical Bulletin, No. 124. (1989, January) The battered woman. Washington, DC: American College of Obstetricians and Gynecologists.

Baker, C., Gilson, G., Vill, M. & Curet, L. (1993). Female circumcision: Obstetric issues. *Am J Obstet Gynecol, 169*:1616–1618.

Berenson, A., Stiglich, N., Wilkinson, G. & Anderson, G. (1991). Drug abuse and other risk factors for physical abuse in pregnancy among white non-Hispanic, black, and Hispanic women. *Am J Obstet Gynecol, 164*(6):[Part I. 1491–99.]

Brownworth, V. (1997, August 9). The other side of sexual assault: When a woman is raped by a woman. *Baytimes.*

Burgess, A. & Hartman, C. (1990, November 9). Violence against women and children. Paper presented at the National Institutes of Mental Health Conference on State of the Art and Science of Psychiatric Nursing: Evaluating Our Progress and Guiding Our Future. Bethesda, MD.

Chez, R. & Jones, R. (1995). The battered woman. *Am J Obstet Gynecol, 173*(3):677–679.

Committee on Adolescence. (1983). Rape and the adolescent. *Pediatrics, 72*(5):738–740.

Committee on Adolescence. (1994). Sexual assault and the adolescent. *Pediatrics, 94*(5):761–765.

Fitzcraft, A. (1995). From public health to personal health: Violence against women across the life span. *Ann Int Med, 123*(10):800–802.

Frazier, P. & Borgida, E. (1985, September). Rape trauma syndrome evidence in court. *Am Psychologist,* 984–992.

Gabbar, I.A. (1985). Medical protocol for delivery of infibulated women in Sudan. *Am J Nurs, 85:*687.

Hibbard, R., Ingersoll, G. & Orr, D. (1990). Behavioral risk, emotional risk, and child abuse among adolescents in a nonclinical setting. *Pediatrics, 86*(6):896–901.

Kaufman, A., Divasto, P., Jackson, R., Voorhees, D. & Christy, J. (1980). Male rape victims: Non-institutionalized assault. *Am J Psychiatry, 137:* 221–223.

Lightfoot-Klein, H. & Shaw, E. (1991). Special needs of ritually circumcised women patients. *J Obstet Gynecol Neonatal Nurs, 20:*102–107.

Morrow, J., Yeager, C. & Lewis, D. (1997). Encopresis and sexual abuse in a sample of boys in residential treatment. *Child Abuse & Neglect, 21*(1):11–18.

Rapkin, A., Kames, L. & Darke, L., et al. (1990). History of physical and sexual abuse in women with chronic pelvic pain. *Obstet & Gynecol, 76*(1):92–96.

Schroeder, P. (1994, September). Female genital mutilation—a form of child abuse. *N Engl J Med, 331*(11):739–740.

Wells, R., McCann, J., Adams, J., Voris, J. & Ensign, J. (1991). Emotional, behavioral, and physical symptoms reported by parents of sexually abused, nonabused, and allegedly abused prepubescent females. *Child Abuse & Neglect, 19*(2):155–163.

3 | Genital Anatomy

A thorough medical examination of both male and female sexual assault victims includes inspection and evaluation of the entire anogenital area. This chapter includes a description of the major anatomic landmarks of genital anatomy of both males and females, followed by changes which occur in the female as a result of menopause. The human sexual response, during consensual sexual activity of men, women, and postmenopausal women, is provided as a theoretical framework for later discussions (in Chapter 4) of the patterns of injury in female sexual assault victims. Finally, some of the salient features of consensual anal intercourse, gleaned from interviews of homosexual men, is provided with the hope that improved understanding of this often "taboo" subject will shed some insight and spur further study into the mechanisms and patterns of injury for victims of sodomy.

FEMALE GENITAL ANATOMY

Sexual assault examiners utilize the numbers on the face of a clock as a uniform method of designating either the location of structures, or particular physical findings within a structure. In this methodology, the 12 o'clock position is always superior (up). The 6 o'clock position is always inferior (down). If the patient is examined in more than one position, it is important to *note* the position used (Fig. 3–1).

The Vulva

The *vulva,* also known as *pudendum,* includes all structures that lie within the boundaries of the mons pubis (anteriorly), to the anus (posteriorly), and within the two genitocrural folds laterally. These structures include the labia majora, labia minora, clitoris, hymen, vestibule, urethral meatus, Bartholin's and Skene's glands, and the vestibulovaginal bulbs (Fig. 3–2). The size, color, hair distribution, and shape of individual structures may vary. Normal pubic hair distribution in the female

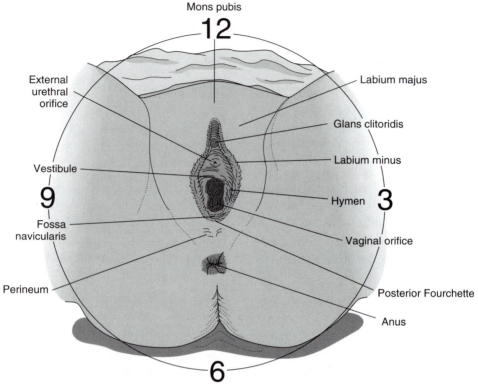

Figure 3–1. O'clock face: external female genitalia. *(Adapted from Krantz, K. [1994]. Anatomy of the female reproductive system. In: DeCherney, A. & Pernoll, M. [Eds.].* Current Obstetric and Gynecologic Diagnosis and Treatment, *8th ed. Stamford, CT: Appleton & Lange, pp. 5–53, Adapted with permission.)*

is an inverted triangle, with the base centered over the mons pubis. In 25% of females, the pubic hair may extend up along the linea alba.

Perineum

The perineum is the part of the genitalia located between the anus and the vulva in the female, and the scrotum and the anus in the male. The pelvic floor lies under the external surface of the perineum, and support is provided by the pelvic and urogenital diaphragms. The levator ani muscles and coccygeus muscles posteriorly, along with their fascial coverings, comprise the pelvic diaphragm. The levator ani form a broad muscular sling. The perineum

supports and surrounds the distal portions of the urogenital and gastrointestinal tracts of the body. The muscle fibers of the pelvic diaphragm insert around the vagina and rectum, forming sphincters. They also insert into a raphe in the midline, between the vagina and rectum, and into a midline raphe below the rectum. Fibers insert into the coccyx as well. The urogenital diaphragm is a triangular-shaped area external to the pelvic diaphragm. The corners of the triangle are formed by the ischial tuberosities and the symphysis pubis. They contain the deep transverse perineal muscles, the constrictor muscle of the urethra, and internal and external fascial coverings. The nerve supply of the perineum is primarily from the

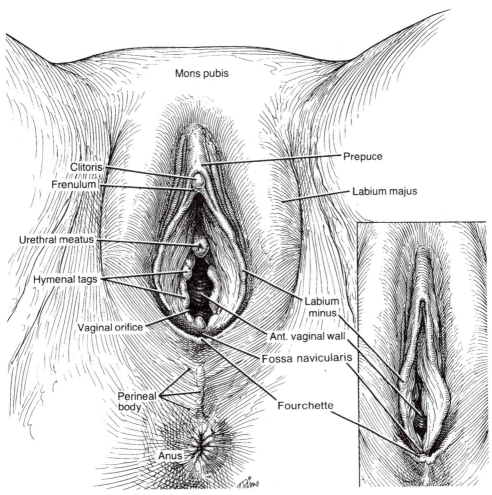

Figure 3–2. External organs of reproduction of women. The lower anterior vaginal wall is visible through the labia minora. In nulliparous women, the vaginal orifice is not so readily visible (*inset*) because of the close apposition of the labia minora. *(From Cunningham, F. G., MacDonald, P., Gant, N., et al. [Eds.]. [1997]. Anatomy of the reproductive tract. In: Williams Obstetrics, 20th ed. Stamford, CT: Appleton & Lange, p. 38, reprinted with permission.)*

pudendal nerve and its branches. The internal pudendal artery and its branches, including the inferior rectal and posterior labial artery provide the major blood supply (Fig. 3–3).

The perineal body, located between the vagina and anus, is the point of convergence of the bulbocavernosus muscles, the superficial transverse perineal muscles, and the external anal sphincter. The perineal body is re-

inforced by the central tendon of the perineum. These structures provide much of the support for the perineum.

Labia Majora

[Singular: labium majus] The labia majora are two rounded mounds or folds of skin-covered adipose tissue. They form the lateral boundaries

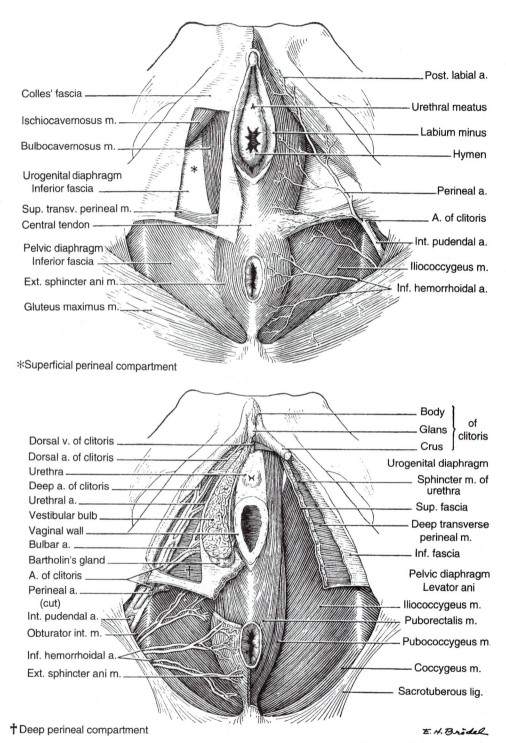

Colles' fascia

Ischiocavernosus m.

Bulbocavernosus m.

Urogenital diaphragm
Inferior fascia

Sup. transv. perineal m.

Central tendon

Pelvic diaphragm
Inferior fascia

Ext. sphincter ani m.

Gluteus maximus m.

Post. labial a.

Urethral meatus

Labium minus

Hymen

Perineal a.

A. of clitoris

Int. pudendal a.

Iliococcygeus m.

Inf. hemorrhoidal a.

*Superficial perineal compartment

Dorsal v. of clitoris

Dorsal a. of clitoris

Urethra

Deep a. of clitoris

Urethral a.

Vestibular bulb

Vaginal wall

Bulbar a.

Bartholin's gland

A. of clitoris

Perineal a.
(cut)

Int. pudendal a.

Obturator int. m.

Inf. hemorrhoidal a.

Ext. sphincter ani m.

Body
Glans   of
Crus   clitoris

Urogenital diaphragm

Sphincter m. of
urethra

Sup. fascia

Deep transverse
perineal m.

Inf. fascia

Pelvic diaphragm
Levator ani

Iliococcygeus m.

Puborectalis m.

Pubococcygeus m.

Coccygeus m.

Sacrotuberous lig.

† Deep perineal compartment

E. H. Bridel

Figure 3–3. The perineum. The more superficial components are illustrated above and the deeper structures below. (m. = muscle; a. = artery; lig. = ligament; Int. = internal; Ext. = external; Inf. = inferior.) *(From Cunningham, F. G., MacDonald, P., Gant, N., et al. [Eds.]. [1997]. Anatomy of the reproductive tract. In: Williams Obstetrics, 20th ed. Stamford, CT: Appleton & Lange, p. 44, reprinted with permission.)*

of the vulva and extend downward and back from the mons pubis to the perineum, joining medially to form the posterior commissure. Embryonically, these structures are homologues of the male scrotum (Krantz, 1994). Their appearance varies, depending on the amount of fat and other characteristics, such as age, height, weight, race, parity, and pelvic architecture. (While less prominent with repeated children, they decrease more in old age.) The labia are covered by hair on the medial surfaces, and have a generous supply of sebaceous glands, which are more numerous on the medial surface. The inner surface is moist, similar to mucous membrane in the nulliparous woman; it is more skin-like, but still hairless, in the multiparous female. Subcutaneous fat provides the bulk of the volume of each labium, and there is a layer of dense connective tissue. The lateral surface of each labium is adjacent to the medial aspect of the thigh. The medial surfaces of the two labia may directly appose each other, especially in the nulliparous female. Protrusion of the labia minora through the opening is also a normal anatomic variant. An extensive venous plexus and lymphatic system supplies the area, with communication to the dorsal vein of the clitoris, veins of the labia minora, perineal veins, and the inferior hemorrhoidal plexus. Rupture of these veins during childbirth or trauma results in a hematoma on the labia. The arterial supply comes from the internal and external pudendal artery. The round ligaments of the uterus terminate at the upper borders. The average size of each labium is 7 to 9 cm in length, 2 to 3 cm in width, and 1 to 1.5 cm in thickness (Cunningham, 1997). They taper posteriorly in the midline, toward the anus. The apocrine (scent) glands of the labia majora are the same as those found in the breast, axillae, and the perianal area.

Labia Minora

[Singular: labium minus] In the adult female, the labia minora form the lateral boundaries of the vulva. These two flat, reddish tissue folds of connective tissue extend from the base of the clitoris to the posterior fourchette. Each labium minus is 4 to 5 cm in length, 0.5 to 1 cm in thickness, and 2 to 3 cm in width. The width varies; in some women the labia minora project through the labia majora. On initial gross inspection, without separation of the labia majora, they may not be immediately visible in the nulliparous woman. *Anteriorly,* the two labium converge, dividing into two lamellae. As shown in Fig. 3–2, the lower lamella fuses to form the frenulum of the clitoris; the upper pair merges to form the prepuce of the clitoris. *Posteriorly,* each labium becomes smaller, and in multiparous women, they may appear to be contiguous or blend with the labia majora. In children, the labia minora appear prominent, as the labia majora do not become well developed until puberty; they tend to atrophy in the postmenopausal woman (Kaufman & Faro, 1994).

A deep cleft forms on each side, between the labium majus and the labium minus. The labia minora are pigmented and moist, with little or no adipose tissue. The surface contains multiple corrugations. The lateral aspects are covered by skin; the medial surfaces partially so. The labia are covered by stratified squamous epithelium, with numerous projections of papillae. The skin on the medial surface of each labium changes into epithelium similar to mucous membrane. Morphologists have debated whether this medial surface is comprised of skin or mucous membrane (Kaufman & Faro, 1994). The epithelium here is less cornified. Hart's line, named after a 19th century Scottish gynecologist, is a line of demarcation between the skin and mucous membrane. The extensions of this "line" run along the base of the inner aspect of each labium minus. Both lines converge medially at the fossa navicularis; this separates the skin of the posterior fourchette from the mucous membrane of the hymen (Kaufman & Faro, 1994). There are no hair follicles in the labia minora, but there are many sebaceous glands and sparse sweat glands. The labia contain highly vascular connective tissue and some smooth muscle fibers, making it an erectile structure. Anastomoses from the superficial perineal artery perfuse the area. Innervation comes from fibers that supply the labia majora and from branches of the pudendal nerve. The many nerve endings make the labia extremely sensitive. The labia minora are homologous to the male penile urethra.

Clitoris

The clitoris is an erectile organ located superiorly in the vulva. It consists of a *glans,* a *body* (corpus), and *two crura* (Fig. 3–3). On the ventral surface of the clitoris is the fused junction of the labia minora, the *frenulum clitoridis* (Figs. 3–2 and 3–4).

The glans is covered by mucous membrane and made up of spindle-shaped cells. It is approximately 0.5 cm in diameter, covered by stratified squamous epithelium, and richly supplied by nerve endings. The erectile tissue that comprises the glans has many large and small venous channels, surrounded by smooth muscle tissue, arranged into the corpora cavernosa. The prepuce is a hood-like integument.

The body is formed by the fusion of the two corpora cavernosa, and is approximately 2 cm in length. The walls of the corpora cavernosa contain smooth muscle fibers. The body extends from the pubic arch to the glans. The two crura are long and narrow. They separate at the inferior border of the pubic arch, and follow the inferior border of the inferior rami of the pubic bones. The crura are attached to the inferior rami and lie under the ischiocavernosus muscles. When these contract, they trap blood within the corpora cavernosa and result in erection of the clitoris.

The blood supply to the clitoris is from the dorsal artery, a branch of the internal pudendal artery. Innervation of the clitoris is from the terminal branch of the pudendal nerve.

Pacinian corpuscles are located in the clitoris and are sensitive to deep or heavy pressure. These corpuscles are an example of a proprioceptor, a receptor that responds to stimuli originating within the body itself, especially pressure, position, or stretch. Pacinian corpuscles are found throughout the glans and body of the clitoris, with highest concentration in the glans.

Vestibule

The vestibule is the almond-shaped area of the vulva. The lateral boundaries of the vestibule are the labia minora; the superior and posterior boundaries are the clitoris and the posterior fourchette. Embryonically, the vestibule is the mature female structure of the urogenital sinus, and is analogous to the male penile urethra. Figure 3–4 shows the six openings of the vestibule: the urethra, vagina, Bartholin gland ducts (2), and paraurethral, or Skene's duct openings (2). The skin covering the vestibule is nonkeratinized, nonpigmented squamous epithelium. The stroma supporting this epithelium contains many mucous secreting glands. These glands drain via ducts, often lined with transitional epithelium. The orifices of these ducts often appear as pits on the surface of the vestibule. The external urethral meatus is slit-like, and generally located 2 to 3 cm posterior to the clitoris, within the vestibule. The edge is everted and may have two or three overhanging lips, occasionally making it difficult to visualize the urethra itself. The urethra generally measures between 3 to 5.5 cm in length, from the neck of the bladder to the external urethra. The upper portion of the urethra is separated by connective tissue from the anterior vaginal wall. The lower half of the urethra is closely adherent to the musculature of the vaginal wall. Skene's ducts may open on the posterior wall of the urethra, just inside the meatus, although they are usually located on either side of the urethra. If an infection occurs in the ducts or glands, the duct outlet becomes obstructed. Abscesses may form on the anterior

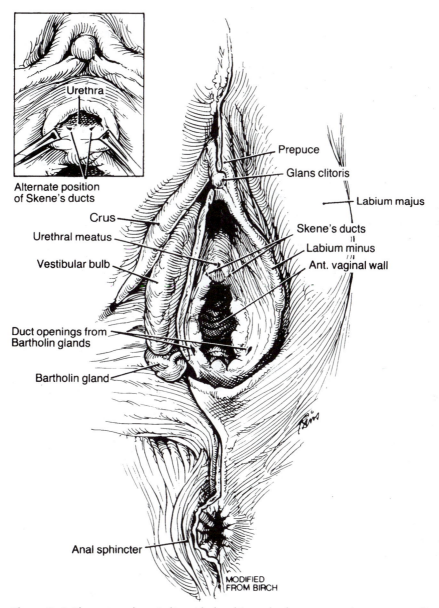

Figure 3–4. The external genitalia with the skin and subcutaneous tissue removed from the right side. *(From Cunningham, F. G., MacDonald, P., Gant, N., et al. [Eds.]. [1997]. Anatomy of the reproductive tract. In: Williams Obstetrics, 20th ed. Stamford, CT: Appleton & Lange, p. 39, reprinted with permission.)*

vaginal wall and rupture into the urethra. These may subsequently enlarge into diverticula (Kaufman & Faro, 1994).

The main ducts of the Bartholin's glands lie on each side of the hymen at about the 5 and 7 o'clock positions. These glands are homologous to Cowper's glands in the male, are lobulated, and are about the size of small peas. The ducts are about 1.5 to 2 cm long and lined by stratified transitional epithelium. The orifices of the Bartholin's glands are not normally visible unless an abnormality exists, such as erythema, exudate, or a mass in or upon the orifice of the gland. Beneath the floor of the vestibule, within the bulbocavernosus muscles, are two oval masses of erectile tissue. These are the bulbi vestibuli. Each Bartholin's gland lies in the base of a vestibular bulb. The rich blood supply to the vestibule comes from branches of the internal and external pudendal arteries. A large plexus of veins drains the vulva. Innervation of the vestibule is primarily from the sacral plexus, through the perineal nerve.

Hymen

The hymen is the thin membrane comprised of connective tissue that overlies the vaginal opening into the vestibule. Both inner and outer surfaces are lined with stratified squamous epithelium. Connective tissue papillae are found on the inside vaginal surface of the hymen and on the free edge. The hymen does not contain glandular or muscular elements and does not have a rich nerve supply. There are no nerve cells or fibers on the free edge. In the newborn, the hymen is vascular and redundant. In pregnancy, the epithelium thickens and the tissue becomes rich in glycogen. The epithelium thins and focal cornification may develop after menopause. In the adult, the hymenal tissue varies in thickness and elasticity.

There are various, normal hymenal shapes:

- Cribriform—multiple openings in the hymen.

- Annular—circumferential in shape; the tissue extends completely around, or encircles, the entire vaginal orifice.
- Septate—the membrane is bisected by a band of hymenal tissue, creating two or more orifices.
- Crescentic—the membrane attaches superiorly, at or near the 11 and 1 o'clock position. No hymenal tissue is present between these two points of attachment.
- Imperforate—occurs rarely (0.014–0.024%; Kaufman & Faro, 1994); the hymenal membrane completely occludes the vaginal opening.

If the hymenal membrane is transected, the torn edges, after healing, will persist as two sections on either side of the laceration. They are separated by a narrow sulcus, and the two edges do not reunite (Cunningham, 1997).

Myrtiform caruncles are tissue remnants formed from cicatrized nodules of various sizes. These result when the hymen has been torn during delivery.

Vagina

The vagina is a tubular, musculomembranous canal or sheath. It extends inward from the vulva to the uterine cervix. It lies behind the urinary bladder and in front of the rectum (Fig. 3–5). The vagina pierces the urogenital diaphragm at its lower end, and is surrounded by the two bulbocavernosus muscles and bodies, which act as a sphincter. In addition to functioning as an excretory canal for uterine secretions and menstrual blood, it is the lower part of the birth canal and the organ of copulation. The uterine cervix enters the anterior vaginal wall. This makes the anterior wall shorter (6–8 cm) than the posterior wall (7–10 cm). These two walls are lax and approximate each other with only a very slight, or potential space between. As shown in Fig. 3–6, the lateral walls of the vagina are more rigid; thus a cross-section of the nondistended vagina has an "H" shape. The va-

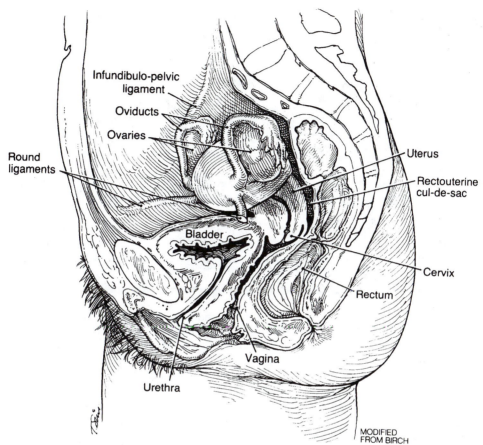

Figure 3–5. Sagittal section of the pelvis of an adult woman showing relations of pelvic viscera. *(From Cunningham, F. G., MacDonald, P., Gant, N., et al. [Eds.]. [1997]. Anatomy of the reproductive tract. In: Williams Obstetrics, 20th ed. Stamford, CT: Appleton & Lange, p. 41, reprinted with permission.)*

gina is capable of marked distention, obvious during childbirth. Four fornices are formed in the upper end of the vaginal vault by the protrusion of the cervix. These are the anterior, posterior, and two lateral fornices. The entrance of the cervix on the anterior wall also makes the posterior fornix deeper. Internal pelvic organs can be palpated through the walls of the four fornices. Three layers comprise the vaginal walls. The outer, fibrous layer is derived from the pelvic fascia. The middle layer is muscular and the inner layer is mucosal. The mucous membrane of the vagina is noncornified, stratified squamous epithelium. Estrogen stimulation at puberty causes the mucosa to thicken as squamous cells mature (Fig. 3–7). For the remainder of the reproductive years, the vaginal mucosa responds to the hormones of the ovarian cycle. Longitudinal ridges project into the lumen of the vagina and transverse ridges, or rugae, extend outward, almost at right angles to these. The rugae form a corrugated surface that is not present before menarche. The surface becomes gradually smoother after repeated childbirth and postmenopause. The uterine, pudendal, and middle hemorrhoidal arteries provide an extensive blood supply.

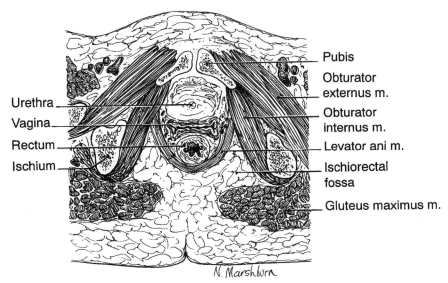

Figure 3–6. Cross-section of the pelvis of an adult woman; the H-shaped lumen of the vagina is apparent (m. = muscle.) (N. Marshburn after E. H. Brödel). *(From Cunningham, F. G., MacDonald, P., Gant, N., et al. [Eds.]. [1997]. Anatomy of the reproductive tract. In: Williams Obstetrics, 20th ed. Stamford, CT: Appleton & Lange, p. 42, reprinted with permission.)*

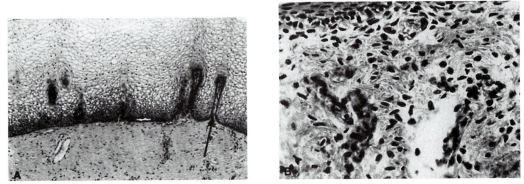

Figure 3–7. A. Photomicrograph of the vagina of an adult woman that is characterized by noncornified, thick, stratified squamous epithelium; note that epithelial appendages are not present. Arrow is pointed to a papilla. **B.** Photomicrograph of typical thin vaginal epithelium of a prepubertal girl. *(From Cunningham, F. G., MacDonald, P., Gant, N., et al. [Eds.]. [1997]. Anatomy of the reproductive tract. In: Williams Obstetrics, 20th ed. Stamford, CT: Appleton & Lange, p. 42, reprinted with permission.)*

These form a plexus around the vagina, sometimes referred to as the azygos vaginal arteries. Venous drainage also occurs through a series of plexuses. The vaginal mucosa is normally continuous and unbroken, with a clear, colorless, odorless secretion. Before menopause, the mucosa is pink; it becomes paler in the postmenopausal state. The pH of adult vaginal secretions is normally between 4 and 5.

Cervix

The cervix is the cylindrical part of the uterus that protrudes 1 to 3 cm into the vagina. In the nulliparous woman the diameter of the cervix is 2 to 3 cm. After vaginal delivery, it may increase to 3 to 5 cm. The shape is usually round and symmetrical. The cervix is composed primarily of collagenous tissue, in addition to elastic tissue, blood vessels, and smooth muscle fibers. The external cervical os lies at the level of the symphysis pubis. The os may have a variety of shapes or appearances. In the nulliparous female, it is small, regular, and oval. This becomes a transverse slit after childbirth, which divides the os into anterior and posterior lips. A deep laceration during delivery may heal in an irregular, nodular, or stellate pattern, with some portions overlapping (Figs. 3–8 and 3–9). The cervical mucosa is normally a uniform pink; the color varies from female to female. The epithelium

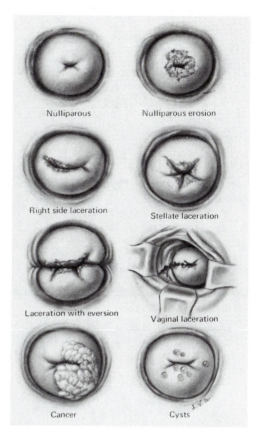

Figure 3–9. The uterine cervix: normal and pathologic appearance. *(From Kawada, C. [1994]. Gynecologic history, examination, and diagnostic procedures. In: DeCherney, A. & Pernoll, M. [Eds.]. Current Obstetric and Gynecologic Diagnosis and Treatment. Norwalk, CT: Appleton & Lange, pp. 613–632, adapted with permission.)*

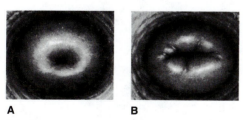

A   **B**

Figure 3–8. A. Cervical external os of a nonparous woman. **B.** Cervical external os of a parous woman. *(From Cunningham, F. G., MacDonald, P., Gant, N., et al. [Eds.]. [1997]. Anatomy of the reproductive tract. In: Williams Obstetrics, 20th ed. Stamford, CT: Appleton & Lange, p. 47, reprinted with permission.)*

is smooth, with colorless secretions. The ectocervix (the part that protrudes into the vagina) is lined with squamous epithelium. The endocervical canal is lined with a single layer of high columnar epithelium resting on a thin basement membrane.

In some women, the columnar epithelium of the endocervical canal extends out onto the surface of the ectocervix. Blood vessels are more easily seen through columnar epithelium than squamous epithelium. This results in an area of redness, or circumoral erythema, around the os. This is a normal finding when the redness is circumscribed, symmetric, and with regular borders. During pregnancy, the ectocervix appears cyanotic. The cervical glands extend into the connective tissue and produce a thick tenacious secretion. If these glandular ducts become plugged, they form retention, or Nabothian cysts, a common and normal finding. The squamocolumnar junction is the line of demarcation between the squamous epithelium of the vaginal part of the cervix and the columnar epithelium of the endocervical canal.

Uterus

The uterus is a pear-shaped, muscular organ located between the base of the bladder and the rectum. It is connected to the uterine tubes above and the vagina below. The two main sections of the uterus are the broad, rounded portion, or *fundus,* and the smaller *cervix* below. These two sections are connected by the narrow *isthmus* portion. The size of the uterus is variable (Figs. 3–10 and 3–11). Before puberty, the uterus is 2.5 to 3.5 cm long, and the body of the uterus is only one-half as long as the cervix. In the nulliparous, adult female, the uterus is 6 to 8 cm long × 3.5 to 5 cm at the widest diameter, and 2 to 2.5 cm in its anteroposterior diameter. The cervix and the body of the uterus are equal in length. Characteristic changes occur during pregnancy, depending on the stage of gestation. The overall size is greater in all dimensions after a woman has been pregnant. The uterus of the multiparous female is 9 to 10 cm long. The cervix comprises slightly greater than one-third of the total length of the organ (Cunningham, 1997).

The position and axis of the uterus also varies. Usually, it forms a sharp angle with the vagina, bending at the isthmus so that the

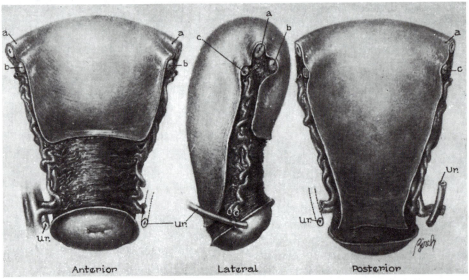

Figure 3–10. Anterior, right lateral, and posterior views of the uterus of an adult woman. (a = oviduct; b = round ligament; c = ovarian ligament; Ur. = ureter.) *(From Cunningham, F. G., MacDonald, P., Gant, N., et al. [Eds.]. [1997]. Anatomy of the reproductive tract. In: Williams Obstetrics, 20th ed. Stamford, CT: Appleton & Lange, p. 45, reprinted with permission.)*

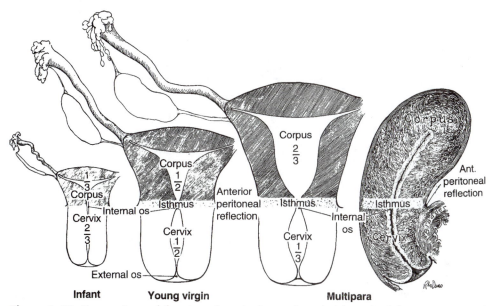

Figure 3–11. Comparison of the size of uteri of prepubertal girls and adult nonparous and parous women by frontal and sagittal sections. *(From Cunningham, F. G., MacDonald, P., Gant, N., et al. [Eds.]. [1997]. Anatomy of the reproductive tract. In: Williams Obstetrics, 20th ed. Stamford, CT: Appleton & Lange, p. 45, reprinted with permission.)*

cervix faces back and the body of the uterus is horizontal in the pelvis. The positional variations of of the uterus are pictured in Fig. 3–12, and are as follows:

- *Midposition*—the cervix points along the vaginal axis; the body lies in the same plane as the vagina.
- *Anteversion*—the cervix points posteriorly; the body is rotated anterior to the vaginal plane.
- *Anteflexion*—the cervix points along the vaginal axis; the body is bent forward.
- *Retroversion*—the cervix points anterior; the body is rotated posterior to the vaginal plane.
- *Retroflexion*—the cervix points along the vaginal axis; the body is bent backward.

The uterine blood supply comes from the uterine and ovarian arteries. The veins form a plexus and drainage is via the uterine vein to the hypogastric vein. Several chains of lymph nodes provide lymphatic drainage. Innervation is from the three divisions of the pelvic autonomic system: the superior, middle, and inferior hypogastric plexuses.

Fossa Navicularis

[Latin, fossa: ditch, trench; navicularis: boat, ship owner] The fossa navicularis is a concavity located on the lower portion of the vestibule. It lies inferior to the vaginal opening and extends to the posterior fourchette (see Fig. 3–2).

Posterior Fourchette

[French, fourchette: fork] The posterior fourchette is the junction of the two labia minora which extend inferiorly as low tissue ridges and fuse in the midline (see Fig. 3–2). This area is referred to as the posterior commissure in the prepubertal child because the labia minora are incompletely developed until puberty.

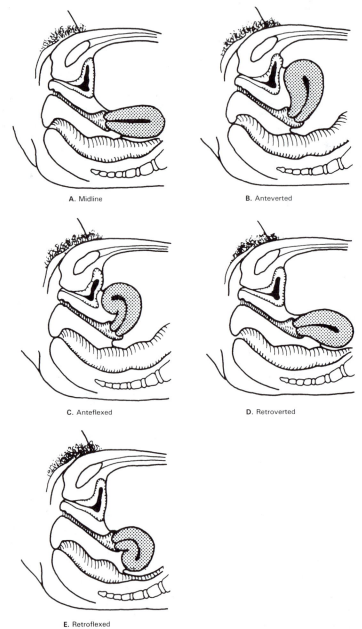

Figure 3–12. Uterine positions. *(From Lichtman, R. & Papera, S. [1990]. Gynecology Well Woman Care. Norwalk, CT: Appleton & Lange, p. 37, reprinted with permission.)*

Anus

The anus lies in the fold between the buttocks and is the lower opening, or orifice, at the end of the digestive tract. The anal canal is 3.8 cm long in the adult, and begins where the lower end of the ampulla of the rectum narrows; the canal passes down and backward, ending at the anus. The anal opening is surrounded and kept closed by two sphincter muscles. The internal anal sphincter is comprised of a smooth muscular ring of circular fibers and is situated at the upper end of the anal canal. It is maximally contracted when the rectal ampulla is at rest or empty, or relaxed to accommodate a distending fecal mass. The external anal sphincter is a spindle-shaped (fusiform) ring of striated muscle. It surrounds the anus and attaches posteriorly to the coccyx and anteriorly to the central tendon of the perineum. The external sphincter is divided into subcutaneous, superficial, and deep portions (Fig. 3–13). The *anal verge* is the tissue that overlies the subcutaneous portion of the external anal sphincter at the area of

the anal orifice. It extends to the anal skin (APSAC, 1995).

The anterior wall of the anal canal is shorter than the posterior wall; it is separated anteriorly from the lower vagina in the female (and the penile urethra in the male) by the perineal body. The mucous membrane lining of the lower portion of the canal is pale pink and semitranslucent, so that underlying rectal blood vessels can be visualized through it. The upper half of the canal lining (15 mm) is plum colored, due to blood in the subjacent internal rectal venous plexus (Williams & Warwick, 1980). The epithelium of the anal canal varies. The epithelium below the pectinate line tends to be stratified squamous epithelium, while that above is stratified columnar epithelium. The mucous membrane of the anal canal is arranged into six to ten vertical folds, called the anal columns. While these are well marked in the child, they are not always as obvious in the adult. A terminal artery and a vein are contained within each column. Primary internal hemorrhoids are caused by enlargements of

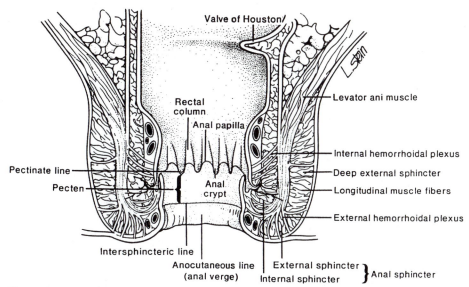

Figure 3–13. Anal anatomy. *(From Giardino, A.P., Finkel, M., Giardino, E. R., Seidl, T. & Ludwig, S. [1992]. A Practical Guide to the Evaluation of Sexual Abuse in the Prepubertal Child. Newbury Park, CA: Sage Publications, p. 50, reprinted with permission.)*

these veins. The lower ends of these columns are joined by small, crescentic valve-like folds of mucous membrane, the *anal valves.* An *anal sinus* lies above each valve.

The *pectinate line,* or dentate line, is a saw-toothed line of demarcation between the lower part of the anal valves and the pectin, a smooth zone of stratified squamous epithelium extending to the anal verge (APSAC, 1995). The pectinate line lies opposite the middle of the internal anal sphincter. It is commonly considered to be the site at which the anal membrane is situated in the early fetus, and represents the junction of the endodermal part of the canal (from the cloaca) and the ecto-dermal part (from the anal pit) (Williams & Warwick, 1980).

During a digital examination of the rec-tum, the muscles of the external anal sphinc-ter will normally close snugly around the ex-aminer's finger. Sphincter tightness may be exhibited when the patient is anxious, or when the tissues are inflamed. Laxity may be noted in some neurologic diseases. The anal tone may also be relaxed when feces are present in the rectum, and can be evaluated with gentle lateral traction on the buttocks. Redundant folds, at 12 and 6 o'clock, are common find-ings. Severe constipation may cause super-ficial anal fissures.

Some of the normative data obtained from a study sample of children screened for nonabuse included a variety of soft tissue anal findings, including:

- perianal *erythema*
- *increased pigmentation* (especially in darker-skinned children)
- *venous engorgement,* seen in 73% of chil-dren 4 minutes in the knee-chest position
- *anal dilation,* when stool was present in the rectal ampulla
- *midline* (6 and 12 o'clock) *smooth areas* at the anal verge
- *anal tags,* or folds (mostly anterior) (Mc-Cann et al, 1989)

Rectum

The rectum is approximately 12 cm in length and is the portion of the large intestine that is continuous with the descending sigmoid colon, proximal to and ending in the anal canal. Above the anorectal junction, the rectum bal-loons out and turns posteriorly into the hollow of the coccyx and sacrum to follow the sacro-coccygeal curve. The wall of the rectum con-tains three transverse semilunar folds, referred to as the valves of Houston. One of these is sit-uated proximally on the right. A second ex-tends inward from the left side, and the third and largest fold projects caudally. Each fold is about 12 mm in width. When the intestine is empty, the folds overlap. In the female, the uterine cervix can usually be felt through the anterior rectal wall. In the male, the prostate gland is palpable anteriorly as a rounded, heart-shaped structure about 2.5 cm in length.

MALE ANATOMY

A review of male genital anatomy is essential to the complete examination of the adolescent and adult male victim of sexual assault. As with the female, it is important to recognize normal variations in anatomy, and discern other manifestations which might be due to aging, disease processes, or trauma.

The Penis

The three parts of the penis are the root, body, and glans. The root is attached via ligaments to the front and sides of the pubic arch. The body is composed of three cylindrical masses of erectile tissue. The top two are the corpora cavernosa and lie parallel to each other. The lower cylindrical mass is the corpus spongio-sum, through which the urethra passes. The corpus spongiosum also forms the glans pe-nis, the thickening at the top of the penis (Figs. 3–14 and 3–15). The foreskin, or pre-

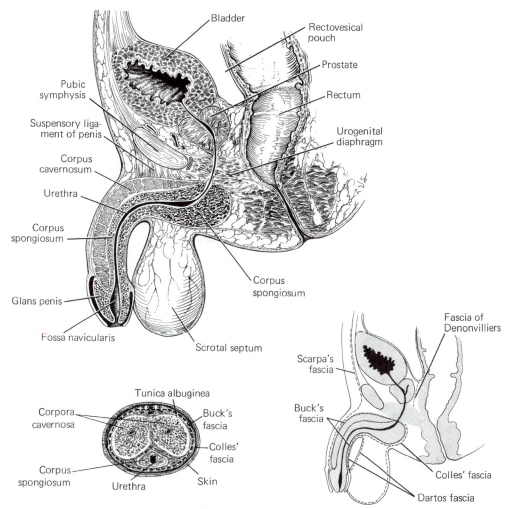

Figure 3–14. Top: Relations of the bladder, prostate, seminal vesicles, penis, urethra, and scrotal contents. **Lower left:** Transverse section through the penis. The paired upper structures are the corpora cavernosa. The single lower body surrounding the urethra is the corpus spongiosum. **Lower right:** Fascial planes of the lower genitourinary tract. (After Wesson.) *(From Tanagho, E. A. & J. W. McAninch [1995]. Smith's General Urology, 14th ed. Stamford, CT: Appleton & Lange, p. 10, reprinted with permission.)*

puce, covers the glans. The frenulum (Latin for bridle), a restraining portion or structure, is a thin fold of tissue that connects the foreskin to the glans dorsally. The corona is the ridge that delineates the glans from the body of the penis. Penile size does not necessarily correlate with a man's height or muscular development. The length of the penis in the flaccid state is usually 8.5 to 10.5 cm[1] (average, 9.5 cm). In the erect state, penises that mea-

---

[1] 1 inch = 2.54 centimeters.

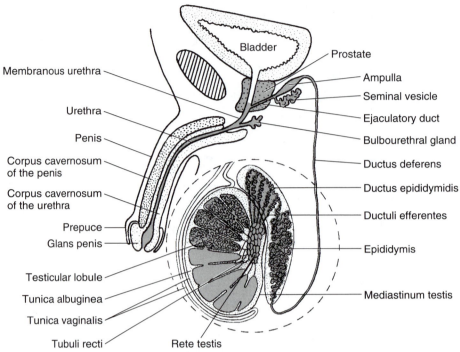

Figure 3–15. Diagram of the male genital system. The testis and the epididymis are in different scales from the other parts of the reproductive system. Observe the communication between the testicular lobules. *(From Junqueira, L. C., Carneiro, J. & Kelly, R. [1999]. Basic Histology, 7th ed. Stamford, CT: Appleton & Lange, reprinted with permission.)*

sured 7.5 to 9.0 cm in the flaccid state, added another 7.5 to 8 cm at full erection. Those penises that were 10 to 11.5 cm in the flaccid state increased by 7 to 7.5 cm in the fully erect state. The greatest change in penile size from the flaccid to the erect state occurs where the flaccid size is 7.5 cm (Masters & Johnson, 1966). The diameter of the penis at the glans is approximately 3.5 cm.

Prostate

The prostate gland surrounds the neck of the bladder and the urethra. It is composed of glandular elements, and its ducts empty into the prostate portion of the urethra, producing the majority of the seminal fluid (Figs. 3–14 and 3–15).

Scrotum

The scrotal pouches contain the testicles and accessory organs. Each scrotal sac contains a testis, epididymis, and lower spermatic cord. The scrotum is divided on its surface into two portions by a ridge that progresses to the undersurface of the penis and posteriorly along the midline, as the midline ridge, or midline raphe. The left side of the scrotum usually hangs lower than the right because of the longer length of the left spermatic cord. The skin and dartos tunic make up the two layers. The skin is thin, brown, corrugated, and contains many sebaceous follicles and scattered hairs (Figs. 3–14 and 3–16). The dartos tunic has unstriated, smooth muscle fibers and projects into the internal septum, which divides the scrotum into

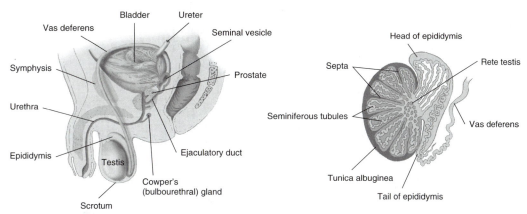

Figure 3–16. Left: Male reproductive system. **Right:** Duct system of the testis. *(From Ganong, W. (1997).* Review of Medical Physiology, *18th ed. Stamford, CT: Appleton & Lange, p. 398, reprinted with permission.)*

two compartments, one for each testicle. The scrotum is highly vascular and contains no fat.

Epididymis

[Greek, plural: epididymes] Each epididymis is a long, tightly coiled duct that carries sperm from the seminiferous tubules of the testes to the vas deferens. They attach the spermatic cord to the posterior portion of the testis on each side. Stretched end to end, they are 20 feet long and lie on the posterior part of each testis (Figs. 3–15 and 3–16).

Vas Deferens

The vas deferens are excretory ducts of the testes, extensions of the epididymis. They ascend from the scrotum and join the seminal vesicle to form the ejaculatory duct. The vas deferens are enclosed by fibrous connective tissue, with blood vessels, nerves, and lymphatics, and pass through the inguinal canal as part of the spermatic cord (Figs. 3–15 and 3–16).

The Testes

[Singular: testis] Each testis is one of a pair of male gonads that produce semen. In the adult, the testis is suspended in the scrotum by the spermatic cord. Early in fetal life, the testes are located in the abdomen; they descend before birth into the scrotum. Each testis is a lateral, oval-shaped body, 4 cm long × 2.5 cm wide, weighing about 12 g. The convoluted epididymis lies on the posterior border. Each testis consists of several hundred conical lobules containing coiled seminiferous tubules, each 75 mm in length. Sperm develop in the walls of the seminiferous tubules. Both ends of each loop of the seminiferous tubules drain into a ductal network in the head of the epididymis. As shown in Fig. 3–16, sperm then pass through the tail of the epididymis and enter the vas deferens, ejaculatory ducts, and the urethra in the body of the prostate at the time of ejaculation (Ganong, 1997). The blood supply to the testes is from the two internal spermatic arteries, arising from the aorta. The testicular veins form the pampiniform plexuses and constitute the greater part of the spermatic cords. Innervation is from the spermatic plexuses, derived from the celiac plexus of the autonomic nervous system.

Sperm

The term sperm is short for spermatozoa. A single spermatozoa is a spermatozoon, and is the mature male germ cell. It develops in the seminiferous tubules and looks like a tadpole, about 50 μm, or $1/_{500}$ inch long, with a head (containing the nucleus), a neck, and a tail. The tail permits propulsion, which may ultimately culminate in impregnation of an ovum, supplied by the female, and result in fertilization (Fig. 3–17).

POSTMENOPAUSAL CHANGES IN ANATOMY

Estrogen functions as the major growth factor of the female reproductive tract. As the level of production of this hormone diminishes during the menopausal years, changes occur in both the anatomy and the pelvic organ. Terminology related to the physiologic phases of aging that the woman experiences are defined by the *Comité des Nomenclatures de la Fédération Internationale de Gynécologie et d'Obstétrique:*

- Climacteric—phase during which a woman passes from the reproductive to the non-reproductive stage. *Climacteric symptoms* may present at this time; if more serious, they are referred to as *climacteric complaints.*
- Premenopause—part of the climacteric phase prior to occurrence of menopause; menstrual cycle likely irregular, and other climacteric symptoms or complaints may be present.
- Menopause—final menstruation; occurs during the climacteric phase.
- Postmenopause—the phase of life after the menopause. Variation occurs in usage of this term, referring at times to the remainder of a woman's life, or only to the period during which climacteric symptoms persist (Smith & Judd, 1994).

During and following menopause, both skin and mucosal surfaces of the vulva become thinner. As a result, these areas may be easily traumatized. The vulva thins and flat-

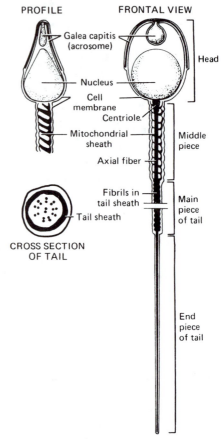

Figure 3–17. Human spermatozoan. *(From Ganong, W. [1997]. Review of Medical Physiology, 18th ed. Stamford, CT: Appleton & Lange, p. 400, reprinted with permission.)*

tens due to the reduced thickness of the keratin and epithelial layers. The eccrine and apocrine glands become attenuated and the sebaceous glands produce less secretions. Hair is more sparse over the labia majora and mons pubis. There is a decreased growth rate of the epidermis, and decreased collagen content and thickness. Wound healing may be slower, and local immune responses impaired.

The earliest signs of estrogen loss occur in the vaginal mucosa; this can precede changes to the vulva by months, or even years. Many postmenopausal women will have no subjective complaints of symptoms, but may notice vaginal spotting after slight trauma, from either a break in the vaginal mucosa or a urethral caruncle (benign tumor).

Ovaries

As the female grows older, the ovaries become more corrugated. The external surface may become markedly convoluted. The oviducts and ovaries decrease in size, making them difficult to palpate during a pelvic examination. The ovaries of some postmenopausal women may secrete estrogens in dwindling amounts for several years. Another source of endogenous estrogen for some women is the peripheral conversion of androstenedione and other precursors.

Labia Majora and Labia Minora

The labia majora tend to atrophy and frequently become lax and wrinkled due to a loss of subcutaneous fat. The labia minora become more prominent as the labia majora tend to atrophy. However, the labia minora also shrink, both in thickness and length. The labia minora may atrophy to the point of disappearance, but this is usually due to an associated disease process, eg, lichen sclerosus (Kaufman & Faro, 1994). Labial adhesions may develop due to the fragility of the mucosal edges of the labia minora.

Vagina

Most postmenopausal women at some point encounter various degrees of atrophic changes in the vaginal epithelium. As the vaginal rugae flatten, the interior of the vagina becomes smoother and more tubular. Vaginal atrophy follows a naturally occurring course that results when the amount of estrogen available to the vagina falls below a certain physiologic level. Some women may have visible thinning of the vaginal mucosa even before the first missed period. Other women continue to produce enough exogenous estrogens for years, and are able to maintain a normal mature vaginal state, or experience only minimal atrophy (Kaufman & Faro, 1994).

As the estrogen supply decreases, the vaginal epithelial cells undergo less maturation. A cytologic smear shows increased shedding of cells from the deeper intermediate and parabasal cell layers. The amount of glycogen present decreases and the pH of the vagina increases. This change in pH acts to discourage the growth of favorable lactobacilli, which may result in an invasion of opportunistic bacteria, pruritis, and discharge. Eventually, the vaginal mucosa, after months to years, thins to only a few cell layers in thickness. Some portions of the epithelium may become denuded, forming patches of granulation tissue; this results in an acute inflammatory process with superinfection. Subepithelial capillaries shine through the thinner epithelium, producing areas of diffuse or patchy redness. Some of these surface capillaries rupture easily on exposure, causing irregular petechiae, or even a brownish discharge. Spotty bleeding can occur with intercourse, digital penetration, douching, or during a speculum exam. Vaginal dryness can also contribute to painful intercourse. This leads to a vicious cycle where pain on coitus reduces the frequency of intercourse, which can lead to further atrophy from disuse. Denuded areas of epithelium can agglutinate. Stenosis may occur from the overall shrinkage of the mucosa. This tends to occur first in the fornices. Pain with intercourse may be exacerbated by stretching of inelastic tissue that surrounds a more stenotic introitus, narrow, and shortened vaginal canal, or in women who have had overly snug repairs of episiotomies or vaginoplasties (Kaufman & Faro, 1994).

While vaginal atrophy is a normal process, it must be differentiated from atrophic vaginitis, which is the presence of vaginal atrophy plus other factors, such as bacterial infection. The differential diagnosis varies, depending on the criteria used by different clinicians for diagnosis. The cytologic and clinical findings in atrophic vaginitis are similar to those in trichomoniasis, namely ecchymoses, petechiae, red and thinning mucosa, mixed bacterial flora, and many polymorphonuclear leukocytes. The presence of trichomonads will differentiate. In atrophic vaginitis, the woman may complain of dysuria, external burning, pruritis, tenderness, and dyspareunia, often from painful areas of ulceration. There may also be a burning, watery discharge due to the bacterial effects on the atrophic vagina (Kaufman & Faro, 1994:368).

Bladder and Urethra

Many elderly women complain of frequency, urgency, and burning on urination. Both the bladder and urethra experience atrophic changes due to decreased estrogen supply to the epithelium of the bladder and urethra. Atrophic cystitis may be manifested by urgency, incontinence, and frequency, without pyuria or dysuria. There may be loss of urethral tone and pouting of the urethral meatus. The thin epithelium favors the formation of a urethral caruncle; this, in turn, can result in dysuria, meatal tenderness, and occasionally, hematuria (Masters & Johnson, 1970).

Other Organ Changes

The glans of the clitoris atrophies slightly and may retract beneath the prepuce. The epithelium of the hymen thins. A regression in breast size usually occurs, due to reduction in adipose and glandular tissue. In the uterus there is atrophy of both the endometrium and the myometrium, caused by cessation of hormone stimulation of the endometrium.

HUMAN SEXUAL RESPONSE

Basic to any discussion of the mechanism of injury in sexual assault is a clear discussion of the dynamics that constitute consensual sexual behavior. All of us who currently practice forensics in the area of sexual assault owe a great deal to the decades of clinical research by William Masters and Virginia Johnson. After establishing a clinic for the treatment of sexual dysfunction at the Washington School of Medicine in 1959, they launched into physiologic research on the human sexual response (Masters & Johnson, 1970).

In 1966, Masters and Johnson discussed with amazing clarity how the human body responds to sexual stimulation. The role of each anatomic part was described in detail, explaining the marvelous way in which the body orchestrates the entire process. Within the sexual experience, stimuli were characterized as *somatogenic* (relating to physical activity), or *psychogenic* in origin. Regardless of the source of the stimulus, the higher cortical centers are involved in the interpretation of the impulse. Located in the large nerve bundles, pacinian corpuscles have a role in the proprioceptor response to deep pressure and in relaying afferent impulses created by somatogenic stimuli (Masters & Johnson, 1966). The pacinian corpuscles are also found in the fingers, mesentery, and tendons. They are small, oval bodies formed of concentric layers of connective tissue. The axon of a nerve fiber runs through the soft core and splits up into fibrils (Stedman's, 1995). The proprioceptor response of these pacinian corpuscles occurs to stimuli originating within the body, eg, pressure, position, and stretch.

For both the male and female, there are two specific total body responses to elevated levels of sexual tension. These are increased muscle tension, or tonus (*myotonia*) and pooling of blood in both the superficial and deep tissues (*vasocongestion*). The sex flush is an example of superficial vasocongestion, while the transient increase in breast size is from deeper tissue engorgement. For both genders, the sexual cycle is comprised of four progressive phases: *excitement, plateau, orgasm,* and *resolution.*

Excitement Phase: Female Response

Both the increased myotonia and vasocongestion begin during this first phase in response to any physical or psychic stimuli. The first physical manifestation of response to sexual stimulation for the female is usually *lubrication,* which occurs early during the excitement phase. This is caused by vasocongestion of the numerous venous plexuses that surround and encircle the vagina, bulbus vestibuli, plexus pudendalis, plexus uterovaginalis, and possibly the plexus vesicalis and plexus rectalis externus. These veins become dilated during sexual stimulation. Within 10 to 30 seconds after the excitement phase begins, drops of mucoid-like material appear in the rugal folds of the vagina. Thus, this transudation process begins with a sweating type of phenomenon throughout the rugal folds, quickly providing complete lubrication with copious amounts of the slippery liquid (Masters & Johnson, 1970; Masters et al, 1994). This lubrication is essential during intercourse and episodes of prolonged coitus to prevent irritation to either partner. According to Masters and Johnson (1970), this ability of the female to achieve sufficient and complete vaginal lubrication is equivalent to the male's attainment of a satisfactory erection. The woman cannot wish or lubricate on demand; rather, the transudation occurs spontaneously when she has achieved that particular state of concentration on the sensual pleasure that arises from participation in the sexual experience.

Prior to the clinical studies of Masters and Johnson, was the notion that female lubrication was due to the secretions of the Bartholin glands. These glands do have a secretory response to sexual tension, but this occurs late in the excitement phase and early in the plateau phase. The amount of secretion is very small; in nulliparous women, it was rarely greater than a drop, and in multiparous women, only 2 to 3 drops. While this tiny amount is sufficient to moisten the introitus, it is inadequate to lubricate the entire vagina. The secretions from the Bartholin glands do appear to augment lubrication during periods of prolonged coitus, when the sexual tension level is kept at late excitement or early plateau levels of response. However, even during automanipulation, participants in the study showed no significant secretion by these glands (Masters & Johnson, 1966:42–43).

The obstetric history of the woman affects the response pattern of individual anatomic sites. Obstetric trauma may preclude the labia majora from closely approximating at the midline, and moreover, the degree to which they move outward and upward during the excitement phase. If the woman has labial varicosities, these become distended and produce a two- to threefold increase in the labial diameter. The labia become pendulous, but may still have some lateral movement away from the midline.

Excitement Phase: Male Response

In addition to generalized tension increase, the male response is characterized by the beginning of erection, scrotal thickening, and testicular elevation.

Plateau Phase: Female Response

During this second phase of the sexual response cycle, tension levels greatly increase. The outer third of the vaginal barrel responds to the deep vasocongestion with a localized response, so that the lumen narrows, forming the cuff-like *orgasmic platform.* The vagina continues to lengthen and expand, preparing a landing for support and containment of the male penis during coitus. In the nulliparous female, the distance from the posterior fourchette to the posterior fornix increases from 7 to 8 cm (unstimulated) to 9.5 to 10 cm (stimulated). The diameter at the transcervical width of the vagina increases from 2 cm (unstimulated) up to 5.75 to 6.25 cm (stimulated).

As demonstrated by normal childbirth, the vagina is capable of essentially unlimited distensibility.

The clitoris enlarges and retracts against the anterior border of the symphysis and withdraws beneath its prepuce, due to engorgement. Using colposcopy at 4 to 60× magnification in the clinical studies, the clitoral response was established. The clitoris was observed to engorge in a time frame that paralleled the venous engorgement of the labia minora (Masters & Johnson, 1966:48–49).

Plateau Phase: Male Response

During the plateau phase in the male, the penile erection increases in rigidity and the head of the penis increases somewhat as well. In some men, preejaculatory fluid may appear. The testes increase in size and pull closer to the body. About one-fourth of men will experience a sex flush. Sexual stimulation can be increased through voluntary contraction of the rectal sphincter. During this phase, and lasting until the resolution phase, there may be diminished visual and auditory acuity (Masters & Johnson, 1994).

Orgasmic Phase: Female Response

This phase of the sexual response cycle is marked by the extremely brief, albeit explosive release of the vasocongestion and muscle tension that has peaked in the previous two phases. During these few seconds of response, the vagina undergoes strong contractions at approximately 0.8-second intervals. Normally, there are from three to four, or as many as ten to twelve contractions with each orgasmic experience. After the first several contractions, the interval between the contractions lengthens and the intensity diminishes. From one female to another, there is variation in both the duration and degree of intensity during orgasm. There is also variance in duration and intensity from one orgasm to another.

Orgasmic Phase: Male Response

Semen collects in a pool at the base of the urethra, below the prostate. At this point, the man has a very clear premonition that ejaculation is imminent. This is known as ejaculatory inevitability, when the testes are fully elevated and drawn tightly against the body, pressing against the perineum. When the male has reached this level, there is no turning back (Masters and Johnson, 1994).

The male orgasm also incorporates powerful, rhythmic contractions of the penis, seminiferous tubules, prostate, and rectum. These contractions recur at similar intervals to the female, and culminate in ejaculation, which occurs shortly after contractions of the prostate begin. The quantity of the ejaculate is from 0.2 to 6 mL.

Resolution Phase: Female Response

This last phase is marked by a physiological return to the preexcitement status. The vasocongestion and myotonia disappear both generally and to the specific target organs in the pelvis. If orgasm was not achieved, there will be some residual sexual tension that needs to gradually dissipate. In addition to the changes noted in Table 3–1, the lumen of the vagina increases again, as the orgasmic platform dissipates. The rugal pattern returns to the folds. As the inner two-thirds of the vagina go back to the collapsed position, the anterior wall of the vagina, plus the cervix, descend first. This creates a tent-like effect in the upper vagina, at the transcervical diameter. The cervix thus becomes immersed in any remaining seminal pool. If the nulliparous woman does not change position from the supine, the portion of ejaculate remaining after penile withdrawal can remain for hours. However, many factors affect the quantity of ejaculate in the sperm pool. In the parous female, obstetric trauma causes ejaculate to escape after the orgasmic platform disappears. Changes in position of the female cause further fluid loss. If coitus continues after the male has

▶ **TABLE 3–1.** PHYSICAL CHANGES IN THE FEMALE DURING THE SEXUAL
RESPONSE CYCLE

Desire Phase	No specific physical changes
Excitement	Vaginal lubrication begins
	Inner two-thirds of the vagina expands
	Color of vaginal wall becomes darker
	Outer lips of vagina flatten and move back from the vaginal opening
	Inner lips of the vagina thicken
	Clitoris enlarges
	Cervix and uterus move upward
	Nipples become erect
	Breast size increases modestly
	Sex flush appears (late and variable)
	Heart rate and blood pressure increase
	General neuromuscular tension increases
Plateau	Vaginal lubrication continues, but may wax and wane
	Orgasmic platform forms at outer third of the vagina
	Cervix and uterus elevate further
	Inner two-thirds of vagina lengthens and expands further
	Clitoris retracts beneath the clitoral hood
	Lips of the vagina become more swollen and change color
	Sex flush intensifies and spreads more widely
	Further increase in breast size; areola enlarges
	Heart rate and blood pressure increase further
	Breathing may become more shallow and rapid
	Voluntary contraction of rectal sphincter used by some females as a stimulative technique
	Further increase in neuromuscular tension
	Visual and auditory acuity are diminished
Orgasm	Onset of powerful involuntary rhythmic contractions of orgasmic platform and uterus
	Sex flush, if present, reaches maximum color and spread
	Involuntary contractions of rectal sphincter
	Peak heart rates, blood pressure, and respiratory rates
	General loss of voluntary muscular control; may be cramp-like spasms of muscle groups in the face, hands, and feet
Resolution	Clitoris returns to normal position within 5–10 seconds after orgasm
	Orgasmic platform disappears
	Vaginal lips return to normal thickness, position, and color
	Vagina returns to resting size quickly; return to resting color may take as long as 10–15 minutes
	Uterus and cervix descend to their unstimulated positions
	Areola returns to normal size quickly; nipple erection disappears more slowly
	Rapid disappearance of sex flush
	Irregular neuromuscular tension may continue, as shown by involuntary twitches or contractions of isolated muscle groups
	Heart rate, respiratory rate, and blood pressure return to baseline (preexcitation) levels
	General sense of relaxation is usually prominent
	Visual and auditory acuity return to usual levels

From Masters, W., Johnson, V. & Kolodny, R. (1994). Heterosexuality. New York: Harper Collins, *reprinted with permission.*

ejaculated, the weight of the penis itself promotes leakage. Seminal fluid also escapes with each penile withdrawal during active stroking or thrusting. The vaginal barrel normally has an anatomic angle 10 to 45° lower than the horizontal plane. Although individual variations exist in both anatomy and physiology, the dipping down of this angle causes the cervix to lie lower than the vaginal outlet (at the area of the posterior fourchette). Thus, gravity assists in formation of the vaginal sperm pool. Women can return to another orgasm at any point in the human sexual response cycle. Specific changes that occur during each phase of the female sexual response are summarized in Table 3–1 and Fig. 3–18.

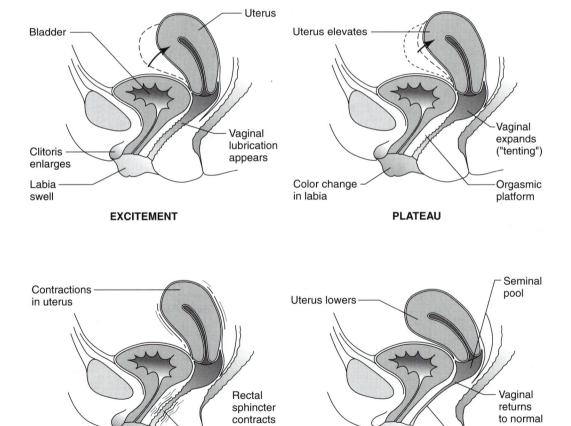

Figure 3–18. Internal changes in the female sexual response cycle. *(From Masters, W., Johnson, V. & Kolodny, R. [1994]. Heterosexuality. New York: Harper Collins, p. 59, reprinted with permission.)*

Resolution Phase: Male Response

During the resolution phase, there is rapid loss of the penile erection. The testes drop down to their normal position and decrease to normal size. The resolution period in the male generally includes a relative refractory period when the next ejaculation is not possible. This refractory period is extremely variable from male to male. In general, the refractory period is shorter in younger males. During this phase, there is a general sense of relaxation, and a return to normal visual and auditory acuity (Masters & Johnson, 1994).

HUMAN SEXUAL RESPONSE IN THE POSTMENOPAUSAL WOMAN

Masters and Johnson (1970) presented the findings of 61 menopausal and postmenopausal women (ages 41–78) who participated in their clinical studies. Their discussion was presented as clinical impressions, rather than biologic facts, but did represent an exhaustive review of the composite physiologic findings of these women within the human sexual response. Although a complete review is beyond the scope of this text, a general summary serves to put the previously discussed anatomic changes in perspective.

As the woman ages, the level of myotonia is generally less intense. Burning on urination after coitus is a common complaint of postmenopausal women. This phenomenon is similar to the honeymoon cystitis that occurs in younger women due to the mechanical irritation of the urethra and bladder caused by the thrusting penis. The vagina of the older woman provides less protection to these anterior structures, and irritation may occur more frequently if the woman does not lubricate well. In the Masters and Johnson study group, the response of the clitoris continued into the 70-year age bracket. In the postmenopausal woman, the clitoris continues to enlarge and

become engorged with blood during arousal. The labia majora, however, lose their ability to flatten, separate, and elevate in response to sexual tension. Thickening and expansion of the labia minora still occur; this was observed in 67% of the women in the 41- to 50-year-old group and 30% in the 51- to 60-year-old group, but not at all in the group of women past age 61 (Masters & Johnson, 1970; Masters & Johnson, 1994).

The previously noted changes that occur in the functional anatomy of the vagina, such as thinning and loss of elasticity of the vaginal lining, can result in painful intercourse for some women. On the whole, vaginal lubrication takes longer in the postmenopausal woman, and is of lesser quantity. The localized vasocongestion that produces the orgasmic platform is also notably decreased. The regularly recurring uterine contractions that occur during orgasm may be quite painful for some older women. Decreased intensity of the orgasms may also be due to neuromuscular factors. Overall decreased blood flow to the pelvic region affects both lubrication in the woman and changes in penile erections that are often problematic for older men. It is important to recognize however that the capacity for orgasm is not automatically diminished by the aging process, excluding other existent physiological problems. Indeed, many older women find they achieve orgasm more easily, feeling less burdened by issues and concerns they may have had when they were younger (Masters & Johnson, 1994).

Some women in the 50- to 70-year age range continued to effectively function in terms of sexual responsivity, without receiving supplemental hormone replacement. Two clear patterns were prevalent in these women. One type of woman typically ceased her menstrual flow in her late 40s or early 50s; she had decreased, but still clinically apparent, production of hormones for years afterward. These women had few, if any, menopausal symptoms. They reported high levels of strength and energy, and this was confirmed by peers. In their 60s, these women had vaginal smears that showed rates of cornification at 10 to 20%. Satisfactory sexual activity for this group of women continued unabated. Their vaginal walls retained some corrugation, and they produced adequate lubrication during sexual excitation. Their labia, clitoris, and mons area retained the configuration of their younger counterparts.

The second pattern that emerged was that of the older woman who enjoyed intercourse 1 to 2 times per week on a regular basis, over many years. There appears to be great physical and psychological value in continuing sexual exposure as a woman matures. This is evidenced by improved efficiency of the vaginal response to sexual stimulation. The findings in these women certainly suggest that the regularity of sexual experiences will help overcome the effects of hormone insufficiency in the female reproductive system (Masters & Johnson, 1970).

HUMAN SEXUAL RESPONSE: IMPLICATIONS

Study into the physiologic basis of the human sexual response provides us with a framework for some comprehension of the mechanism of genital injury in sexual assault. Comparisons of findings in female rape victims with women engaging in consensual intercourse have yielded valuable information on the types of injury that result from nonconsensual penile/vaginal penetration. The dynamics of human sexuality, as described by Masters and Johnson, are based on a thorough study of the physiologic processes that occur during each phase of the sequence. In addition to the significance of consent in the prevention of injury, the mechanism of injury in genital trauma is also influenced by anatomic design. The pelvic musculature tethers in the area of the perineal body, which lies subjacent to the posterior fourchette, the most frequent site of

injury in rape (Lauber & Souma, 1982; Slaughter, Brown, Crowley, and Peck, 1997).

When we study the dynamics of the human sexual response, we can draw inferences that help explain how genital injuries result from a forced sexual situation. The synchrony of the consensual experience is such that participants both respond to the physical changes that occur within their own bodies, *and* they accommodate to the desires, wishes, and movements of their partners. For example, the female tilts her pelvis at the beginning of coitus. This prevents the fully erect penis from entering her vagina at an angle that might cause pain or injury on insertion. Likewise, because the response to excitement in the female is lubrication, she is well prepared for coital activity. If certain actions or maneuvers do cause discomfort to one or the other, adjustments or adaptations can once again bring harmony. Herein is the difference between a consensual sexual experience and forced nonconsensual sexual acts, where the victim may simply comply with the demands of the rapist. Although the acts may be the same, the dynamics of the experience are vastly different.

ANAL INTERCOURSE

The incidence of anal trauma in cases of nonconsensual sodomy is about 50% for both male and female children (McCann, 1993) and adults (Slaughter, Brown, Crowley and Peck, 1997). In discussing child sexual assault, Heger and Emans (1992) note that most victims of anal trauma will not present with medical findings. However, penetrating blunt force trauma may cause abrasions, lacerations, edema, and bruises. Healing time varies, but is generally within weeks. Anal scarring is rare. If trauma has altered the anal tone, it will resolve with time (Heger & Emans, 1992:82).

The acute victim of sodomy who has no evidence of anal trauma is neither unusual nor inconsistent. Of the adult women rape victims in the study by Slaughter, Brown, Crowley and Peck (1997), who reported anal contact, 56% had anal findings. Moreover, even those victims who had a *normal* anal examination sustained some genital trauma. Those adult victims who experienced anal contact also had a higher mean number sites (3 vs. 2.4 sites) of injury to the anogenital area, when compared to those who experienced penile/vaginal penetration. Although 57% of the rape victims had nongenital trauma overall, it was sustained by *87%* of those who had experienced anal contact (Slaughter, Brown, Crowley and Peck, 1997). Preference of some rapists for anal sex has been related to increased violence and aggressive, even brutal acts inflicted on the victim (Hazelwood et al, 1989; Hazelwood & Warren, 1990). Forced sodomy may be an expression of a desire to humiliate and degrade the victim, especially if these acts occur prior to other sexual acts, such as fellatio or vaginal penetration.

With regard to the human sexual response, there is a paucity of information on consensual anal intercourse. Anecdotal information regarding salient features of anal sex was sought from "experts" in the practice, namely a group of gay men. This volunteer group strove to provide some insight into some of the involved dynamics. Of the five homosexual men interviewed, 40% had been previously married to a woman. Ages ranged from the mid-30s to 63 years old. The age at first anal intercourse varied; a few were as young as 11 to 12 years old (with a similar aged peer); the others were considerably older (late adolescence and older). The most critical factor expressed by these men was that *trust* is of paramount importance. This theme was woven throughout, in the information and stories they recounted, as well as during the interview process.

Techniques associated with anal intercourse are as personal and individualized as for penile/vaginal intercourse. Douching prior to anal sex is based purely on personal preference and practice. Some of the men felt that this was an essential preliminary component, for aesthetic reasons. Frequency of anal intercourse is an individual choice and as variable for homosexual men as for heterosexual individuals. Likewise, gay couples may face the same disparity in their sexual appetites as their heterosexual counterparts, with one partner desiring anal sex at a different frequency than the other. More important than a prescribed technique is to proceed *slowly* and *gently*. This was reiterated by all; it serves both to alleviate fear or apprehension with any partner and it helps avoid injury. Positions used for anal intercourse vary. All those interviewed felt that the least comfortable and enjoyable for the recipient was the prone (lying face down) position. Lubricants are important, especially to ease and promote comfortable penile insertion. Those men who had been the recipient of anal penetration by an uncircumcised partner felt that this was more highly pleasurable. One uncircumcised man reported that he has consistently been told by partners (male, and a former wife), that they received greater sensation from the increased friction provided by his foreskin.

Deep penetration that approaches the prostate is thought to produce a more intense orgasm, with more forceful ejaculation. All of the men reported that, at times, pain associated with anal intercourse was not uncommon. The experience of soreness after the event was also not unusual. The men felt that pain was far more likely to occur with a larger penile size. There was a greater likelihood of apprehension at the prospect of penetration by a male with a larger penis. Pain during anal intercourse most often occurs during the first contact, with insertion of the penis at the position of the anal verge. Once the rectum has been entered, the coital connection becomes more comfortable for the recipient. Despite precautions and comfort measures, there is occasional scanty bleeding, usually subsiding after a few hours, and is usually noticed on wiping. Soreness is more likely to persist longer.

All of these men interviewed shared intensely private thoughts, feelings, and events in the hope that it might in some way be useful to forensic examiners; in short to provide us with more insight, information, and a reality based description of what goes on during consensual anal sex. Armed with this type of information, we can begin to understand what then goes "awry" in a nonconsensual case of sodomy. We can begin to discern implications and sequelae in the absence of those consensual behaviors. While this should seem obvious, experience has shown us that there are many subtle factors that exist between two people in a relationship, whether that relationship is a mutually attracted couple or the real, albeit coerced relationship between the rapist and the victim.

These men also hoped to make a difference in the pain and suffering experienced by victims. That which is poorly understood is often poorly dealt with. It is often quite difficult to elicit from victims details related to sodomy. While victims will usually respond to the examiner's questions, they may be extremely uncomfortable, and thus unlikely to volunteer information. To some extent, this is because they have been subjected to a humiliating and violent physical and emotional assault. It may also be difficult for the nurse examiner to know which questions to ask. Understanding the dynamics of both consent and nonconsent situations can help us explain subsequent physical findings (or lack thereof) during a medical exam.

SUMMARY

In conclusion, the mastery and application of principles of functional anatomy provide a sound foundation for the complete anogenital examination of the victim of sexual assault. A solid background in this content area is essential to later proficiency in the recognition of the wide range of normal variations in anatomy, and the discernment of anatomic variants from benign gynecologic conditions and traumatic lesions.

The interplay of anatomic and physiologic factors and the concomitant changes that occur in response to sexual arousal have major implications for the examination of the rape victim. The examiner who incorporates this body of knowledge into clinical practice is a more competent examiner and is better able to meet the needs of a sexual assault victim. The examiner will also use this knowledge base for testifying in court.

Finally, the forensic examiner must be cognizant of the relevant changes that occur as we age, to better assess normal changes as well as trauma findings in the older victim of a sexual assault.

REFERENCES

APSAC. (1995). *Practice Guidelines: Descriptive Terminology in Child Sexual Abuse Medical Evaluations.* American Professional Society on the Abuse of Children, Chicago, Illinois.

Cunningham, F.G., MacDonald, P., Gant, N., et al. (Eds). (1997). Anatomy of the reproductive tract. In: *Williams Obstetrics,* 20th ed. Stamford, CT: Appleton & Lange, pp. 37–47.

DeCherney, A. & Pernoll, M. (Eds.) *Current Obstetrics and Gynecologic Diagnosis and Treatment*, 8th ed. Stamford, CT: Appleton & Lange.

Ganong, W. (1997). *Review of Medical Physiology,* 18th ed., Stamford, CT: Appleton & Lange.

Hazelwood, R. & Warren, J. (1990, February). The criminal behavior of the serial rapist. *FBI Law Enforcement Bulletin, 59.* Washington, DC.

Hazelwood, R. & Reboussin R. & Warren J. (1989). Serial rape: Correlates of increased aggression and the relationship of offender pleasure to victim resistance. *J Interpersonal Violence, 4*:65–78.

Heger, A. & Emans, J. (1992). *Evaluation of the Sexually Abused Child.* New York: Oxford University Press.

Kaufman, R. & Faro, S. (1994). *Benign Diseases of the Vulva and Vagina,* 4th ed. St. Louis: Mosby-Year Book, pp. 1–13.

Krantz, K. (1994). Anatomy of the female reproductive system. In: DeCherney, A. & Pernoll, M. (Eds.). *Current Obstetric and Gynecologic Diagnosis and Treatment,* 8th ed. Stamford, CT: Appleton & Lange, pp. 5–22.

Lauber, A. & Souma, M. (1982). Use of toluidine blue for documentation of traumatic intercourse. *Obstet & Gynecol, 60*(5):644–648.

Masters, W. & Johnson, V. (1966): *Human Sexual Response.* Boston: Little, Brown & Co.

Masters, W. & Johnson, V. (1970). *Human Sexual Inadequacy.* Boston: Little, Brown & Co.

Masters, W., Johnson, V. & Kolodny, R. (1994). *Heterosexuality.* New York: Harper Collins.

McCann, J., Voris, J., Simon, M. & Wells, R. (1989). Perianal findings in prepubertal children selected for nonabuse: A descriptive study. *Child Abuse & Neglect, 13*(2):179–193.

Smith, K. & Judd, H. (1994). *Menopause & Postmenopause.* In: DeCherney, A. & Pernoll, M. (Eds.) *Current Obstetric and Gynecologic Diagnosis and Treatment, 8th ed.* Stamford, CT: Appleton & Lange, pp. 1030–1050.

Slaughter, L., Brown, C., Crowley, S. & Peck, R. (1997). Pattern of genital injury in female sexual assault victims, *Am J Obstet Gynecol, 176*(3): 609–616.

Stedman's Medical Dictionary. (1995). 26th ed. Baltimore: Williams & Wilkins.

Williams, P., & Warwick, R. (Eds.). (1980). *Gray's Anatomy,* 36th ed. Edinburgh: Churchill Livingstone, p. 1358.

SUGGESTED READINGS

Anderson, K., Anderson, L. & Glanze, W. (Eds.). (1994). *Mosby's Medical, Nursing, and Allied Health Dictionary.* St. Louis: Mosby-Year Book.

Bates, B. (1983). *A Guide to Physical Examination,* 3rd ed. Philadelphia: J.B. Lippincott Co.

McCann, J. & Voris, J. (1993). Perianal injuries resulting from sexual abuse: A longitudinal study. *Pediatrics, 91:*390–397.

Netter, F. (1984). *Reproductive System.* Vol. 2 of *The Ciba Collection of Medical Illustrations.* Summit, NJ: Ciba-Geigy Corp.

Netter, F. (1989). *Atlas of Human Anatomy.* Summit, NJ: Ciba-Geigy Corp.

4

The Medical–Legal Examination

This chapter explores the medical examination of adult and adolescent victims of sexual assault. Discussions related to adolescents refer to postpubertal stages of growth and development. Because of the strong emphasis on careful evaluation for evidentiary purposes, the focus of this chapter is on the *acute* medical–legal examination, that is within 72 hours from the time of the assault. In no way should it be construed that only victims who report a sexual assault within that time frame be examined. Rather, the same basic principles apply, without consideration of biological evidence.

With these considerations in mind, a current discussion of the full scope of the medical–legal exam should encompass the following:

- A general patient assessment and physical examination, with evaluation of any nongenital trauma.
- A thorough anogenital examination, using both traditional methods of gross inspection, colposcopy, and any adjunctive technology which augments visualization of genital trauma.
- Collection of all physical evidence on the person and/or clothing of the victim.
- Collection of reference standards, according to local crime lab protocol.
- Documentation on appropriate forms of the physical exam and all specimens and samples collected and submitted to the crime lab.
- Pregnancy and sexually transmitted disease testing, or prophylaxis, according to local, state, and Centers for Disease Control (CDC) guidelines (see Appendix I).
- Interpretation of the findings for the victim and other members of the multidisciplinary team.
- Referral of the victim for follow-up medical care and counseling services to community resources.
- Arrangement for follow-up medical exam to document the resolution of any genital (or nongenital) trauma.

DEVELOPING A STYLE

All clinical forensic examiners eventually develop a style or approach to the medical–legal examination. The average, complete, adult, evidentiary exam takes about 2 to 4 hours to complete and document. The numerous procedures, protocols, equipment, and collection of minutiae of physical evidence require fastidious preparation and implementation. To extrapolate an example from a more universal, perhaps everyday experience, we can scrutinize the steps involved in the preparation of a gourmet multicourse meal for a special occasion. Concomitant with the efficiency required to plan and implement all the tasks, is the need to oversee the whole process and keep things running smoothly by ensuring that everyone involved is as comfortable as possible and leaves satisfied. Obviously not all styles of cooks can deliver the chef's touch. It can be orchestrated, however, if one steps back and attempts to perceive the total picture. After arming yourself with the necessary skills and knowledge, you would devise a master plan. Within the framework of this master plan, you would ensure that everything was organized down to the smallest detail, and you would be flexible enough to allow for spontaneous interjections of the unexpected. After seeing to all the details, you would again look at the process as a whole, to see that nothing was missed, and form a basis to evaluate outcome and plan for future events.

Similarly, a methodology that incorporates all the many facets of the examination process helps ensure completion of the myriad responsibilities of the forensic examiner. Although different jurisdictions and programs may vary in *how* they implement specific procedures and protocols, there is usually room for individualized styles within those requirements. A suggested methodology is one based on a sequential approach, that proceeds in a logical and organized manner. This will minimize omissions, avoid errors, and yield a more satisfactory outcome.

In this style, the examiner goes from general survey to detailed inspection for each segment of the exam, and then back to an overall evaluation of the total picture. Minute details are viewed within the context of the whole body, and in relation to the dynamic events of a sexual assault. This will not only guide the examiner to initial areas of inspection, but also afford an evaluation to help ensure that nothing overt has been overlooked during a careful search for minute details. Although this seems obvious, it is common for new forensic examiners to become very focused on all of the *things* that need to be done. We can get so entrenched in all the necessary details; but we must not forget the importance of grasping the total picture.

Many sexual assault cases may not reach the adjudication process for months—or even longer—after the actual physical exam. It is useful for the forensic examiner to develop a *consistent* approach. By drawing upon an established pattern, the examiner may enhance credibility in future cases or at trials, when called upon to explain how a particular examination technique or procedure was carried out. When questions are asked in court about exam details, the examiner can relate his or her routine method of examination, based on a particular *style*.

GENERAL PATIENT ASSESSMENT

Many aspects of the patient's overall physical status can be assessed during the investigative interview, or medical history. While conversing, the examiner can observe and note gait and coordination, level of consciousness, orientation, appropriateness of responses, and eye contact. If the examiner shakes hands during introductions, skin temperature and strength of grip can be noted at that time. It is vital to approach physical contact with a rape victim slowly, allowing time to build a rapport, and always assessing the victim's level of comfort and safety. Gait and coordination can be evaluated while measuring height and weight. At that time, notation can also be made of eye and hair color and use of glasses or contact lenses or any other assistive devices. Note physical stature and any obvious physical limitations or use of prosthetic or assistive devices.

Not infrequently, the forensic examiner is called upon in court to describe the demeanor that the victim displayed during this exam. It is imperative to be *objective* and remember that every patient will respond uniquely to the immediate stress of a sexual assault. A victim may need frequent reassurance that her behavior is normal for what she has experienced. When noting behavioral responses, observe when they occurred and what seemed to elicit them. For example, if a patient cries, is it throughout the interview, or only during specific portions of the history and physical? Behaviors and demeanor should be described briefly and succinctly.

Protocols vary greatly as to what information is recorded on the medical–legal form. A separate medical record is often used to record other features of the history and physical, such as general medical information and gynecologic history. These areas should be thoroughly planned and implemented with recommendations from local agencies, and legal input from the district attorney's office.

VICTIM INTERVIEW

The interview can be an extremely difficult and exhausting ordeal for the victim. It is hard enough to remember horrid events that are emotionally charged and painful. We ask victims not only to remember, but to recount all the details to strangers, who need to both hear and write down what is said. A combination of professionalism and warmth enables the victim to supply this vital information. Victims of a sexual assault need to know we are aware of the difficulty involved in this process. Be sure to convey that your probing questions serve a twofold purpose: they are necessary to complete the investigation, but they also help you, as an examiner to perform a better exam. The examiner who is an experienced interviewer and clinician picks up valuable, often subtle clues that can guide further inquiry and focus the physical exam. With younger victims, it may be helpful to tell them there are no right or wrong answers, that being unsure is also an acceptable response. All victims have the right to know that although many of the questions are highly intimate, and may even appear "nosy," our intent is not to judge, but to establish facts about the assault. If a break is needed during the interview, it should be offered. This is a good opportunity for the advocate to spend some time with the victim to help relieve some of the stress before proceeding.

One way to ease into the interview is to explain the process of the exam and have all necessary consents signed. Generally, patients sign consents for examination, treatment, evidence collection, and photography, which includes the genital area. Additional consents may be required for HIV status, acknowledgment of eligibility for crime victim compensation, and permission to use anonymous data for scientific and health research purposes.

General categories of the patient history are:[1]

- Pertinent medical and gynecologic history: this includes last menstrual period (LMP), recent gynecologic injuries, procedures, or treatments, preexisting medical conditions, consenting intercourse within the last 72 hours, and drug or alcohol ingestion (within time frame of evidence collection).

---

[1] Sample state examination forms are included in the appendices.

- Postassault hygiene (within 72 hours).
- Assault-related medical conditions (injuries, loss of consciousness, pain, bleeding).
- Acts committed by the assailant: weapons, physical force, injuries, restraints, threats, forced drug use.
- Injuries inflicted by the victim to the assailant.
- Sexual acts committed by the assailant (this includes "frequency", "sequence", "attempts", and "unsure" categories):
    ◆ penetration of the vagina by penis, finger, object
    ◆ penetration of the rectum by penis, finger, object
    ◆ oral copulation of the genitals by suspect to victim or by victim to suspect
    ◆ oral copulation of anus, by suspect to victim or by victim to suspect
    ◆ biting, licking, kissing
    ◆ ejaculation (location)
- Positions used during the assault.
- Chronologic order of sex acts.

PHYSICAL EXAMINATION

Clothing

Some programs provide a change of clothing, such as a sweatsuit, for the victim to wear after his or her own clothes are collected. If this is not available, have the victim, friend or family member bring a change of clothing to the hospital or Sexual Assault Response Team (SART) facility. The purpose of clothing collection should be explained to the victim, as taking belongings at this point may elicit different feelings in different individuals. For instance, some may never want to see the outfit they were assaulted in again, while for others, the item you are collecting for evidence may be an expensive or cherished article that signifies yet another loss. Although careful inspection of the clothing is important, the victim's sense of modesty and privacy should be maintained as much as possible. When the patient is undressing or when 35-mm photographs of the breasts and genital anatomy are being taken, it is still possible to appropriately drape the patient.

Collection of Clothing [2]

- Have the patient remove their shoes and step onto two sheets of white exam paper, one on top of the other.
- Wearing gloves, examine, then carefully fold each article of clothing, and place each item in a separate paper bag.
    ◆ do not shake clothing
    ◆ avoid folding *across* a stain
- Observe clothing for rips, tears, stains, or foreign matter.
- Collect top sheet of paper into a *bindle,* and place in separate, labeled paper bag.
- Document on the medical–legal form. (Refer to Chapter 5 for further processing of clothing as physical evidence.)

A *bindle* is a leakproof envelope/container constructed from a folded sheet of paper so that small particles of collected debris or evidence will not fall out. One can be easily constructed from a sheet of paper utilizing the following steps:

1. fold paper in half
2. fold half-sized paper into thirds
3. fold over right flap
4. fold over left flap
5. fold in half; seal open end of bindle, not folded end. Initial tape.

Head and Neck

Check the scalp for signs of forced hair removal, lacerations, scratches, or areas of bruising or tenderness. Measure and carefully

---

[2]Clothing can be scanned with a Wood's lamp or alternate light source (ALS); this can be done either immediately after collection, or just after scanning the victim's body, when the room is already darkened.

document the location on a traumagram, if possible. *Collect* any foreign debris present in the hair into an envelope or bindle; label and seal. Collect reference standards[3] by having the patient tug, or pull 15 to 20 hairs from various locations on the head.

The Eyes

Check the pupils for size, reaction, and accommodation to light. Observe extraocular eye movements. Examine conjunctivae for discharge or petechiae.

Attempted strangulation may result in subconjunctival or retinal hemorrhages. Both may occur spontaneously. *Subconjuctival hemorrhages* are bright red, due to rupture of the small conjunctival vessels. They usually, but not always occur in one eye, in any age group. These are alarming to the patient (Schwab & Dawson, 1995). Blood leaks outside the vessels, as a small conjunctival blood vessel ruptures, and is seen in the substantia propria of the conjunctiva (Yanoff & Fine, 1975). The pupils will appear normal in size and shape, and there is no effect on visual acuity. Gradually, subconjunctival hemorrhages will fade and absorb in 2 to 3 weeks. Suspected *retinal hemorrhages* should receive medical evaluation, and be referred to an ophthalmologist. Retinal perfusion is via the retinal and choroidal blood vessels. The retinal arteries function as end arteries, and correspond to the systemic arterioles. The choroidal circulation contains most of the blood within the eye. Retinal hemorrhages are caused by diapedeses from veins and capillaries by any condition that alters the integrity of the endothelial cells of the blood vessels. Morphology of retinal hemorrhages is dependent on size, site, and extent of damage to the blood vessel (Sanders & Graham, 1995). Retinal hemorrhages are a salient feature of acceleration-deceleration injuries (shaken baby syndrome). In the adult, they may occur whenever there is a sudden increase in venous congestion, eg, strangulation

maneuvers (Cress, 1998). Blunt trauma to the head may produce ocular manifestations, such as subconjunctival hemorrhages, hyphema (blood in the anterior chamber of the eye), cataracts, lens subluxation, glaucoma; retinal, vitreous, intrascleral and optic nerve hemorrhages; and papilledema (Frederick, 1995).

With all assault-related trauma, the examiner must make a thorough assessment and evaluate the need for appropriate medical referrals. This is especially relevant in the victim who has received blows to the head, or sustained a loss of consciousness. All nongenital trauma should be carefully evaluated. Figure 4–1 shows normal retinal vasculature. Figure 4–2 shows retinal hemorrhages.

Assess the patency of the nose and examine the nasal turbinates. Note the condition of the mucous membrane, and any discharge. Inspect the external ear and behind the ear for trauma. Using an otoscope, examine the ear canals and observe the eardrum.

If there is a known or suspected history of forced oral copulation of the victim by the suspect, this is a good time to darken the room and scan the victim's head and body with the Wood's lamp or alternate light source (ALS) for signs of dried semen secretions. At this point, the patient has become accustomed to the examiner's touch and may feel comfortable in a dark room as the examiner shines a light over his or her body including the anogenital area. It is also timely. The examiner can proceed to take any swabs of foreign matter and control samples, starting with the head. If suspicious areas are noted on other areas of the body, they can be outlined for future swabbing by circling upon illumination, using a child's *washable* marker (verify that this is okay with the patient first). Samples and controls can be collected later, while examining that particular part of the body. *Do not* use markers on areas that contain nongenital trauma as the marker will introduce artifact into the photo.

---

[3] Note: This step varies with local crime lab protocol.

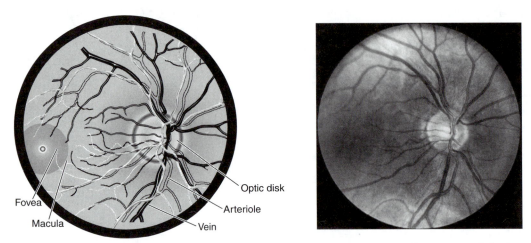

Figure 4–1. Retina seen through the ophthalmoscope in a healthy human eye. Diagram at left identifies the landmarks in the photograph on the right. *(From Vaughan, D. & Asbury, T. [1999]. General Ophthalmology, 15th ed., Stamford, CT: Appleton & Lange, reprinted with permission.)*

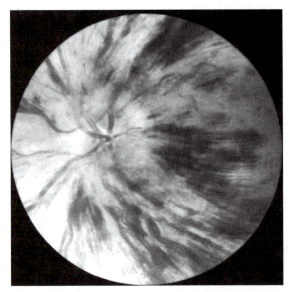

Figure 4–2. Flame-shaped retinal hemorrhages in the nerve fiber layer radiate out from the optic disk. Three days before the photograph was taken, the patient experienced sudden loss of vision, which left him with light perception only. *(From Vaughan, D. & Asbury, T. [1999]. General Ophthalmology, Stamford, CT: Appleton & Lange, p. 296, reprinted with permission.)*

The Mouth

Note the breath odor. Examine the perioral area for evidence of injury and, if a recent history of fellatio, for evidence of seminal fluid. If dried stains are noted, swab the area around the mouth and collect dried secretions with a swab moistened *slightly* with distilled water. Collect any moist secretions with dry swabs, to avoid dilution. Make a control swab of an unstained area. Inspect lips and mucous membranes for color and integrity. Explore the oral cavity. Carefully inspect the frenulum, the inside of the lower lip, and pharynx for exudate, lacerations, ecchymoses, or petechiae. Note recently chipped teeth, which may require magnification for adequate visualization and photographs. Palpate the trachea and thyroid gland.

Trauma resulting from forced oral copulation that *may* be visible with magnification of the mouth includes petechiae in the posterior pharynx. The frenulum under the tongue can tear. Oral trauma from voluntary fellatio has been discussed in the dental literature. In 1948, Barthelemy reported palatal lesions as an occupational mark in a professional fellatrice (Damm et al, 1981). Many reported cases have presented with purpura or petechiae of the soft palate. The classic picture of palatal hemorrhage is described as ecchymotic, non-ulcerated, and nonpainful, with irregular borders. Papular elevations may be noted in the center of the lesion. The subepithelial hemorrhage in the highly vascular soft palate results from negative pressure, concomitant with palatal musculature elevation and tension of the area. Ecchymosis results from severe suction. Most fellatio does not produce clinical lesions, trauma, or involve heavy negative pressure (Damm et al, 1981:420).

Up to 6 hours postassault, collect two swabs from the oral cavity by carefully swabbing the area from the gums to the tonsillar fossae, the upper and second molars, behind the incisors, and the fold of the cheek. Prepare two dry mount slides from these swabs. If done at the time of the exam, collect the saliva reference sample *after* swabs for evidence of semen. Three common methods of collection of this sample are:

- liquid saliva sample
  or
- two dry swabs inserted into mouth, like a lollipop until saturated
  or
- cotton gauze or pledget, placed under the tongue until saturated (use forceps to handle)

Some criminalists advise *against* collecting a saliva reference sample at the initial examination if there has been a recent history of oral copulation (Devine, 1997).

If sexually transmitted disease (STD) testing is done in conjunction with the exam, collect an oral gonorrhea culture *after all* forensic samples are obtained (see Appendix I).

The Neck

Check the carotid pulses, one at a time, and palpate the cervical lymph nodes. Closely inspect for signs of any nongenital trauma. Photograph any trauma using a 35-mm camera and L-shaped scale (Fig. 4–3). Measure and document; the metric system is preferred, although either metric or apothecary may be used as long as there is consistency throughout. Do not document suction ecchymoses as *"hickeys"* on a medical–legal form.

Routinely inspect the neck, ankles, and wrists for signs of sexual bondage. This is typically manifested by the elaborate, excessive use of binding material and ligatures that are characteristically neat and symmetrical in appearance. If suspected or known by history, photograph the marks or bindings using a macrolens and Alternate Light Source, if available (see "Evaluation of Nongenital Trauma" later in this chapter). If duct tape or other binding tape was used, there may be adhesive residue present on the skin which can be scraped into a paper bindle using the edge

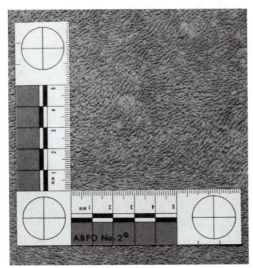

Figure 4–3. L-shaped ABFO scale. *(Courtesy of Lightning Powder Co., Inc. Salem, OR; 1-800-852-0300.)*

of a clean glass slide. Submit slide for evaluation as well.

Upper Extremities

Check the brachial and radial pulses, skin temperature, and look for any edema. Inspect for nongenital trauma, such as scratches, bruises, abrasions, bitemarks, and lacerations, as well as tattoos or scars. If the victim reports that he or she scratched the assailant, collect fingernail scrapings by gently scraping under the tips of each nail with a manicure stick or toothpick, and package the tool and scrapings from each hand separately. Alternately, obtain fingernail cuttings. Traces of tissue or blood may be present under the nails.

Chest and Trunk

Auscultate heart sounds and breath sounds (anterior and posterior). Note the point of maximum cardiac impulse. Indicate any abnormal sounds such as murmurs, wheezes, or crackles. Percuss the lungs; inspect and palpate the spine, checking for bruises or scratches. Look for non-

genital trauma over the entire area, and possibly a patterned injury if the victim was lying on her back on a patterned surface during the assault. This will be more easily seen if an ALS is used.

Breasts

For adolescents, note the Tanner stage (see Appendix C). Inspect for any signs of trauma. Measure and photograph, as described for nongenital trauma (see p. 91). Drape the breast(s) as much as possible, while permitting adequate visualization of the entire area of injury. At times, it may be necessary to expose the entire breast for the *orienting* photographs in order to show a wound in relation to the entire body part (see "Photography," p. 89). Most other photos of wounds on the breast(s), however, can be draped. This is true for pictures in the anogenital area as well. Palpate the breasts and axillary lymph nodes. Inspect the nipples for discharge. If sex acts included licking or biting of the breasts or nipples, make two swabs of the relevant areas for presence of saliva (see "Procedures for Collection of Evidence from Bitemarks," p. 92). Make a control swab from unstained area.

Abdomen

Auscultate bowel sounds. Gently palpate each quadrant, and observe for rigidity, abdominal pain, enlarged organs, and rebound tenderness. Record any pelvic tenderness or abdominal pain, notably in the suprapubic area. Inspect for bruising in the umbilical area.

Lower Extremities

Check strength of femoral, popliteal, and pedal pulses. Note any pedal edema, as well as the color and temperature of the skin. Check carefully for bruises, scratches, or abrasions. Note if the bruises appear to be of varying ages. Carefully examine bony prominences. Determine strength and sensation by having the patient bend his or her lower leg and push hard against your hand. Check the soles of the feet.

THE GENITAL EXAMINATION

The genital examination can be quite difficult for the victim of a sexual assault, even when the patient accepts the necessity of this procedure and has initiated the request for a medical evaluation. Because the genital area is probably the place the patient will be least comfortable having examined and probed, it is paramount for the examiner to build a rapport during the interview and initial portions of the physical to ensure a smooth and more comfortable genital exam. Tell the victim you realize the implications and difficulty of this process, and suggest that you will do everything possible to help her through it. It may be helpful to have the advocate or other support person sit at the head of the exam table during the pelvic exam to quietly talk, hold the victim's hand, or help her breathe deeply to relax. Tell her you will keep her informed of your moves, and that you will not suddenly grab her or insert anything. This is important, as she may experience flashbacks of the rape during the pelvic examination. Do not apologize for performing the pelvic exam; help her see it in a positive manner. Although she may dread being touched in the genital area, she is now in control. Your touch is part of a total assessment that can promote her physical well being and help prevent infections. The routines of the gynecologic exam are an accepted part of every woman's health care. Going through many of these motions can help the victim of a sexual assault, in a sense, bring her body back to her. She does not have to be left with the feeling that the exam is another violation, but it may seem so at the time, unless the examiner enlists the support and trust of the most valuable participant, the victim.

To promote a smooth exam and calm atmosphere, assemble all necessary equipment beforehand, and place it conveniently within reach. It is helpful to arrange everything on top of a clean towel, on a movable exam stand or tray. In this manner, the examiner working alone does not need to interrupt the flow of the exam, and needed items will not be forgotten. Necessary equipment may include:

- New sexual assault evidence kit, with unbroken seal.
- Evidence envelopes from kit for reference standards, evidence specimens (swabs and slides), and Wood's lamp swabs.
- Paper for bindles, or envelopes from kit, to contain foreign matter and trace evidence.
- One or two sizes of metal or plastic speculums.
- Emesis basin with warm water, for lubrication.
- *Swabs:* vaginal, cervical, and rectal swabs from evidence kit (3–4 vaginal; 2 external-genital; 1–2 cervical; 2 rectal).
  - ◆ Male victim: one swab from glans penis (include area under foreskin, if uncircumcised); one swab from urethra (if local protocol).
- Slides: external genital slides (2)
  - ◆ Vaginal: three glass slides; one with drop of saline for wet mount slide; cover slip for wet mount slide
  - ◆ Cervix: 1 slide
  - ◆ Rectal: 2 dry mount slides
- One or two procto swabs (plain and balloon covered).
- Extra cotton- or Dacron-tipped swabs.
- Urine specimen cup.
- Blood specimens: for blood alcohol, conventional serology, and DNA (do not use alcohol swab during collection).
- Post-it notes (small).
- Colposcope identification tag; note magnification setting on colposcope.
- Rubber bulb syringe.
- *Optional: Xylocaine jelly* (to probe hymenal borders after evidence collection).

- *Optional: One percent Aqueous Toluidine blue dye* (recommended use: only after conclusion of the genital and anal exam, and collection of all forensic specimens). Dacron swab and solution to apply. To remove excess dye: use dilute acetic acid and water solution, witch hazel, or water-based lubricant and 4″ × 4″ gauze squares. Can also use baby wipes.

Optional STD Testing

The following STD tests may be conducted, depending on local protocol:

- Gonorrhea and chlamydia: (mouth, cervix, rectum, urethra). For specificity of results, a *rectal* chlamydia test must utilize *culture* medium.
- Wet prep: pipette and small vial of sterile saline for aspirate, or one swab and culture tube containing a few cc's of saline.
- Blood: tube(s) for syphilis serology, HIV (needs separate consent).
- If indicated: herpes culture, vinegar solution (acetowhitening of questionable lesions).

Prior to the exam, the patient should urinate. Although some protocols advise urine collection after the exam, specimens for possible testing of drugs should be collected as soon as possible. Recent drugs used in the commission of rape are excreted quickly, especially gamma hydroxy butyrate (GHB); only 5% of this substance is excreted in the urine, the rest is converted to CO_2. Late collection of the specimen not only risks the drug sample, but may make the patient uncomfortable during the pelvic exam. If this is the first voiding since the rape, and there is concern over loss of semen by wiping or urinating, the victim can be instructed to use only a minimal amount of tissue to wipe (this can be saved and dried). If sufficient quantity is obtained for the urine sample (≥30 cc), a portion can be saved for a urine pregnancy test. If used, a urine pregnancy test should have a sensitivity of less than 50 mIU/mL of human chorionic gonadotropin (HCG).

Examination Positions

The following positions may be utilized during the pelvic exam:

- lithotomy, or supine
- left-lateral (may be easier for elderly victims during prolonged exam)
- knee-chest (used by some examiners for adolescents, in *addition* to supine)

Drape the patient appropriately in the lithotomy position. Have her bring her buttocks as far down to the edge of the table as possible. Adjust the stirrups for maximum visualization and patient comfort. Potholders placed on the stirrups make the stirrups more comfortable. Clean white socks keep the feet warm and are a comforting touch. A simple technique that promotes relaxation can be helpful with patients who are fearful or distressed about the pelvic exam. Have the patient place one of her hands on her lower abdomen, with your hand on top of it. Show her how to breathe deeply and slowly. To help her relax, have her concentrate on the movement of her hand up and down with each respiration. She can imagine a balloon inside her pelvis that inflates on inspiration and deflates on expiration. Let her know that deep breathing and keeping her legs open as wide as possible, will serve to make her exam more comfortable, especially if she has any tender or painful areas. If possible, subdue any bright, overhead lights, especially if the victim has a headache. Provide a bath blanket to keep her warm.

Inspect the medial thighs for trauma. Swab any areas of dried or moist secretions, and areas of positive (+) fluorescence, using only distilled water. A control swab should also be taken, and labeled "*W.L. control,*" to correlate it to the evidence swabs. Semen can sometimes be detected by the mucoid appearance of smears, streaks, or splash marks. It has a characteristic tendency to flake off the skin. Under ultraviolet illumination, it may exhibit blue-white or orange fluorescence. Fresh semen, however, may not fluoresce with a Wood's lamp. Therefore, any suspicious areas or areas consistent with the history should be swabbed. While some criminalists request only one body control for multiple stains, others prefer to have a control for each site sampled. The examiner should inquire as to the needs and preferences of the local crime lab.

Pubic Hair

Place a sheet of paper beneath the patient's buttocks to capture any debris or foreign matter that falls from the body. The pubic hair may contain dried semen from vaginal drainage, or ejaculation outside of the vagina. If the pubic hair is matted, representative samples should be cut and packaged separately. The pubic hair should then be combed or brushed with the comb/brush supplied by the evidence kit. Foreign fibers or hairs from the assailant might have transferred during the rape. Some patients may wish to do this themselves and should be instructed to comb so that any debris will fall directly onto the paper towel. The contents of the paper towel, plus the comb or brush, should be folded, with the towel wrapped over the brush/comb, and placed carefully into a bindle or bag.

If reference samples are collected, 15 to 20 pulled, or tugged hairs, from different pubic areas should be obtained. Have the victim do this *herself.* She can drop the pulled hairs into a bindle or envelope held by the examiner. Explain the reason for *pulling* the hairs, that is, to include the hair root, which permits a more accurate analysis of the hair by the crime lab. As a last resort, or for a young adolescent, the examiner may cut some hairs *close* to the skin, but should then carefully denote on the bindle and chart that the samples were *cut,* not pulled. (see "Reference Standards" for pubic hair, Chap. 5).

At this point, the examiner sits on the exam stool facing the patient. Encourage the patient to keep her legs open wide. Tell the patient what you are going to do, and then touch her inner thigh with a gloved hand, to accustom her to your touch. Using an external light source, or the colposcope light, begin the exam. Simple gross visual inspection should always precede palpation or colposcopy, for consistency, and to allay allegations of iatrogenically induced trauma. Any findings noted with only gross visual inspection (ie, without magnification) should be documented as such. Approach the entire anogenital area in a *sequential manner.* Progress from top to bottom, and side to side. The more superficial areas are inspected first, followed by deeper, or recessed structures. This will ensure that none of the anatomic sites are omitted.

An elderly patient may not tolerate any exam position for a prolonged time. Promote circulation and provide comfort measures. Try using small pillows, or folded bath blankets or towels under bony prominences. Small chunks, rolls, or blocks of foam can be kept handy for this. Position them in the small of the back, under the buttocks, or lateral to the hips. Cushion the stirrups. Allow the patient to change position as needed. A short, narrow, Pederson speculum may be more easily tolerated. A large otoscope can be substituted for a speculum, if necessary.

Using gross visualization and magnification, *inspect* the following anatomic landmarks. Use gentle *separation* of the labia minora and gentle *traction* to expose more recessed structures.

- Labia majora
- Clitoris and clitoral hood
- Periurethral area
- Labia minora—both aspects, inner and outer
- Hymen
- Vaginal barrel, distal portion
- Perineum
- Fossa navicularis
- Posterior fourchette

Minute particles of foreign debris or other trace evidence may sometimes be found in the genital area upon viewing with colposcopy.

These are extremely small and can best be gathered by looking through the colposcope, catching the particle on the tip of a swab, and placing it (along with swab, if adherent) onto the sticky edge of a small post-it paper. As soon as possible, place the post-it in a bindle to avoid loss.

Labial Separation

With the patient supine, gently separate the labia, using the tips of the fingers. Separate laterally and slightly downward, until the introitus is exposed, using one or both hands.

Labial Traction

This technique is also done with the patient supine and in stirrups. Each labium is grasped between the thumb and index, or thumb, index, and middle finger of the examiner's hands. Both labial edges are then gently pulled *outward,* and slightly *upward,* in a direction toward the examiner, with *slight* lateral traction on both edges. This serves to widen and open the vaginal orifice, exposing most of the hymenal rim and distal vagina.

Some crime labs, eg, Los Angeles County Sheriff's Department and Los Angeles Police Department, have included the collection of external genital swabs, in addition to the routine vaginal pool samples. These two swabs are slightly moistened with distilled water and collected simultaneously, by swabbing the labia and vulva. Two slides are then made from the swabs.

Inspection of the Hymenal Borders

The normal redundancy of the estrogenized hymen may necessitate gentle probing of the hymenal borders to thoroughly inspect all surfaces for microtrauma. Petechiae from blunt trauma may be obscured in the hymenal folds. Inspection of the hymenal rim can be accomplished in different ways.

- One or two Dacron, cotton, or even tiny nasopharyngeal swabs can be used to gently lift and separate the hymenal folds, or sections, if there are old tears. The swabs can be moistened with distilled water, if the tissues appear dry. The internal aspect of the hymenal rim and all "creases" can then be seen.

- Hymenal transections, both partial and complete, can be clearly delineated when gently splayed over a procto swab, which can be *slightly* moistened with distilled water. A dry procto swab is useful when the patient is menstruating, as it serves to absorb the blood flow that so often collects in the folds of tissue, preventing a clear view of the area.

  In the adolescent or adult experiencing significant distress from trauma or anxiety, probing of the hymenal borders can be deferred until after the speculum exam and collection of *all* forensics. Perform colposcopy and obtain preliminary photos of the exposed hymenal area *before* the speculum is inserted and any manipulative techniques are used. At this point, a few additional techniques may facilitate adequate visualization.

- In 1993, the author had a brainstorm while chastising her 8-year-old daughter for making water bomb balloons in the house. At the San Luis Obispo SART program, we had been searching for a method to provide visual and photographic contrast of both old and new hymenal lacerations, and had experimented with Foley catheters and different swabs. I borrowed my daughter's bag of balloons and began slipping different colored balloons over the procto swabs. The bright colors provided excellent visual contrast against the mucous membrane. The small size of the balloon was a perfect match for the large swab. (*Note:* This should be done after collection of the forensic specimens is completed. It is only recommended for use in the postpubertal female.)

♦ Xylocaine jelly (1%) can be applied to the hymenal area. Wait a few minutes, and resume the exam. Dacron or cotton swabs can be used to explore the rim. The jelly even serves to "add volume" to the tissue, so that it is easier to probe the projections looking for microtrauma, which can then be photographed.

♦ Another technique that is useful for children and adolescents is to take a baby's rubber mouth and nose bulb syringe (Fig. 4–4). Fill with warm water from an emesis basin, and gently squirt over the introitus, from directly above the area (best accomplished by a second person). Then, using labial traction, inspect and photograph. The hymenal edges "float" inward and outward, often exposing areas that were previously hidden in redundant folds of tissue.

The internal portions of the female genital anatomy—the *vagina, cervix,* and *rectum*—are inspected during the speculum exam and anoscopy.

THE SPECULUM EXAMINATION

For the internal exam of the sexual assault victim, use the smallest size speculum possible which still permits adequate visualization. The victim is often uncomfortable from geni-

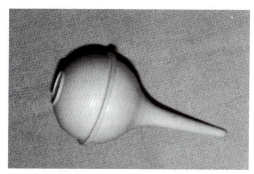

Figure 4–4. Rubber bulb syringe, for irrigation of water onto hymenal borders.

tal trauma, anxiety, or a combination of both. The vertical distance between the top and bottom blades of the speculum influences patient comfort via the amount of introital stretching during insertion. Lubricate the speculum with water only; lubricating jellies are spermicidal and interfere with evidence collection. Hold the speculum with one hand, while the other hand is used to spread the labia majora from above. This technique will avoid obscuring the visual field. Table 4–1 discusses techniques of speculum insertion. Examples of various specula are shown in Figs. 4–5, 4–6, and 4–7. Correct placement of the speculum is shown in Fig. 4–8 on page 79.

Before collecting any samples, carefully inspect the following internal landmarks, using gross visualization, followed by photocolposcopy:

• vaginal walls
• cervix
• os

Simultaneously insert three to four swabs from the evidence kit between the speculum blades and collect a sample from the vaginal pool, in the posterior fornix. From these swabs, two dry mount slides and one wet mount slide will be prepared after the speculum has been removed. The *wet mount* slide is prepared with either normal saline or a buffered nutrient medium. If 48 hours has elapsed, *or* the victim has had consensual sexual activity within the last 72 hours, also collect one or two evidence swabs from the cervical os, and prepare slides. If the crime lab requests a vaginal *aspirate,* or *lavage,* instill a few cc's of normal saline or sterile water through the speculum blades into the posterior fornix. Use a pipette to aspirate the sample. (Collection of forensic swabs is summarized in Appendix B, "Sexual Assault Examination: Evidentiary Checklist.")

After collection of forensic samples, cervical cultures for STDs may be collected (if local protocol). Gonorrhea and chlamydia cultures should be obtained from the cervical

► **TABLE 4–1.** SPECULUM INSERTION

Types of Specula

Graves	Pederson	Plastic
Standard Graves; relatively deep and wide; also available in larger and smaller size Graves.	Blades relatively flat, narrow, and long.	Disposable; contoured similar to a Pederson. Available in small and medium.
Standard size suitable for sexually active female with average size vaginal orifice. May need larger Graves if multiparous or gaping orifice, to visualize cervix.	Standard Pederson available in two smaller sizes.	Some varieties accommodate light for illumination of vaginal barrel.
Huffman-Graves: as long as adult Graves and as narrow as short pediatric Graves ($\frac{1}{2}'' \times 4 \frac{1}{4}''$).	Good for sexually active females.	
Good for adolescents.	Smallest size Pederson suitable for young or virginal adolescents, and postmenopausal women. $\frac{7}{8}'' \times 4 \frac{1}{2}''$	

Insertion of Speculum

- Lubricate speculum with water only.
- Hold speculum in one hand while other hand is used to spread the labia majora (from above, to avoid obscuring view). Examiner can hook index finger over base of upper blade to increase firmness of grasp before insertion.
- Position blades along axis of vagina.
- Insert blade tips with both tips and bases closed.
- Ask patient to relax; give time to do so. Rotate speculum handle to 4 o'clock (or 8 o'clock) position to decrease effective width of vagina, and gently insert tips. During insertion, press lower blade uniformly against the posterior vaginal wall; watch space between upper blade and urethra.
- Insert speculum up to base, with base of lower blade pressed against (but not compressing) perineum. With most women, this lands the tips in the posterior fornix.*
- Rotate the handle back to 6 o'clock.
- Depress the lever to open the blades and distend the vaginal walls, allowing visualization of the cervix.
- If using a metal speculum, tighten the lever nut to secure the position. To open the bases of the speculum, push upward on the Y-shaped component of the handle and secure in this position (if necessary, due to laxity of the vaginal walls).
- Position the light source to shine through the speculum blades. (Can use colposcope light).

Partial Obstruction of Cervix

This may be due to a marked posterior orientation of the cervix or laxity of the vaginal walls. Attempt insertion a second time: insert the speculum more deeply and posteriorly by compression of the perineal tissues. If the cervix is now seen, but walls obscure the view, try a larger speculum. A markedly anterior cervix (retroverted uterus), may also preclude visualization of the cervix. Position the speculum more horizontally (anteriorly) to bring the cervix into view.

Withdrawal of Speculum

- Inspect and photograph the cervix and vaginal walls.
- Collect all evidentiary and STD specimens.
- Close base of speculum, if they have been opened.
- Inspect vaginal wall mucosa as speculum is being withdrawn.
- Keeping the tips partially open, rotate the speculum obliquely (decreases effective width), and view once on each side. Do not close tips while they surround the cervix.
- Close tips after they are withdrawn past cervix.
- Keep tips closed during withdrawal to avoid irritation of urethra.
- Continue to maintain downward pressure along posterior vaginal wall throughout withdrawal.
- Check for visible space between upper blade and anterior vaginal wall.

*If necessary, apply gentle pressure of blade tips against fourchette to prompt patient to relax vaginal opening; try to avoid this step, as fourchette is most frequent site of injury in the rape victim.

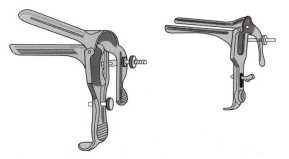

Graves vaginal speculum   Pederson vaginal speculum

Figure 4–5. Specula. *(From Benson, RC:* Handbook of Obstetrics & Gynecology, *8th ed. Los Altos, CA: Lange Medical Publications, 1983. In DeCherney, A. & Pernol, M. [Eds.]. [1994].* Current Obstetric and Gynecologic Diagnosis and Treatment, *8th ed. Norwalk, CT: Appleton & Lange, p. 621, reprinted with permission.)*

os. For a wet prep culture, obtain a specimen as for vaginal aspirate, or insert a single swab into the posterior fornix until saturated. Immerse this swab into a culture tube containing a *small* amount of saline. Break off the external end of the swab and seal the culture tube.

Preparation of Vaginal Swabs and Slides

Prior preparation of the vaginal slides and swabs beforehand prevents mix-up during collection or drying. Swabs can be lined up in a Lucite air drying box in slots prelabeled for each body cavity. Slides should be prelabeled

or marked with a pencil or slide marker. Vaginal swabs are all collected simultaneously from the vaginal pool in the posterior fornix and arbitrarily designated as #1, #2, #3, and #4. Make two dry mount slides (#1 and #2) to correspond with swabs #1 and #2. The third swab is correlated to the vaginal wet mount slide, eg, "*Vag. wet mount, #3.*" If collected, the fourth swab is extra; label as "*Vag. #4.*" *All slides are labeled to correspond to the swab they are prepared from.* Place a drop of normal saline or buffered nutrient medium on the third vaginal slide to preserve any sperm motility. Roll the third swab of the vaginal pool back and forth in the

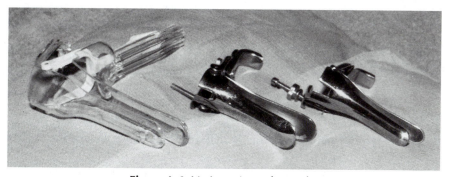

Figure 4–6. Various sizes of specula.

Figure 4–7. The Huffman-Graves speculum (middle) is as long as the adult Graves speculum (right) and as narrow as the short pediatric Graves speculum (left). *(From DeCherney, A. & Pernol, M. [Eds.]. [1994]. Current Obstetric and Gynecologic Diagnosis and Treatment, 8th ed. Norwalk, CT: Appleton & Lange, p. 639, reprinted with permission.)*

drop to transfer the cellular debris to the drop. Place a cover slip on the slide and examine within 5 to 10 minutes, using a biological microscope. Scan first at 100 power (10×) to discern sperm. Then, examine more closely at 400 power (40×) to determine if sperm are present. Motility can only be observed in an unstained wet mount specimen. Living sperm dry out and become immotile. A phase contrast microscope is useful for this. This slide, along with other swabs and slides for the evidence kit are then air dried for 60 minutes and packaged for the crime lab. Nonmotile sperm are best visualized after fixing and staining by the criminalist.

ANAL AND RECTAL EXAMINATION

An examination of the anus and entire perianal region should be done routinely, in conjunction with the genital examination, regardless of history. An additional examination of the rectum should be performed whenever there is reported or suspected history of anal penetration. A thorough rectal exam includes insertion of an anoscope (Fig. 4–9) and is recommended if there is known or suspected sodomy in an adolescent or adult victim.

The anal portion of the exam can be done with the patient in various positions, depending on patient comfort and adequacy of visualization during inspection and photocolposcopy. Common positions employed include left lateral (side-lying), with the patient's legs flexed at hips and knees. The lithotomy position may also be used for the anal portion of this exam. An additional method which affords excellent visualization for the examiner is a modified supine, with legs flexed onto the abdomen. The patient lies supine, as for lithotomy, but instead of having her legs in the stirrups, they are flexed and drawn up over the abdomen. The patient can provide stability by using her arms to hold the lower legs flexed in place ("hugging" her knees). Tell patients that this portion of the exam may make them feel as though they need to move the bowels, but that will not occur. Remind patients to use the relaxation methods employed during the speculum exam. Rhythmic breathing and relaxation techniques during the anal exam may enable the examiner to see up to the pectinate line *prior* to any instrumentation. The anal and rectal examination of the male sexual assault victim is conducted in a similar manner. Refer also to Table 4–2 for the adult male victim evidentiary exam.

Examine and photograph the anal area. Note any trauma seen on gross visual inspection. Because there are normal folds in the perianal area, the examiner must carefully and systematically apply gentle lateral traction to the perianal area to separate and allow for a complete view of the anal verge and anus. Systematically separate the anal folds, going from 12 to 3 to 6, back to 12 o'clock positions. Tears can easily be obscured in these folds of tissue. Be cognizant of normal perianal pig-

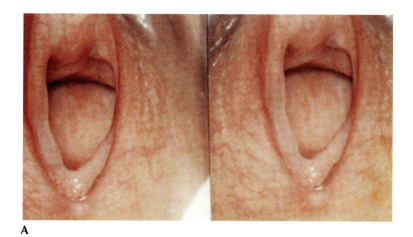

A

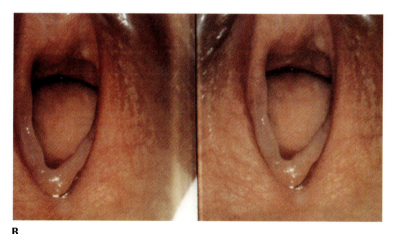

B

Figure 1. Diaphragm settings with Leisegang Model 3B Photocolposcope. **A.** Diaphragm Setting 3″ (optimal with clear filter) **B.** Diaphragm Setting 4″. (Reproduced with permission, Nancy Kellogg, MD., Alamo Children's Advocacy Center. In: *The Use of Colposcopy in the Assessment for Sexual Abuse/Assault.* [1997]. Leisegang Medical, Inc. Boca Raton, Fla., page 20.)

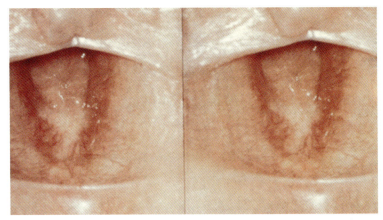

Figure 2. Labial separation in a pre-pubertal child. (Reproduced with permission, Nancy Kellogg, MD., Alamo Children's Advocacy Center. In: *The Use of Colposcopy in the Assessment for Sexual Abuse/Assault.* [1997]. Leisegang Medical, Inc. Boca Raton, Fla., page 13.)

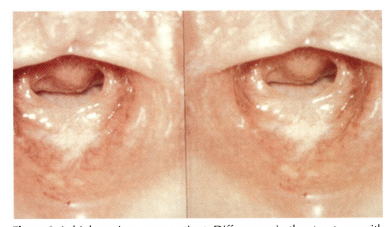

Figure 3. Labial traction; same patient. Differences in the structures with labial separation and labial traction. (Reprinted with permission, Nancy Kellogg, MD., Alamo Children's Advocacy Center. In: *The Use of Colposcopy in the Assessment for Sexual Abuse/Assault.* [1997]. Leisegang Medical, Inc. Boca Raton, Fla., page 13.)

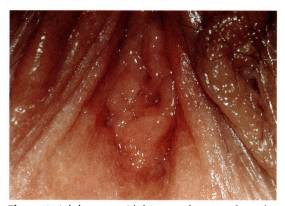

Figure 4. Adolescent with history of repeated penile-vaginal penetration by stepfather × 4 years duration. Using *labial separation*, no healed tears visible within the hymenal folds. (Courtesy, Nancy Kellogg, MD., Alamo Children's Advocacy Center.)

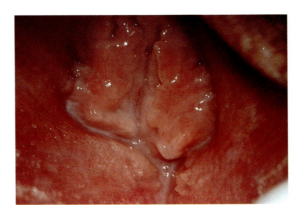

Figure 5. *Labial separation*, 15 year old. (Courtesy, Nancy Kellogg, MD., Alamo Children's Advocacy Center.)

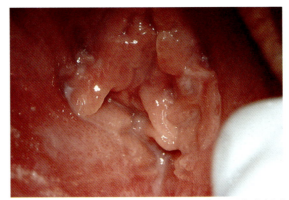

Figure 6. Same patient as in Figure 5, but with *labial traction*. This maneuver allows visualization of a healed tear in the hymen at 6–7 o'clock. (Courtesy, Nancy Kellogg, MD., Alamo Children's Advocacy Center.)

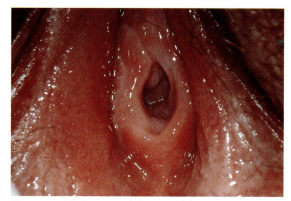

Figure 7. Adolescent with normal hymen. (Courtesy, Nancy Kellogg, MD., Alamo Children's Advocacy Center.)

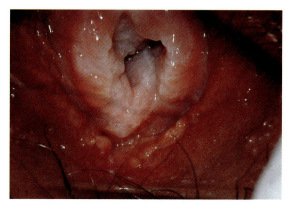

Figure 8. Twenty-two year old female 13 days post-rape. No previous history of sexual contact. Healed, partial tear at 5 o'clock. External vaginal ridges and benign papillomatosis within the posterior vestibule extend from 4–8 o'clock (normal findings). (Courtesy, Nancy Kellogg, MD., Alamo Children's Advocacy Center.)

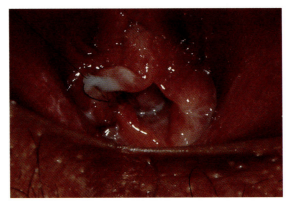

Figure 9. Adolescent with history of rape 5 days previously. Slide shows submucosal hemorrhage at inner hymenal margin, at 8 o'clock. (Courtesy, Nancy Kellogg, MD, Alamo Children's Advocacy Center.)

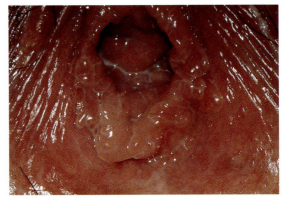

Figure 10. Adolescent with history of sexual assault 15 days previously. History of consensual sexual activity for some years. (Courtesy, Nancy Kellogg, MD, Alamo Children's Advocacy Center.)

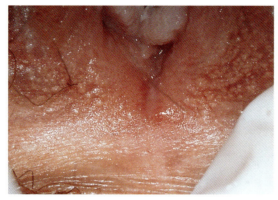

Figure 11. Adolescent 2 weeks post-rape. Healed tear in the fossa navicularis. (Courtesy, Nancy Kellogg, MD, Alamo Children's Advocacy Center.)

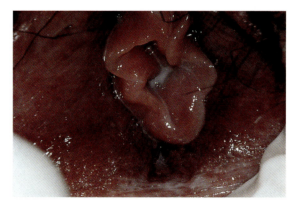

Figure 12. Adolescent with normal hymen; no evidence of previous hymenal lacerations. Tissues of hymen and vestibule are engorged; 8 months pregnant by stepfather. Example of normal hymenal exam with evidence of penile vaginal contact. (Courtesy, Nancy Kellogg, MD, Alamo Children's Advocacy Center.)

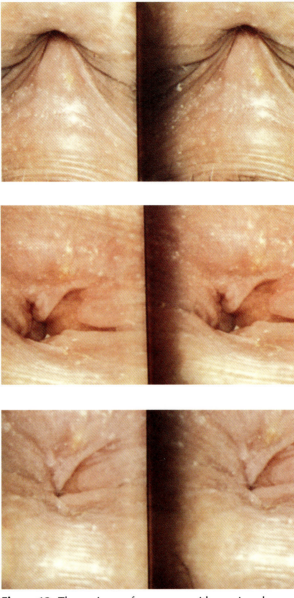

Figure 13. Three views of one anus with varying degrees of gluteal separation. Excessive or uneven tension can distort the anatomy significantly. The examiner's thumbs or forefingers should be placed a few inches from the anal folds with gentle tension applied evenly. The knee-chest position offers the best visualization of the anus, and gluteal separation is not usually necessary when the position is utilized correctly. (Reproduced with permission, Nancy Kellogg, MD., Alamo Children's Advocacy Center. In: *The Use of Colposcopy in the Assessment for Sexual Abuse/Assault.* [1997]. Leisegang Medical, Inc. Boca Raton, Fla., page 14.)

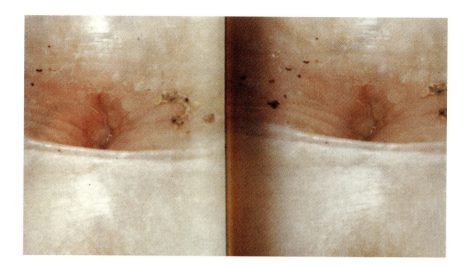

Figure 14. Incorrect positioning of patient and/or photocolposcope for knee-chest position resulting in an inadequate photograph of anus. Note that if the patient's lower back is not lordotic, the upper half of the anus will be inadequately visualized; if the photocolposcope is too low, the lower half of the anus will be inadequately visualized. The photocolposcope neck will need to be raised and the head of the colposcope tilted to the correct angle by the fine focus handle.

A. *Incorrect* Patient Position (Lower back not lordotic) Or,

B. Photocolposcope Position (Colposcope not high enough)

C. *Correct* (lens is at right angle to photograph object)

(Reproduced with permission, Nancy Kellogg, MD., Alamo Children's Advocacy Center. In: *The Use of Colposcopy in the Assessment for Sexual Abuse/Assault.* [1997]. Leisegang Medical, Inc. Boca Raton, Fla., page 16.)

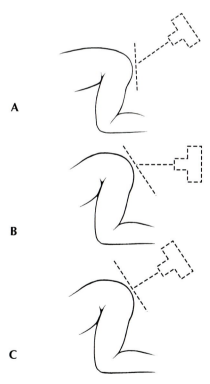

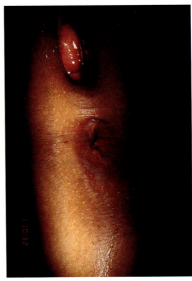

Figure 15. Use of 7.5 colposcopic magnification to view and photograph the perianal area. The 7.5 setting is sometimes better able to depict anal findings due to the larger field of focus. Changes such as fixed anal dilatation, perianal hypopigmentation and perianal venous congestion may be better demonstrated at lower magnification. (Reproduced with permission, Nancy Kellogg, MD., Alamo Children's Advocacy Center. In: *The Use of Colposcopy in the Assessment for Sexual Abuse/ Assault.* [1997]. Leisegang Medical, Inc. Boca Raton, Fla., page 26.)

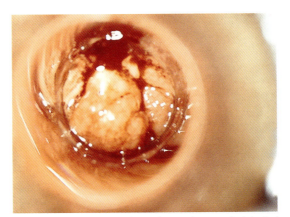

Figure 16. Rectal bleeding due to hemorrhoid. Colposcopy at 15 × magnification is used to view through the anoscope.

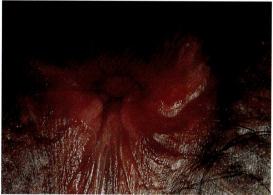

Figure 17. Adolescent female, 36 hours after history of forced sodomy; Wide anal laceration at 3 o'clock. Lateral decubitus position. (Courtesy, Nancy Kellogg, MD, Alamo Children's Advocacy Center. Reproduced with permission.)

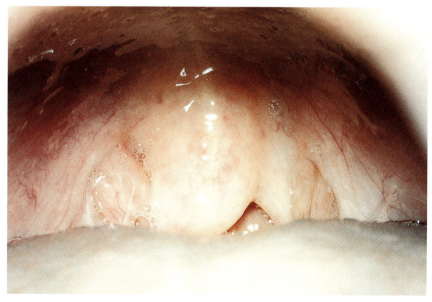

Figure 18. Colposcopic view of normal oral cavity (15 × magnification).

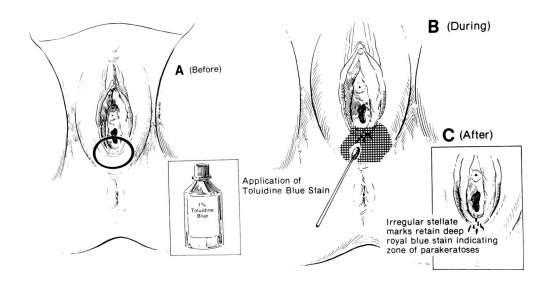

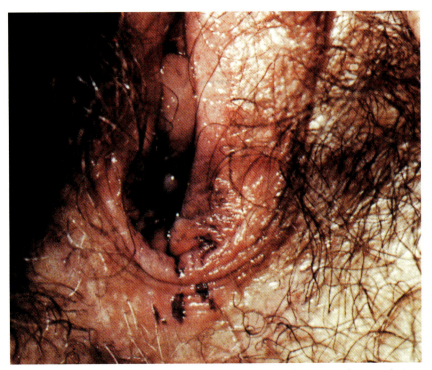

Figure 19. **(Top)** Toluidine blue dye application procedure: **A.** Before, **B.** during, **C.** after. **(Bottom)** Toluidine blue dye retained in postcoital perineal laceration. (Reprinted with permission from *The American College of Obstetricians and Gynecologists* [Obstetrics and Gynecology], 1982. Vol. 60, page 646.)

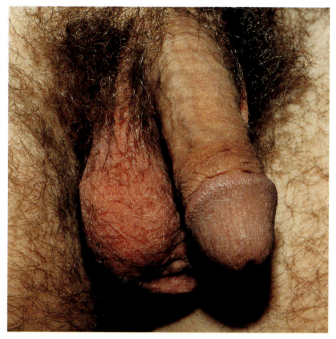

Figure 20. External male genitalia: Caucasian adult.

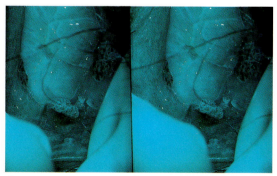

Figure 21. Detecting early Human Papilloma Virus lesions. The green filter can accentuate the blood vessels within the condylomatous growths, facilitating detection of these lesions. (Reproduced with permission, Nancy Kellogg, MD., Alamo Children's Advocacy Center. In: *The Use of Colposcopy in the Assessment for Sexual Abuse/Assault.* [1997]. Leisegang Medical, Inc. Boca Raton, Fla., page 24.)

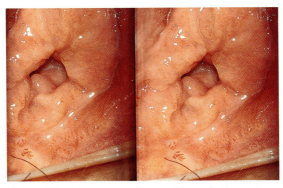

Figure 22. Human Papilloma Virus lesions: Two weeks s/p sexual assault (note vascular lesions at 6 o'clock in posterior vestibule). (Reproduced with permission, Nancy Kellogg, MD., Alamo Children's Advocacy Center. In: *The Use of Colposcopy in the Assessment for Sexual Abuse/Assault.* [1997]. Leisegang Medical, Inc. Boca Raton, Fla., page 25.)

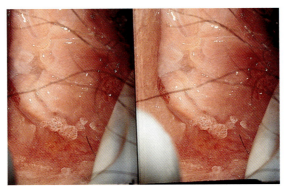

Figure 23. Human Papilloma Virus lesions: Six weeks s/p assault (HPV lesions seen at 3, 6, 9 o'clock locations within the vestibule). (Reproduced with permission, Nancy Kellogg, MD., Alamo Children's Advocacy Center. In: *The Use of Colposcopy in the Assessment for Sexual Abuse/Assault.* [1997]. Leisegang Medical, Inc. Boca Raton, Fla., page 25.)

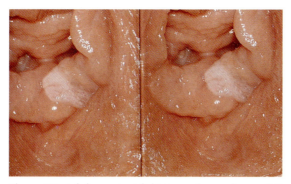

Figure 24. Adolescent with history of sexual assault 5 months earlier. HPV lesion at 4 o'clock in hymenal tissue. (Courtesy, Nancy Kellogg, MD., Alamo Children's Advocacy Center.)

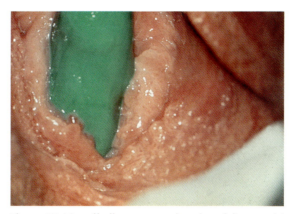

Figure 25. Use of balloon-covered swab to delineate old hymenal tear (Colposcopy, with 15 × magnification).

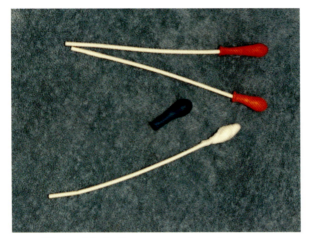

Figure 26. Balloon-covered swabs. Large rectal/procto swabs covered with tiny balloons.

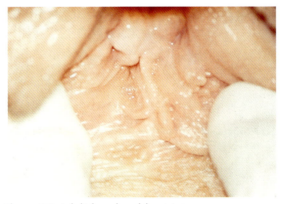

Figure 27. Adult female; old episiotomy scar.

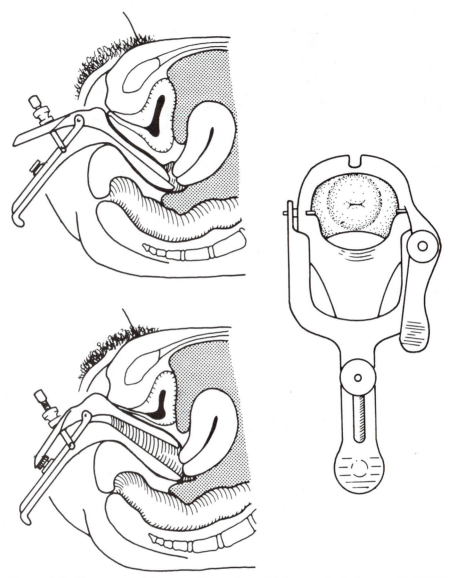

Figure 4–8. Placement of the speculum. *(From Lichtman, R. & Papera, S. [1990]. Gynecology Well Woman Care. Norwalk, CT: Appleton & Lange, p. 35, reprinted with permission.)*

mentation and venous pooling in the dependent position. The venous pooling may become quite pronounced if the patient has been in the exam position for any length of time; this should not be confused with swelling or bruising due to trauma.

The anus is normally free of blood, and no tissue should be seen protruding through it. Check for the presence of an abnormal mass within or upon the orifice. Abnormal findings consist of blood in the orifice, or protrusion through the orifice of a red, swollen mass

Figure 4–9. Anoscope.

(hemorrhoid), or a brownish, velvety mass (prolapse of the rectum). Skin tags and folds of anal tissue may generally be considered normal findings. Collect any dried secretions seen grossly, or with the use of the Wood's lamp or ALS, using distilled water to moisten the swabs. Label the swabs as "perianal," to differentiate from rectal samples.

Prior to collection of the rectal swabs in the female patient, gently *clean the perianal area with water* to avoid contamination of the rectal swabs from any runoff vaginal drainage present on the perianal skin. This helps ensure that semen found on the rectal swabs was indeed deposited into the rectum during the assault, and not transferred to the swabs from contaminated skin.

Two rectal swabs should be collected and two dry mount slides prepared. The rectal swabs can be made by slightly moistening them with water and inserting them one at a time through the rectal sphincter to a distance of about 2 cm. However, if the anus is first dilated with an anoscope, collect all forensic specimens, followed by STD samples during the same procedure, and simultaneously examine the rectum as well.

Insertion of the Anoscope

With the pad of a gloved finger over the anus, ask the patient to bear down, or strain. As the sphincter relaxes, the anoscope should be gently inserted into the anal canal, in a direction pointing toward the umbilicus. If the sphincter tightens, pause to reassure the patient.

After relaxation, proceed again. Note the tone of the anal sphincter. It is normally firm, but not rigid. The anal sphincter muscles usually close snugly around the anoscope. The sphincter tightens with anxiety, and may spasm after acute sodomy. Visually inspect the rectal mucosa for bleeding or tears. Inspect with the colposcope and photograph. Insert rectal swabs from the evidence kit. When using the anoscope, both swabs can be collected at the same time. (If STD testing is local protocol, collect a rectal gonorrhea culture and a chlamydia culture specimen.) As you withdraw the anoscope, inspect and photograph the mucosa at different levels. Make two dry mount slides from the corresponding rectal swabs.

PHYSICAL FINDINGS IN SEXUAL ASSAULT

At the conclusion of the medical–legal examination, the forensic examiner is asked to make a determination that compares the physical exam with the history provided. All of the earlier discussed techniques, protocols, and technology are incorporated into the exam to assist in the detection of any observable injuries that might have been inflicted during the assault. Sometimes, further evaluation is needed, such as interpretation of lab results to rule out coexisting benign conditions (see Figs. 4–10 through 4–14 on pages 82–84 for some examples). At times the examiner may wish to have colposcopic photographs reviewed, or see the patient in follow-up, before rendering a final decision. However, in most cases, the examiner will describe their findings after completion of the history and physical. Generally, the salient features are:

- Are there physical findings?
- Are these findings consistent or inconsistent with the history and time frame provided?

Since the growth of the rape crisis movement in the 1970s, more attention has been

▶ **TABLE 4–2.** ADULT MALE VICTIM: EVIDENTIARY EXAMINATION

1. Notify *advocate.*
2. Obtain patient *consents* on medical–legal exam form.
3. Obtain joint *history* with law enforcement.
    Describe threats, use of physical force, episodes of physical brutality (increased likelihood of multiple assailants).
4. *Clothing:* Undress on two sheets of paper.
5. *General physical appearance:* Objective data:
    affect, behavior, demeanor
    vital signs, height, weight, allergies, medications
    drug and/or alcohol use by victim and/or suspect(s)
6. *Wood's lamp* or *alternate light source (ALS):* Scan body; use swabs slightly moistened with distilled water to collect dried secretions that fluoresce. Indicate sites of positive fluorescence and collection of control swabs on body traumagrams.
7. *Nongenital trauma:* Measure, document, and photograph all bruises, lacerations, abrasions, and bitemarks. Use photographic L-scale and 35-mm camera. Swab bitemarks for saliva; refer to forensic odontologist as soon as possible, and cast, per local protocol.
8. *Head/oral:* Collect any foreign matter/debris in hair. If local protocol, collect *hair reference samples (20–30 pulled hairs from representative areas).* Inspect perioral area and swab if positive fluorescence. Inspect oropharynx for signs of trauma/petechiae. Photograph with magnification. If history of oral copulation within 6 hours, take two oral swabs and prepare two dry mount slides.
    Saliva reference sample (per local protocol): Gauze square, or two swabs saturated with saliva, or liquid sample. (Check with crime lab re: saliva reference sample if history of recent oral copulation.)
    Body/facial hair reference samples: 20 to 30 pulled hairs.
    STD tests: Oral gonorrhea culture from oropharynx.
9. *Fingernail scrapings:* Package Right and Left hand samples separately.
10. *Genital:* Collect any foreign material and/or matted pubic hair combings. Collect any dried and moist secretions, using swabs moistened with distilled water. Comb pubic hair and package comb/brush into envelope. Collect 20 to 30 *pubic hair reference samples.* Inspect penis and scrotum for signs of trauma or other lesions. Inspect for injuries/abrasions of glans or tearing of meatus. Photograph any trauma with colposcope. If uncircumcised, collect any retained foreign materials or secretions. Collect two penile swabs: one from glans and one from shaft of penis, using swabs lightly moistened with distilled water. If STDs: Collect urethral swabs for gonorrhea and chlamydia cultures.
11. *Anal:* Inspect for anal/perianal trauma and photograph with colposcope. Collect dried and moist secretions, using swabs lightly moistened with distilled water. Collect two rectal swabs and prepare two dry mount slides from these swabs. Insert anoscope, lubricated with water. Inspect rectum and photograph with colposcope.
    STD tests: Rectal gonorrhea and chlamydia culture. (Note: both evidence and STD swabs can be collected through anoscope after evidentiary swabs.)
12. *Laboratory:* (per local protocol):
    Reference sample (Blood): lavender top tube (for DNA) for crime lab and/or yellow top tube (conventional serology)
    Urine toxicology
    Blood alcohol (prep with nonalcohol swab)
    Syphilis serology
    HIV (separate consent)
    Hepatitis panel (optional)
13. *Specimens to crime lab:* Swabs and slides must all be individually labeled and coded to show which slides were prepared from which swabs. Note time collected. All biological material must be preserved by air drying × 60 minutes in stream of cool air and properly packaged. Biological samples should be frozen after drying. Whole blood is refrigerated. All containers for individual items must be properly labeled with name, contents, location of body, exam site, and initials of collector.

(continued)

▶ **TABLE 4–2.** (*Continued*)

14. *Summary of findings:* Note following:
    a. Time frame compatible with history given by victim.
    b. Physical findings (genital/nongenital).
    c. Findings are consistent with history provided.
15. Schedule acute patients with positive findings for follow-up exam to document resolution of trauma and/or any follow-up STD tests.
16. Administer appropriate STD prophylaxis (refer to Appendix I).
17. Follow up with advocate and/or refer for counseling.

paid to the rape victim, from both the psychosocial and medical perspectives. As the references at the end of this chapter show, numerous authors have studied different categories of rape victims. Some have focused on specific populations, such as elderly, pregnant, or postmenopausal victims. Earlier research relied on gross visualization alone to study both patterns of nongenital and genital trauma. In the mid-1980s, a few authors utilized nuclear stains to more clearly delineate genital trauma. In the latter half of the 1980s, we borrowed technology from the arena of child sexual abuse experts, and began to incorporate colposcopy

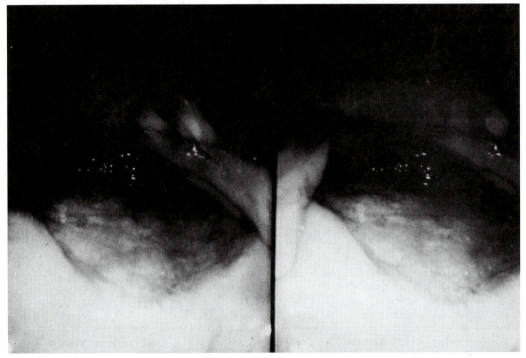

Figure 4–10. Colposcopic view of ulcer anterior to cervix caused by prolonged use of vaginal tampon. (*From DeCherney, A. & Pernol, M. [Eds.]. [1994]. Current Obstetric and Gynecologic Diagnosis and Treatment, 8th ed. Norwalk, CT: Appleton & Lange, p. 693, reprinted with permission.*)

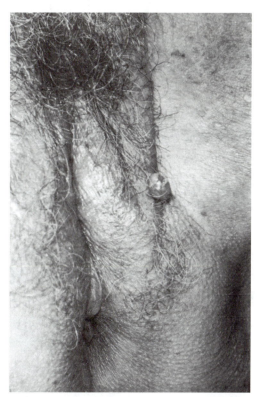

Figure 4–11. Pyogenic granuloma. *(From DeCherney, A. & Pernol, M. [Eds.]. [1994]. Current Obstetric and Gynecologic Diagnosis and Treatment, 8th ed. Norwalk, CT: Appleton & Lange, p. 701, reprinted with permission.)*

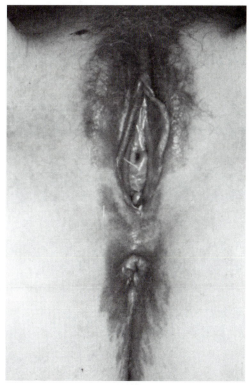

Figure 4–12. Typical lesions of psoriasis with a sharp outline. Surface will appear bright red. *(From DeCherney, A. & Pernol, M. [Eds.]. [1994]. Current Obstetric and Gynecologic Diagnosis and Treatment, 8th ed. Norwalk, CT: Appleton & Lange, p. 702, reprinted with permission.)*

into the physical examination of the adult rape victim.

The following discussion focuses attention on some of the studies that have examined the frequency of injury in rape, for both nongenital and genital trauma. Before doing so, however, it is paramount that no assumption be made, directly or indirectly, that the veracity of a report of rape be based on the discovery of physical findings. Even when the victim reports promptly for an exam, there are no studies where injury has been found 100% of the time. As we enthusiastically pursue our endeavors to find more efficacious methods of

uncovering physical evidence, we must keep this in mind.

INJURY IN SEXUAL ASSAULT

The human sexual response has been presented in Chapter 3. Concomitant with the many facets of the human sexual response is the anatomic layout of genital anatomy. To reiterate, some of the physiologic variables include:

- Lubrication, due to the tremendous transudation from surrounding venous plexuses.

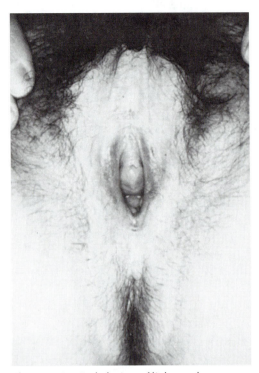

Figure 4–13. Early lesion of lichen sclerosus tatrophicus, typical hourglass configuration. *(From DeCherney, A. & Pernol, M. [Eds.]. [1994]. Current Obstetric and Gynecologic Diagnosis and Treatment, 8th ed. Norwalk, CT: Appleton & Lange, p. 708, reprinted with permission.)*

- Vasocongestive changes to individual anatomic sites. Individual structures swell and increase in size, due to the vasocongestive influence. Depending on age and parity of the female, these structures move laterally, away from the vaginal opening.
- Upward tilting of the female pelvis in preparation for coitus.
- Formation of a sperm pool due to the tenting effect of the cervix.
- Elongation and distention of the vaginal barrel.

Other factors exist in relationships that may be responsible for physiologic changes during the sexual experience. Emotional factors, age, prior sexual experience, and previous sexual encounters with a particular partner may further influence a particular sexual experience in *physical* ways that are not completely understood at present. Rape is a dynamic event. Although the encounter between the two involved parties may be brief, each individual brings to the situation a very unique synthesis of variables. While we study observable events, we must remember that this very fact may also account for some of these different outcomes. Some of these subtle variables may be reflected in cases of spousal

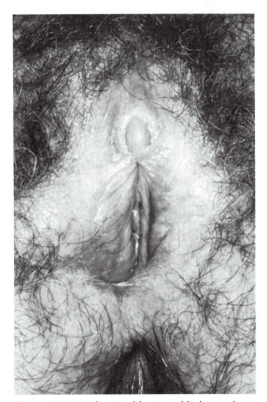

Figure 4–14. Advanced lesion of lichen sclerosus et atrophicus. The labia minora and prepuce of the clitoris have blended into the labial skin. Focal dysplasia was present in the posterior third of the right labium majus. *(From DeCherney, A. & Pernol, M. [Eds.]. [1994]. Current Obstetric and Gynecologic Diagnosis and Treatment, 8th ed. Norwalk, CT: Appleton & Lange, p. 708, reprinted with permission.)*

rape, or where the assailant is an ex-spouse or ex-boyfriend with whom the victim has had some type of prior consenting sexual relationship. Another example may be a victim who is compliant, but not truly consensual.

In Tintinalli et al's (1985) study of 372 rape victims, 68% of the victims had no injury, and 32% had injury to at least one anatomic site. The head, neck, and face sustained the most injuries (41%). Extremities were the site of 26% of the injuries. The vaginal and perineal areas comprised 19% of all injuries. Of note, every case of trauma to the vagina and/or perineum was accompanied by pain, bleeding, or both (Tintinalli et al, 1985:449).[4] The fourth site of injury was to the trunk, with 12% of victims sustaining injury to this area. Injury was unknown in 2%. The mean age of the group was 25 years old, with a range of 13 to 78 years. Women over age 50 accounted for 3% of the group (11/372). Although they were injured more often (63% vs. 32%), there were no vaginal or perineal injuries in this group.

In 405 of the 440 cases studied by Cartwright et al (1986), nongenital trauma was observed in 41%. This was considered objective evidence of nonconsent. The overall incidence of genital injury in this group was 16%. The genital trauma consisted of vulvar contusions and hymenal and vaginal lacerations.[4]

Lauber and Souma (1982), examined a group of 22 rape victims and compared them with 22 women who had engaged in voluntary sexual intercourse. All exams were done within 48 hours of intercourse. Their study included application of a 1% solution of aqueous toluidine blue dye to the area of the posterior fourchette. The use of this dye, a nuclear stain, was described by Richart (1963), for outlining cervical neoplasia. Use of this dye is based on the fact that, as a nuclear stain, it would adhere to areas of abraded skin and microlacerations, where squamae in the deeper layers of the epidermis are nucle-

ated. Lauber and Souma found a 40% incidence of genital trauma in the rape victims using this technique. Of those with lacerations, 70% of the victims were nulliparas. Only one woman in the consent group (5%) had these findings. This individual complained of dry, painful intercourse and had three radial fourchette lacerations. Another member of the consent group had a diffuse dye uptake that persisted for 52 hours, which was attributed to vulvitis. These authors proposed that the posterior commissure offers the initial resistance during forceful penetration, and that this is accompanied by contraction of the bulbocavernosus muscles (Lauber & Souma, 1982:644).

Also using toluidine blue dye, McCauley et al (1987) reported a 58% incidence of injury in a study of 24 victims The number of lacerations seen after application of the dye increased from one in 24, to 14 in 24. All victims were seen within 48 hours. Out of 48 control subjects, 10% had lacerations noted with toluidine blue. Of interest were two women in the control group who had sexual intercourse more than five times in the week prior to presentation. Both of these women were negative for dye uptake.

Collins et al (1966) described 23 categories of benign vulvar diseases. Because the dye is specific for zones of parakeratosis, false-positive tests can be due to any inflammatory causes, including benign or malignant diseases. Columnar epithelium, which lines the cervical os, may also give a false-positive result. The dye tends to give a more patchy and diffuse uptake with inflammatory processes. Slaughter and Brown (1992) found no trauma with toluidine blue that was not already seen with the colposcope. The dye is spermicidal in vitro. Lauber and Souma (1982) found no effect in vitro on acid phosphatase levels. In their description of exam technique, Lauber and Souma (1982) recommended that a sample be

---

[4] Note: Genital exam done using gross visualization; no nuclear stains.

aspirated from the vaginal pool for a hanging drop exam *prior to the application of toluidine blue dye, in order to exclude the possibility of contamination* (from the dye). However, this practice is not generally taught in training programs where use of the dye is advocated. Thus, utilization of the dye should be deferred until *after* the collection of forensic specimens. Adequate photocolposcopy can demonstrate that any trauma was preexisting, and not due to speculum insertion or manipulation of tissues.

Toluidine blue can be a useful adjunct to the acute exam, especially where photocolposcopy is not available. To be effective, it must be carefully and judiciously applied and conservatively interpreted. It can be quite useful in providing good visual depictions of genital microlacerations during courtroom presentation of genital trauma. The jury is able to "see" more clearly the areas of injury to the genital area.

A protocol that incorporated routine use of colposcopy for all sexual assault victims formed the basis for the study by Slaughter and Brown (1992). In their group of 131 rape victims seen within 48 hours of assault, there was an 87% incidence of genital trauma. Injuries were centered in the area of the posterior fourchette and consisted primarily of lacerations, abrasions, ecchymoses, and swelling. Nongenital trauma was present in 55% of the victims.

GENITAL INJURY IN ADOLESCENT FEMALE VICTIMS

Adolescent rape victims were compared with adults to study any differences in experiences and outcomes. Of 126 adolescents (13–18 years old), 60% had positive genital findings. Out of 189 adults, the incidence was 61%. The groups were similar with regard to knowledge of the assailant, multiple sex acts, use of alcohol, the proportion of single to multiple sites of injury, and the distribution of injuries. Adolescents

were less likely to be assaulted in their homes, and twice as likely to report the assault within at or greater than 72 hours. The only significant difference in the two groups was the frequency of hymenal tears, which occurred in 24% vs. 3% in the adult group (Slaughter & Crowley, 1993).

Crowley and Slaughter (1995) documented the status of hymenal tissue and studied the nature of old hymenal findings in adolescent girls. The incidence of nonacute hymenal trauma was 16% in 134 girls. Hymenal tissue was present in all cases, even though 79% had a known history of either consensual sexual activity, history of molest, or both. Single hymenal tears were present in 86% of those with old hymenal trauma, and were located at 3, 5, 6, and 7 o'clock. Multiple hymenal tears were present in 10%, at 5 and 7 o'clock, and 3 and 9 o'clock. Other, older findings included attenuation of the hymen and posterior concavity. Normal variants included anterior hymenal notches, or clefts, and hymenal tags. Hymenal tears were associated with pain 71% of the time, and bleeding 43% of the time. The most frequent location of hymenal tears was at 5 and 7 o'clock. (Note: genital exams done utilizing colposcopy at 15 times)

Adams and Knudson (1996) studied genital findings in pubertal girls, ages 9 to 17, who had been victims of probable or definite abuse. Abnormal genital findings were present on colposcopy in 32% of the patients overall, but were seen more often in those who were examined within 72 hours (69% vs. 26%), or who reported bleeding (50% vs. 26%). Hymenal transections occurred in 8% of the sample. (Note: genital exams done utilizing colposcopy)

FINDINGS IN POSTMENOPAUSAL RAPE VICTIMS

Ramin et al (1992) studied 129 cases of postmenopausal rape (≥ 50 years old), and compared them to 129 younger women between the ages of 14 and 49. Extragenital trauma was more prevalent in the younger group (66% vs. 49%), with more trauma to the head and neck. Injury to the trunk and extremities was common in both groups. Genital trauma was more frequent (43% vs. 18%), and more severe in the postmenopausal women.[5] Ramin and colleagues noted more genital edema, abrasions, and lacerations in the older group. Almost one in five had perineal or vaginal lacerations, with one in four requiring surgical repair. In Cartwright and Moore's study of 740 rape victims, women between the ages of 60 and 90 comprised 3% of the sample. In this older group of women, 52% had nongenital injury, and 52% had genital injury (Cartwright & Moore, 1989). Factors influencing increased prevalence of trauma in the older victim include connective tissue atrophy, lessening of soft tissue elasticity, and atrophy of the vaginal epithelium.

FALSE ALLEGATIONS OF RAPE

It is recognized by all professionals working in the field of sexual assault that there are false reports of rape, just as with other crimes. Ultimately, it is the jury that will decide on outcome and credibility of the victim. While the forensic examiner's role is to perform each exam as objectively as possible, we are asked to render an opinion as to the consistency of any physical findings with the history provided. While a full review is beyond the scope of this text, there are salient features of false allegations that have been recognized and studied. The distinguishing features described in these cases do deserve a cursory review. According to U.S. Bureau of Justice statistics (Greenfeld, 1997), 8% of rape cases in 1995 were determined to be unfounded.

McDowell and Hibler (1987) studied the dynamics of false reports of rape. They found, that in most cases, the solicitude and support given to these individuals from the criminal justice system, family, and friends fulfilled a desperate need for attention. In contrast, for actual rape victims, no amount of external support could fully alleviate the horror they had been through. The individual who makes a false report creates a history and exhibits behaviors based on what he or she believes would be the response of an actual victim. In these accounts the assailant is mostly a stranger and the pseudovictim claims to have used physical resistance, or describes a situation where resistance is impossible. The reported sex acts do not usually include oral or anal sex, unless these acts are included in the individual's personal repertoire of sex acts. The pseudovictim is often unable to recall or otherwise give an accurate account of the assault. Wounds may be numerous and varied, often made by fingernails or sharp instruments *not* found at the crime scene by police. While injuries may be extensive, they generally do not involve exquisitely sensitive areas, such as the nipples, genitals, lips, or eyes. The wounds tend to be present in areas of the body within reach, or at odd angles, which may be consistent with the individual's range of motion. The injuries may appear more severe than they actually are, reflecting a sophisticated understanding of anatomy. Extremely painful injuries may be reported with an indifferent, almost nonchalant air. No defense wounds are present, but hesitation wounds may be evident from an earlier rehearsal (McDowell & Hibler, 1987). In a study by Slaughter, Brown, Crowley, and Peck (1997), all false allegations were reported within 24 hours. In their experience, McDowell and Hibler found the reporting of these cases to be *delayed.*

---

[5]Note: Both groups were examined using gross visualization, no nuclear stains were used.

PATTERNS OF GENITAL INJURY

Using a protocol that routinely included colposcopy, Slaughter, Brown, Crowley, and Peck (1997) studied the nature of genital trauma. Positive genital findings were found in 213 out of 311 rape victims. These were compared with 75 females examined within 24 hours of consensual sexual intercourse, and evaluated using the same exam protocol. The mean age of the group of rape victims was 24, with a range from 11 to 85 years. Anogenital trauma was present in 68% of the group of rape victims; this contrasted with 11% in the consensual sex group. Of the 213 women with positive anogenital trauma, the majority were adults at or over 19 years of age (62%); adolescents comprised 38% of the group and women over 50 years of age, 2%. Most of the women with positive genital trauma reported within 24 hours.

Injuries were confined to a single site in 26% of the victims, and multiple sites of injury were present in 76%. The mean number of sites was 3.1. This was true for both adults and adolescents. Injuries were independent of lubrication; nine of the women were on their periods, and *all* of these had injuries. Genital injuries consisted of a localized pattern of injury, consisting of *tears, ecchymoses, abrasions, redness, and swelling* (TEARS). Table 4–3 lists the 11 anatomic sites studied and the most frequent type of injury to each site. Localized hypervascularity persisted on follow-up in five of the rape victims.

The most frequent sex act (80%) associated with genital injury was penile penetration. This was followed by digital penetration, at 43%. In those cases evaluated *within 24 hours,* where the victim reported *penile penetration,* the incidence of positive genital trauma was 89%. The mean number of sites of injury in this group was 2.3. In the group of rape victims with negative genital exams, 45% reported no penile penetration, and 37% were examined after 72 hours.

There was no difference in the mean number of sites of injury for adults vs. adolescents. The only contrast was in the frequency of hymenal tears, which were present in 18 adolescents, but only 4 adults. The incidence of combined hymenal–vaginal tears was 2%, and vaginal tears alone, 4%. Lacerations to the hymen and vagina were predominantly located in or near the midline. All but one were associated with penile penetration; one was from a foreign object. All were accompanied by vaginal bleeding.

Nongenital trauma was present in 57% of the 311 rape victims. Of this 57%, 74% also

▶ **TABLE 4–3.** SITES AND TYPES OF GENITAL INJURY IN RAPE VICTIMS

Anatomic Site	Frequency of Injury (%)	Type of Injury
Posterior fourchette	70	Tears
Labia minora	53	Abrasions
Hymen	29	Ecchymosis
Fossa navicularis	25	Tears
Anus	15	Tears
Cervix	13	Ecchymosis
Vagina	11	Ecchymosis
Perineum	11	Tears
Periurethral area	9	Ecchymosis
Labia majora	7	Abrasion, redness (equal)
Rectum	4	Tears

From Slaughter, L., Brown, C., Crowley, S. & Peck, R. (1997). Patterns of genital injury in female sexual assault victims. Am J Obstet Gynecol, 176(3):609–616.

had genital trauma. This contrasts with a 61% incidence of genital trauma in those who had no nongenital injuries. Of interest was a subgroup of 41 women who were raped by either a spouse/ex-spouse or boyfriend/ex-boyfriend. Fifty-six percent of these women had nongenital trauma, and 49% had anogenital trauma. In comparing this group with victims who had no previous sexual relationship to their assailant, there was no difference for the incidence of nongenital trauma. However there was a difference in the incidence for anogenital trauma; 74% of the victims with no prior relationship to their assailant had physical findings vs. 49% for those who had a prior relationship with their assailant.

A total of 38% of the victims with positive genital trauma returned for follow-up exam; the mean time to follow-up was 25 days. All injuries were resolved by this exam in 87% of the victims. Tears to the hymen and fossa navicularis did not reunite.

The mean age of the consent group was 25 years old. The 11% incidence of trauma was confined to one anatomic site. Hypervascularity was present in 11% (n = 8), and persisted on follow-up exam at 48 hours in six of the women. Hypervascularity was considered to be a normal variant (Slaughter, Brown, Crowley, & Peck, 1997).

The high incidence of positive genital trauma in victims with a history of nonconsensual intercourse suggests that exam protocols involving colposcopy favor a greater yield of positive genital findings in this population.

TECHNOLOGY TO EVALUATE TRAUMA

Photography

While photographs do not recreate original subject matter, they do preserve a visible record of that moment in time. Photographic distortion is relative to reality, and the replication is a two-dimensional reproduction of a three-dimensional object. A 35-mm single lens reflex camera, ideally with interchangeable lenses, is best suited for forensic photography during the medical–legal examination, both to provide less distortion and longevity of film life. Instant picture cameras lack sufficient sharpness in the print and a negative from which to make enlargements (Smerick, 1992). Instant autofocusing cameras are suitable for rapid preservation of a crime scene prior to intervention by emergency medical personnel.

Camera Functions

Exposure, depth of field, focus, flash synchronization, and motion blur are controlled by *aperture* (lens opening), *shutter speed,* and *focus* (Eastman Kodak Co., 1976). Each of these three camera functions is interrelated.

1. Lens opening (aperture)—controls the intensity of light that reaches the film. The opening is calibrated in "*f*" numbers. The smaller the number, the larger the lens diameter and light gathering power. Each successive number indicates a lens opening with one-half the light of the preceding number.
2. Shutter speed—controls the time that light is allowed to fall on the film. The exposure time is marked with the shutter speed series. The numbers are expressions of fractional seconds, eg, ⅛, ½, ¼. (Each is one-half the previous level and allows for doubling or halving of the time interval.)
3. Focus—controls focal length; sharpness of the image at the focal plane (object in the viewfinder forms a sharp image).

Different combinations of aperture and shutter speed are used to adjust the total amount of light which reaches the film. The aperture also controls the *depth of field,* which is the range of distances in a picture wherein the object looks sharp. A smaller lens opening provides more depth of field. The series of apertures allow for doubling or halving of the intensity of the light. The depth increases with distance, smaller apertures, and lenses of shorter focal length.

Photographic Protocols and Techniques

Each sexual assault program must develop protocols for collection, storage, duplication procedures, and documentation of all photographic evidence. Consult with other members of the multidisciplinary team so that collaboration in case management is optimized, chain of custody is maintained, and patient confidentiality is preserved. Table 4–4 is a sample photographic log which can be used for colposcopy as well as alternate light source (ALS) photography. Smerick (1992) recommends that the first photograph at a crime scene be of an identification card with salient data about the case, so that if film is ever misfiled or misplaced, the first negative contains identification information. This practice would work with all forms of photographic documentation, including colposcopy.

For most crime scenes, the camera should be held at eye level, from a standing position. A small lens opening (f/11 or f/16) guarantees that most of the scene will be in sharp focus. When using a macrolens, ensure that the film plane is *parallel* to the object of the photo to reduce distortion. Take at least one photo without the measuring scale, and keep the scale at the same distance from the film plane as the piece of evidence. Measuring scales will accurately depict the relationships of size and distance of objects.

Bracketing is a technique where additional pictures are taken at other exposure settings, eg, one or more f stops on either side; this is useful where reliable readings are difficult to obtain. A *macrolens* is a lens with an exceptionally close focus capability; the optics are designed to give high quality images at short distances. *Resolution* is the ability of the lens or film to reproduce fine details. A *single lens reflex camera* (SLR) is a camera that has a common lens for viewing and for taking the picture. It gives the same image in the viewfinder as the one formed on the film.

Prior to initiating photography of the victim, his or her entire body should be carefully assessed to discern any nongenital trauma that the assailant(s) may have inflicted during the rape. The history or interview may suggest the possibility of trauma; the examiner should look for it in all recent assaults. In the stress of the situation, the victim (or suspect) may not realize that they were bruised or hurt. Depending on the postassault interval, some of this trauma may not yet be clearly defined. Bruises may appear more demarcated and definitive in a day or two rather than in the first few hours after an assault. Swelling of some areas may hide the true margins or patterns of a wound. As a result, each area should be systematically inspected.

▶ **TABLE 4–4.** PHOTOGRAPHIC LOG

35-mm Camera	Colposcope	Alternate Light Source
Name:	I.D. tag:	Type ALS:
Subject (victim or suspect):	Magnification setting for	Type of camera and lens:
Photographer:	photos:	Type of film:
D.O.B./medical record or case	Number of rolls of film taken:	Band size used for
number:		photography:
Date/time:		Filter used:
Location/hospital:		Number of rolls of film
Description: Scene, body part:		taken:
Type of camera:		

Optional data to include in the log are: light source, camera to subject distances, environmental conditions, shutter speed, lens opening, and film type.

Note: Retain all original negatives, regardless of quality or subject matter (Smerick, 1992).

Inspect the head, neck, upper and lower extremities, chest, abdomen, and back for scratches, lacerations, bruises, erythematous areas, or bitemarks. The color of bruises is a general guide to their age. Recent bruises are more deeply colored. They fade over time, beginning at the peripheral margins and progressing to the center. The following information should be noted and documented on a body traumagram, if available, in addition to 35-mm photography:

- color of lesion
- size of lesion (metric or apothecary, but uniform throughout)
- location of lesion on the body

Refer to "hickeys" as "suction injury" or "suction ecchymosis." Bruises may appear with more clarity if the body part is photographed against a blue background. Blue surgical towels are ideal for this.

During inspection and photography of nongenital trauma, observe for:

- Damage to the teeth, gums, or buccal aspect of the cheeks from blows, wounds, bruises, or bindings.
- Signs of sexual bondage. Inspect and photograph neck, ankles, and wrists using a macrolens. Look for adhesive residue and/or ligature marks.
- Tears in the victim's clothing caused by stab wounds, may correspond to wounds on the victim's body. Backlighting the victim's clothing may help confirm this.

Photography at the actual crime scene may show criminal sophistication, evidenced by planned escape routes, offender activity pre-, post-, and during the assault, disabling of the phone, removal of bed linens and clothing, or removal of bondage material from the scene. Photography is often useful in the identification of two categories of sex offenders. Both the serial *sexual sadist* and those who *sexually exploit children* have a proclivity for taking photographs of themselves with their victims during sexual acts. The offender may cover his face or crop the photo (Smerick, 1992). However, identification may still be made via identifying birthmarks, moles, wrinkles, pimples, freckles, etc. A subsequent medical–legal suspect exam with photography that "captures" these features can offer side-by-side comparisons.

Evaluation of Nongenital Trauma

The victim of sexual assault can have a variety of nongenital wounds inflicted. In this text, bitemarks will be discussed as a model for the evaluation of nongenital trauma by the clinical forensic examiner. This is due in large part to the tremendous amount of clinical experience, research, and the development of protocols and procedures for the evaluation of these wounds that has been accomplished by forensic odontologists. The information presented herein is formulated on bitemarks, but is applicable to other wounds and patterned injuries.

Various factors may alter the appearance of the bitemark site at the time of the initial evaluation. The interval of time since the infliction of the bitemark, and anything done to the injured area either by the victim or emergency personnel may alter the physical appearance of the wound and recovery of biological evidence from the site. The wound may be cleansed, or contaminated by other substances. In the deceased victim, postmortem lividity, embalming, decomposition, and changes of position in the body can affect the appearance of a bitemark. The following will primarily cover evaluation of the bitemark in living victims.

Description of Bitemarks

The prototypical human bitemark is "a circular, or oval (doughnut, ring-shaped) patterned injury consisting of two opposing (facing) symmetrical, U-shaped arches separated at their bases by open spaces. Following the periphery of the arches are a series of individual abrasions, contusions, and/or lacerations reflecting the size, shape, arrangement, and distributions of the class characteristics of the contacting surfaces of the human dentition" (Bowers & Bell, 1995:347).

There are several variations to this prototype. These variations may serve to add to, subtract from, or distort the classic picture of a bitemark. *Additional features* may be present, including a central ecchymosis, caused either by the positive pressure of the teeth closure, or negative pressure from suction and tongue thrusting. *Linear abrasions, contusions, or striations* may present as drag marks (movement between skin and teeth), lingual markings, double bites, weave pattern (interposition of clothing), or peripheral ecchymosis. *Partial bitemarks* may be half bites, one or few teeth, or unilateral marks, caused by uneven dentition or pressure, or skewed bites. Bitemarks may be *indistinct, or fading.* These may present as fused arches, solid marks, closed arches, or be latent marks, and seen only with special imaging techniques. *Multiple bites* may be superimposed on each other. The final variation of the prototypical bitemark is the *avulsed bite* (Bowers & Bell, 1995:334–353). Table 4–5 summarizes basic features of bitemark documentation for the forensic examiner.

Procedures for Collection of Evidence from Bitemarks

Take orienting photographs *before* cleansing, wiping, or swabbing the area of the wound. These photographs illustrate the relation of the bitemark to the rest of the body, or body part. Keep camera parallel to the plane of the bitemark.

Swabs of Bitemarks

These may be analyzed for DNA (unless already washed or postemergency treatments). If swabbing the area would damage or alter wound pattern, it should not be done, or done only after all other preservation methods have been employed (Bowers & Bell, 1995). Use the following protocol when swabbing a bitemark:

- Use distilled water to collect dry secretions.
- Work from periphery toward center.
- Use either cotton swabs or cigarette paper to gather evidence.
- Take control swabs from other, unbitten region.

The examiner can take a final, additional dry swab and go over the bitemark area, to "mop up" any residue remaining on the skin, eg, and such. Label this swab accordingly.

▶ **TABLE 4–5.** BITEMARK DOCUMENTATION

Patient I.D.	Location	Shape	Color	Size	Type Injury	Other
Name	Anatomic site	Description of essential shape, eg, round, ovoid, crescent irregular	Note color, eg, red, purple, etc.	Note vertical and horizontal dimensions; preferably in metric	Describe type: petechial hemorrhage, contusion (ecchymosis), abrasion, laceration, incision, avulsion, artifact	Note if surface of skin is smooth, or indented
D.O.B.						
Sex						
Race						
Case No.						
Examiner	Surface contour (flat, curved, irregular)					
Date of Exam						

Data from Bowers, C. M. & Bell, G. (Eds.). (1995). Manual of Forensic Odontology, 3rd ed. Montpelier, VT: Printing Specialists. © American Society of Forensic Odontology.

Photography of Bitemarks

The American Board of Forensic Odontologists (ABFO) recommends that actual photography be done by a forensic dentist or under direction of an odontologist, if possible, following these guidelines:

- Start with conventional photography and equipment to obtain good quality photographic resolution.
- Both black and white and color print or slide film are recommended. If using color film, assure the accuracy of color balance.
- Both orientation and close-up photographs should be taken first.
- Take the most critical photographs in a manner that eliminates distortion, eg, 35 mm at right angles to various curves of the bite.
- A scale or ruler should be used in most shots (see Fig. 4–3). The scale should be kept on the same plane and placed adjacent to the bitemark, without obscuring it. Do not use a flexible rule or tape measure; this can cause distortion, especially on curved areas of the body. It is desirable to include a circular reference, in addition to a linear scale. More than one scale can be used to demonstrate a lack of distortion. Some photographs should be taken without the scale.
- Take a number of close photographs, with the scale in close proximity to the bitemark. Place the camera lens perpendicular to the bite. This is especially important for wounds on curved body surfaces, such as breasts, shoulders, arms, or legs (Sperber, 1981; Bowers & Bell, 1995).

Color or specialty filters may be used in addition to unfiltered photos. Alternative methods of illumination, video/digital imaging, tripods, focusing rails, bellows, or other devices may be used in addition to conventional photos.

If the victim is alive, it may be beneficial to obtain serial photographs if possible, for 5 days, at 24-hour intervals. Deceased victims should be refrigerated, but not embalmed as this washes out bitemarks.

Lighting

Whenever possible, use *off-angle lighting,* using a point flash (most common form of lighting). To complement or augment off-angle lighting, use a ring flash, natural light, and/or overhead diffuse light. A light source perpendicular to the bite site can be used in addition to off-angle lighting, but care must be taken to prevent reflection of light from obliterating details of the bitemark, secondary to washout. A light source parallel to the bite site may also be added (Bowers & Bell, 1995:334–353).

Bitemark Impressions

These are taken from the surface of the bitemark. Standard dental impression materials should be used. Materials should meet American Dental Association (ADA) specifications, be prepared in accordance with instructions of the manufacturer, and be identified by name in the report. Support the impression material to reproduce body contour accurately. Pictures, impressions, and wax bites of the suspect should also be obtained, by a forensic odontologist, when available, pending informed consent or court order (Sperber, 1981; Bowers & Bell, 1995:340).

For a thorough description of the point system used by forensic odontologists in the evaluation of bitemark evidence from victims and suspects, refer to the *Manual of Forensic Odontology* (Bowers & Bell, 1995).

The suggested procedure for taking a bitemark impression is as follows:

1. Load cartridges of impression material (vinyl polysiloxane) onto automix gun.
2. Attach automix syringe onto tip of cartridge of impression material.
3. Place part of body with bitemark in horizontal position.
4. Disperse or inject impression material over the bitemark (gently). Allow to set; this generally takes 1.5 to 5 minutes. (Manor, 1998). Take care not to trap air bubbles, these can ruin the impression. (Barsley, 1998).

5. Place backing material (such as Hexcelite orthopedic tape) over the impression material to provide rigidity without distortion and maintain the contour of the site.

6. Disperse another mix of impression material on top of the backing material (orthopedic tape). This secures it in place and produces a lifted impression.

Setting times vary, depending on equipment, impression materials, and temperature. The finished impression should be rigid enough for a model. Place in a secure, protective container for transport to the forensic odontologist.

Remember, human bites can be highly infectious. Ensure that the patient is either provided with or referred for medical evaluation, possible debridement, and treatment with antibiotics. Determine the patient's tetanus immunization status. Depending on the nature and severity of the bite, a booster of tetanus toxoid, and for more severe wounds, passive protection with tetanus immunoglobulin, may be indicated.

Colposcopy

Woodling and Heger (1986) described the use of the colposcope for the medical diagnosis of sexual abuse in children. The first to describe the use of the colposcope in forensic evaluations was a physician in Brazil, Wilmes Teixeira, who reported on the medical examinations of 500 patients between the ages of 4 and 51 years (Woodling & Heger, 1986). Colposcopy is a modality of magnified visual inspection, using a binocular system with 5 to 30× (or greater) magnification potential. Figures 4–15 and 4–16 illustrate both colposcopy with 35-mm photographic capability and videocolposcopy, respectively. In the past, colposcopy was used almost exclusively by gynecologists to study cervical pathology and help diagnose early carcinomas in situ. It has since been adapted and used for the evaluation of both child and adult sexual abuse victims. In addition to providing magnification, colpos-

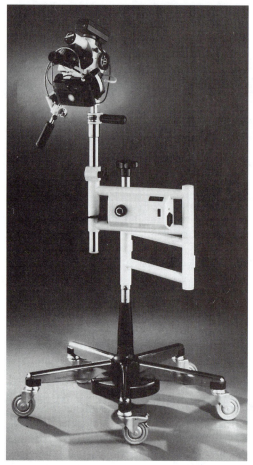

Figure 4–15. Leisegang colposcope *(Courtesy of Leisegang Medical, Inc., Boca Raton, FL; 561-994-0202/800-448-4450).*

copy is an excellent light source for use during the genital exam. Utilization of the colposcope to augment the genital exam of the sexual assault victim is a noninvasive technique. Any trauma seen grossly is depicted even more clearly; previously undetected microtrauma can often be seen. Years of clinical usage has vastly increased our body of knowledge of normal genital anatomy, both of adults and children. Muram and Jones (1993) have found videocolposcopy useful for adolescents, who are not often familiar with their own anatomy.

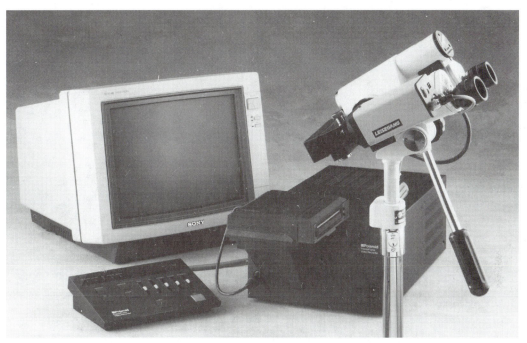

Figure 4–16. Videocolposcopy. *(Courtesy of Leisegang Medical, Inc., Boca Raton, FL; 561-994-0202/ 800-448-4450)*

The visual representation afforded by video-colposcopy simplifies explanations for patients in this age group. The photographic capability provides documentation of genital trauma, which can be called upon for court purposes as the photographs become part of the evidence in a particular case. It is important to manage strict preservation of custody over photographic evidence, as well as other physical evidence. Some varieties of colposcopes have a wide range of magnification possibilities. While these provide variety for viewing purposes, the colposcope should have certain fixed settings that enable the examiner to note which magnification setting was used during photography. This information is vital if these pictures are to be used for evidentiary proceedings. Figure 4–17 shows the use of video technology to allow networking and peer consultation/review via modem lines, using actual colposcopic images.

The Electromagnetic Spectrum

The use of reflective ultraviolet (UV) radiation has been widely studied for the photographic documentation of wound patterns. The mastery of UV photographic documentation evolved into the study of tissue illumination and fluorescent photography using other wavelengths of the electromagnetic spectrum. Table 4–6 shows the range of the electromagnetic spectrum of light. Since using lasers in the late 1970s, crime scene investigators have taken advantage of the fluorescent property of fingerprints. West and colleagues first adapted these principles and techniques to evaluate and photograph the fluorescence of patterned skin wounds, calling the process alternate light imaging, and later, narrow band illumination (West, 1996). The phenomenon of the Stokes shift (where fluorescent light is less intense and has a longer wavelength), makes possible

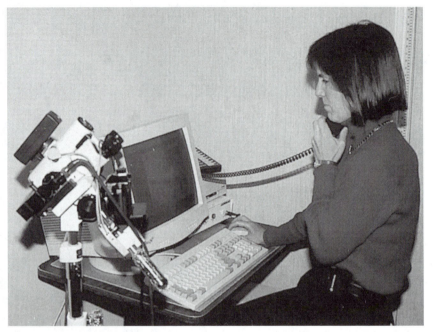

Figure 4–17. Using modems, videotechnology permits consultation with experts using colposcopic images. *(From Kellogg, N. [1997].* The Use of Colposcopy in the Assessment for Sexual Abuse/Assault. *Boca Raton, FL: Leisegang Medical, Inc., reprinted with permission.)*

► **TABLE 4–6.** THE ELECTROMAGNETIC SPECTRUM

Wavelength (nm)	Ultraviolet	Visible Light	Infrared	Alternate Light Source
14–310	14–400 nm, short UV light	400–700 nm	>700 nm	
310–400				
365–450	400+ nm, long UV light	violet		
450–485		blue		Narrow bands: 450, 485, 525, 570
485–530		green		
530–600		yellow		
600–650		orange		Two Wide Bands: <530 nm and All White Light*
650–700		red		
>700			infrared	

*The human eye accepts a wide range of light sources as "white" light, eg, the variance in appearance of daylight from dawn to dusk. If there are not conflicting light sources of widely variant color quality, any light source with fairly uniform distribution of visible wavelengths is perceived as white (Eastman Kodak Co., 1976). White light reflects all light rays, without absorption.
Data from West, M., Barsley, R., Hall, J., Hayne, S. & Cimrmancic, M. (1992, July). The detection and documentation of trace wound patterns by use of an alternate light source. J Foren Sci.

the application of high intensity light sources to observe the fluorescence of trauma. Light striking human skin is either reflected, transmitted to deeper layers, scattered, or absorbed by chromophores (molecules in the tissues). Absorption of a portion of the light energy causes these molecules and atoms to become excited. Within these atoms, the electrons may move to higher energy orbits. The energy they release on their return to the normal, non-excited state may be a photon, a quantum of light energy. This light energy causes a glow, or fluorescence. This fluorescent light is less intense and has a longer wavelength. It is less energetic and not observable with the eye; it is observable, however, if viewed through a filter that blocks the return of excitation light, causing visualization of tissue fluorescence. Hemoglobin, melanin, fibrous proteins, collagen, and fat absorb UV radiation due to protoporphyrin. Other substances, such as carotenoids also absorb UV radiation. Spectroscopic (absorptive) differences exist between healthy and damaged tissues. This forms the basis for tissue illumination by other wavelengths of the electromagnetic spectrum (West et al, 1992).

The Wood's Lamp

A Wood's lamp is used during the evidentiary examination to scan the victim's body and clothing for dried or moist secretions, stains, fluorescent fibers, or foreign materials not readily visible in white light. The American physicist, R.W. Wood, studied UV light during World War I. A disclosure of his experiments and attempts to manufacture beacons of invisible light for use as secret signaling devices for the war effort was published in France in 1919, after the war was over. Wood referred to the UV radiation as "black light;" the device used to illuminate it became known as the *Wood's lamp.* Long UV radiation encompasses wavelengths from 310 to 400 nanometers (nm). This light, while not visible to the naked eye, will cause certain substances to emit visible fluorescence, and has the least potential for causing biological damage (West, Barsley & Frair, 1992). Dermatologists were the first practitioners to use the Wood's lamp for the diagnosis of skin lesions. Ultraviolet light only minimally penetrates the epidermis, where it is either absorbed or reflected by compounds that are actually part of the healing process of wounds to the skin (Barsley et al, 1990).

Because it is a long-wave UV light, this portion of the exam needs to done in a darkened room. White cotton fibers are so prevalent that they rarely are considered forensically useful. Other dried biological material may represent blood stains, semen, saliva stains, traces of skin from the offender, lubricant used during sexual acts, fibers from the clothing of the offender, or debris from the locale of the crime, eg, carpet fibers, vegetation, grass, or soil.

Long-wave UV light has been successfully incorporated into UV photography, which is well described in the literature (Barsley et al, 1990). Immediately after a wound is sustained, the body initiates the healing process. The wound may become distorted, obscuring its pattern, due to inflammation, swelling, scarring, or other reasons, eg, a bitemark can be obscured or "buried" under a large, disfigured, bruise. While it is ideal for an expert, such as a forensic odontologist, to view a wound at the initial exam, this is not often possible, especially for living victims. Several cases have been reported where the wound was examined using UV light and photography. Even when observed days following infliction, images of bitemarks neither visible to the naked eye, nor manifested as a bruise or other *visible* mark were found (Barsley et al, 1990). A Wood's lamp is useful to locate the source of tissue fluorescence. This can then be photographed using UV photography. These techniques have proved quite successful, especially in cases where the patterned injury is older, eg, in child abuse injuries (Barsley, 1998).

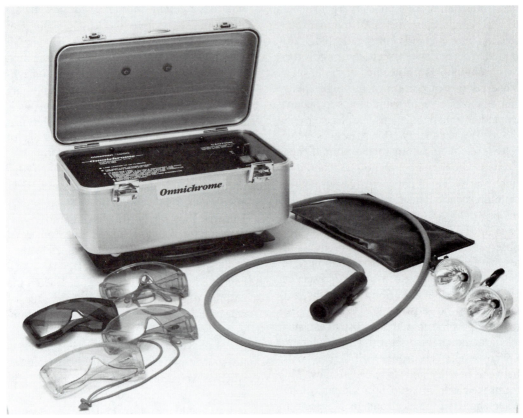

Figure 4–18. Omniprint 1000 alternate light source. *(Courtesy of Omnichrome, Inc., Chino, CA: 909-627-1594, 800-525-OMNI)*

The Alternate Light Source (ALS)

The alternate light source is a high intensity, tunable, forensic light source (Fig. 4–18). It was developed for forensic use in the evaluation of trace evidence, such as hair and fibers, questioned documents, shoeprints, and latent fingerprints. Illumination is delivered either through a 6-foot fiberoptic cable or directly through the light aperture. Selection by a rotary switch provides a choice of four narrow bands and two wide bands of light. The narrow bands are about 30 nm wide each: 450, 485, 525, and 570 nm, respectively (*Omniprint 1000,* 1996). Colored goggles block the reflected light and pass only the fluorescent light emitted by the tissues. The two wide bands are *white light* and all *wave lengths less than 530 nm.* The ALS may be combined with a manual 35-mm single lens reflex camera (SLR) with a 50-mm macrolens for reflective and fluorescent photography. West, Barsley & Hall (1992) and Golden (1994) described specific film types and speeds that have worked well for them in their clinical studies and experiences. Each camera system must be individually calibrated for best results.

The study of absorption and fluorescence of human skin and the application of the ALS has demonstrated wound pattern injuries in both living and deceased victims. West, Barsley and Hall (1992) and Golden (1994) studied bitemark pattern images as they appeared with alternate light imaging and compared them to the full spectrum of light. Many of these wounds were subclinical, that is, not clearly visible under normal visible light (West, Barsley & Hall, 1992). Using alternate light imaging, or *narrow band illumination,* cutaneous and subcutaneous tissue changes were visible. Optimal results were achieved with long-wave (450-nm) *visible blue light;* this is the optimum absorption frequency for traumatized skin (West et al, 1996). This enhanced the reflective and absorptive images of injured tissues, and more clearly defined and delineated wound patterns than did conventional lighting and photography techniques. In addition to the 450-nm narrow band, a yellow blocking filter to eliminate blinding excitation frequencies appears to be ideal for use at that wavelength (West, Barsley et al, 1996).

Narrow band illumination (NBI) includes ultraviolet, visible, and infrared light. Photographically, it includes reflective and fluorescent photography. The light source may be a laser, alternate light source, electronic flash, or flood lamp (West, Barsley et al, 1996). A *wound* can be defined as "an injury to the body of a person or animal, especially one caused by violence, by which the continuity of the covering, as skin, mucous membrane, or conjunctiva is broken" (Black, 1990:1607). A *wound pattern* is a lesion that suggests a particular object or mechanism by virtue of its location or configuration (Davis, in West et al, 1996). Wounds may be chronic, acute, or subclinical and are defined as follows:

- Chronic—eg, scars; can be seen with visible light.
- Acute—visible lesions, eg, bruises; can be seen with visible light.
- Subclinical—can also be acute; may or may not have symptomatology; not visible under normal light (West, Barsley et al, 1996).

Historically, fluorescent photography has been used for several areas of crime scene in-

vestigation. The alternate light source is often used during the medical exam for scanning the body (living and deceased) for possible semen stains and other bits of trace evidence. However, semen is not the only substance that fluoresces; so do food products, bacteria, and urine, to name a few others. Stains on material often have a halo effect, with fluorescence greater at the periphery than in the center of the stain (Devine, 1997). The ALS remains a valuable screening tool. It has also been used during the genital examination of both living and deceased victims of sexual assault to help discern patterns of genital trauma (Crowley, 1998).

The alternate light source presents tremendous possibilities in the arena of sexual assault investigation. West, Barsley and Hall (1992) recommend it for the examination of suspects as well, to denote patterned injuries that may link a particular weapon used in the commission of the crime to the suspect. It is also a tool for scanning for other defining characteristics of the suspect, eg, bitemarks from the victim, that may help identify and link a suspect to a particular crime.

SUMMARY

This chapter started at the top and proceeded all the way through the medical–legal examination of the rape victim. A sequential methodology for the medical exam of both the female and male victim has been presented, and can be adapted to meet the needs of different programs. Evidentiary considerations are correlated to various aspects of the physical exam, and can be tailored to individual crime lab needs and requirements. A partial review of the literature on physical findings in sexual assault provides a foundation to discuss and incorporate the significance and scope of injuries in this population. New and traditional technology assists us in the evaluation and documentation of both genital and nongenital injuries. Finally, it should be clearly evident to the clinical forensic examiner, that while we usually conduct the exam in a unique and independent style, we are interdependent on the diverse expertise and knowledge of the multidisciplinary team in order to realize the full potential of this process.

REFERENCES

Adams, J. & Knudson, S. (1996). Genital findings in adolescent girls referred for suspected sexual abuse. *Arch Pediatr Adolesc Med, 150:*850–857.

Barsley, R., D.D.S., D.A.B.F.O. (1998). Personal communication.

Barsley, R., West, M. & Fair, J. (1990). Forensic photography: Ultraviolet imaging of wounds on skin. *Am J Foren Med & Pathol, 11*(4):300–308.

Black's Law Dictionary, 6th ed. (1990). St. Paul, MN: West Publishing Co.

Bowers, C. & Bell, G. (1995). *Manual of Forensic Odontology,* 3rd ed. Montpelier, VT: Printing Specialists. ©American Society of Forensic Odontology.

Cartwright, P. & Moore, R. (1989). The elderly victim of rape. *Southern Med J, 82:*988–989.

Cartwright, P., Moore, R., Anderson, J., et al. (1986). Genital injury and implied consent to alleged rape. *J Reproduct Med, 31:*1043–1044.

Collins, C., Hansen, L. & Theriot, E. (1966). A clinical stain for use in selecting biopsy sites in patients with vulvar disease. *Obstet & Gynecol, 28*(2):158–163.

Cress, J., MD, Ophthalmologist. (1998). Personal communication.

Crowley, S. (1998). Genital Exam of the Sexual Homicide Victim by Forensic Nurse Examiners. Paper presented at the American Academy of Forensic Sciences. San Francisco, CA.

Crowley, S. & Slaughter, L. (1995). Hymenal Findings in Adolescent Victims of Sexual Assault. Paper presented at American Academy of Forensic Sciences. Seattle, WA.

Damm, D., White, D. & Brinker, M. (1981). Variations of palatal erythema secondary to fellatio. *Oral Surg, 52:*417–421.

Devine E, Supervising Criminalist. Los Angeles Co. Sheriff's Dept., Scientific Services Bureau (1997). *Evidence Issues: Sexual Assault Investigations Course.* Los Angeles: Robert Presley Institute of Criminal Investigation.

Eastman Kodak Company. (1976). *Using Photography to Preserve Evidence.* Standard Book No. 0-87985-166-X.

Frederick, D. (1995). Special Subjects of Pediatric Interest. Chapter 17. In: Vaughan, D., Asbury, T. and Riordan-Eva, P. *General Ophthalmology.* 14th ed. Norwalk, CT: Appleton & Lange, p. 346.

Golden, G. (1994). Use of alternate light source illumination in bite mark photography. *J Foren Sci, 39*(3):815–823.

Greenfeld, L., (1997). An analysis of data on rape and sexual assault. *Sex Offenses and Offenders* (NCJ-163392). Bureau of Justice statistics. U.S. Department of Justice. Washington, DC.

Lauber, A. & Souma, M. (1982). Use of toluidine blue for documentation of traumatic intercourse. *Obstet & Gynecol, 60*(5):644–648.

Manor, V., C.D.A., R.D.A. (1998): Personal communication.

McCauley, J., Guzinski, G., Welch, R., Gorman, R. & Osmers, F. (1987). Toluidine blue in the corroboration of rape in the adult victim. *Am J Emerg Med, 5*(2):105–108.

McDowell, C. & Hibler, N. (1987). False allegations. In: Hazelwood, R. & Burgess, A.W. (Eds.). *Practical Aspects of Rape Investigation: A Multidisciplinary Approach.* New York: Elsevier.

Muram, D. & Jones, C. (1993). The use of video-colposcopy in the gynecologic examination of infants, children, and young adolescents. *Adolesc Pediatr Gynecol, 6:*154–156.

Omniprint 1000, (1996). fsl-0001-2M5C-9502. Omnichrome, Chino, CA.

Ramin, S., Satin, A., Stone, I. & Wendel, G. (1992). Sexual assault in postmenopausal women. *Obstet & Gynecol, 80*(5):860–864.

Richart, R. (1963). A clinical staining test for the in vivo delineation of dysplasia and carcinoma in situ. *Am J Obstet Gynecol, 86*(6).

Sanders, M. and Graham, E. (1995). Ocular disorders associated with systemic diseases. Chapter 15 in Vaughan, D., Asbury, T. & Riordan-Eva, P. *General Ophthalmology* 14th ed. Norwalk, CT: Appleton & Lange, pp. 296–329.

Schwab, I. & Dawson, C. (1995). Conjunctiva. Chapter 5 in Vaughan, D., Asbury, T. & Riordan-Eva, P. *General Ophthalmology,* 14th ed. Norwalk, CT: Appleton & Lange, pp. 95–122.

Slaughter, L. & Crowley, S. (1993, February). *The Adolescent Victim of Sexual Assault.* Paper presented at the California Consortium of Child Abuse Councils Conference. San Diego, CA.

Slaughter, L. & Brown, C. (1992). Colposcopy to establish physical findings in rape victims. *Am J Obstet Gynecol, 166*(1):83–86.

Slaughter, L., Brown, C., Crowley, S. & Peck, R. (1997). Patterns of genital injury in female sexual assault victims. *Am J Obstet Gynecol, 176*(3): 609–616.

Smerick, P. (1992). Crime scene photography. In: Douglas, J., Burgess, A., Burgess, A. & Ressler, R. (Eds.). *Crime Classification Manual.* New York: Macmillan, pp. 269–298.

Sperber, N. (1981, July). Bite mark evidence in crimes against persons. *FBI Law Enforcement Bulletin,* p. 16–19.

Tintinalli, J., Hoelzer, M. & Oak, R. (1985). Clinical findings and legal resolution in sexual assault. *Ann Emerg Med, 14*(5):447–453.

Vaughan, D. & Asbury, T. (1995). *General Ophthalmology.* Stamford, CT: Appleton & Lange, pp. 296–297.

West, M., Barsley, R., Hall, J., Hayne, S. & Cimrmancic, M. (1992). The detection and documentation of trace wound patterns by use of an alternate light source. *J Foren Sci, 37*(6):1480–1488.

West, M., Barsley, R., Frair, J. & Stewart, W. (1992). Ultraviolet radiation and its role in wound pattern documentation. *J Foren Sci, 37*(6):1466–1479.

West, M., Barsley, R., Hayne, S. & Cimrmancic, M. (1996). Narrow band illumination and fluorescence and its role in wound pattern documentation. *J Biologic Photog, 64*(3):67–75.

Woodling, B. & Heger, A. (1986). The use of the colposcope in the diagnosis of sexual abuse in the pediatric age group. *Child Abuse & Neglect, 10:*111–114.

Yanoff, M. & Fine, B. (1975). *Ocular Pathology: A Text and Atlas.* New York: Harper & Row, Publishers, Inc.

SUGGESTED READINGS

A subtle sign of rape. (1992, May). [Editorial]. *Emergency Medicine,* 311A–312B.

Alpert, E. (1995). Violence in intimate relationships and the practicing internist: New "disease" or new agenda? *Ann Intern Med, 123:*774–781.

Augenbraun, M., Feldman, J., Chirgwin, K., et al. (1995). Increased genital shedding of herpes simplex virus type 2 in HIV-seropositive women. *Ann Int Med, 123*(11):845–847.

Baker, C., Gilson, G., Vill, M. & Curet, L. (1993). Female circumcision: Obstetric issues. *Am J Obstet Gynecol, 169:*1616–1618.

Bassford, T. (1992). Treatment of common anorectal disorders. *Am Fam Phys, 45:*1787–1793.

Bays, J. & Lewman, L. (1992). Toluidine blue in the detection at autopsy of perineal and anal lacerations in victims of sexual abuse. *Arch Pathol Lab Med, 116:*620–621.

California Medical Protocol for Examination of Sexual Assault and Child Sexual Abuse Victims. (1987). Sacramento, CA: Office of Criminal Justice Planning (OCJP).

California Medical Protocol for Examination of Sexual Assault and Child Sexual Abuse Victims: Training Curriculum. (1991). Sacramento, CA: Office of Criminal Justice Planning.

Cartwright, P. & the Sexual Assault Study Group. (1987). Factors that correlate with injury sustained by survivors of sexual assault. *Obstet & Gynecol, 70:*44–46.

Cohen, S., Beebe, J. & Duperret, M. (1978). Patient assessment: Examination of the female pelvis, part I. *American Journal of Nursing, 78*(10):1–28.

Crowley, S. (1996). Prevalence of Fossa Navicularis Disruptions in Adolescent Victims of Sexual Assault. Paper presented at the American Academy of Forensic Sciences Annual Meeting. Nashville, TN.

Edwards, L. & Dunphy, E. (1958). Wound healing, injury and normal repair. *N Engl J Med, 259:* 224–233.

Emans, S., Woods, E., Allred, E. & Grace, E. (1994). Hymenal findings in adolescent women: Impact of tampon use and consensual sexual activity. *Adolesc Med, 125:*153–160.

Embree, J., Lindsay, D., Williams, T., et al. (1996). Acceptability and usefulness of vaginal washes in premenarcheal girls as a diagnostic procedure for sexually transmitted diseases. *Pediatr Infect Dis J, 15:*662–667.

Finkelhor, D. & Wolak, J. (1995). Nonsexual assaults to the genitals in the youth population. *JAMA, 274:*1692–1697.

Ganong, W. (1981). *Review of Medical Physiology,* 10th ed. Los Altos, CA: Lange Medical Publications.

Gilliland, M., Luckenbach, M. & Chenier, T. (1994). Systemic and ocular findings in 169 prospectively studied child deaths: Retinal hemorrhages usually mean child abuse. *Foren Sci Intl, 68:*117–132.

Hampton, H. (1995). Care of the woman who has been raped. *N Engl J Med, 332*(4):234–237.

Jenny, C. (1990). Sexually transmitted diseases in victims of rape. *N Engl J Med, 322*(11):15.

Kaufman, R., Faro, S., Friedrich, E. & Gardner, H. (1994). *Benign Diseases of the Vulva and Vagina,* 4th ed. St. Louis: Mosby-Year Book, Inc.

Kecman, M. (1995, March). Who has time for a head-to-toe assessment? *Nursing, 95:*59.

Kellogg, N. (1997). *The Use of Colposcopy in the Assessment for Sexual Abuse/Assault.* Boca Raton, FL: Leisegang Medical, Inc.

Kellogg, N. & Parra, J. (1995). The progression of human papillomavirus lesions in sexual assault victims. *Pediatrics*, *96*(6):1163–1165.

Lichtman, R. & Papera, S. (1990). *Gynecology: Well-Woman Care.* Norwalk, CT: Appleton & Lange, pp. 35–38.

McCauley, J., Gorman, R. & Guzinski, G. (1986). Toluidine blue in the detection of perineal lacerations in pediatric and adolescent sexual abuse victims. *Pediatrics, 78*(6):1039–1043.

McCauley, J., Kern, D., Kolodner, K., et al. (1995). The "battering syndrome": Prevalence and clinical characteristics of domestic violence in primary care internal medicine practices. *Ann Intern Med, 123:*737–746.

Nyirjesy, P., Seeney, S., et al (1995). Chronic fungal vaginitis: The value of cultures, part 1. *Am J Obstet & Gynecol, 173*(3):820–823.

Rambow, B., Adkinson, C., Frost, T. & Peterson, G. (1992). Female sexual assault: Medical and legal implications. *Ann Emerg Med, 21:*727–731.

Roye, C. & Coonan, P. (1997). Adolescent rape. *AJN, 97*(4):45.

Satin, A., Hemsell, D. & Stone, I. (1991). Sexual assault in pregnancy. *Obstet & Gyncecol, 77*(5): 710–714.

Slaughter L., & Brown, C. (1991). Cervical findings in rape victims. *Am J Obstet Gynecol, 164*(2): 528–529.

Smith N., Van Coeverden de Groot, H. & Gunston, K. (1983). Coital injuries of the vagina in non-virginal patients. *S Afr Med J, 64:*746–747.

Smith, W., Alexander, R., Judisch, G., Sato, Y. & Kao, S. (1992). Magnetic resonance imaging evaluation of neonates with retinal hemorrhages. *Pediatrics, 89*(2):332–333.

Young, W., Bracken, A., Goddard, M., Matheson, S. & the New Hampshire Sexual Assault Medical Examination Protocol Project Committee. (1992). Sexual assault: Review of a national model protocol for forensic and medical evaluation. *Obstet & Gynecol, 80:*878–883.

5 Physical Evidence in Sexual Assault Cases

Early in the 20th century, Locard proposed that when two objects come in contact, traces from one will be transferred to the other, in both directions (Locard Transfer Theory). Most of what is discussed in this chapter evolves from this principle. Rape is a crime in which two people have intimate contact. From the forensic perspective, everything we do during the medical examination is aimed at the detection, collection, and preservation of any and all indicators of this contact. We employ procedures and incorporate technologies that will enhance our ability to be a medical "detective" at the very real crime scene of the victim's body. The fruits of this labor are then entrusted to the criminalist, who is responsible for the examination and analysis of this evidence. In turn, the criminalist will interpret all the evidence that is obtained.

This chapter discusses the implications of the physical evidence collected during the medical exam, including biological evidence of the sexual assault evidence kit. The role of DNA in sexual assault cases and problems that have emerged from the use of the rape drugs, Rohypnol and gamma hydroxy butyrate (GHB), are accented because of the tremendous impact and timeliness they present to the forensic examiner approaching the new millennium.

As an additional resource and reference, Appendix A, *"Physical Evidence for Submission to Criminalistic Laboratories,"* should be reviewed.

THE NATURE OF PHYSICAL EVIDENCE

Forensic science, the merging of science and law, deals with the questions of what happened, where it happened, when it happened, and who was involved. According to Inman and Rudin (1997), it is the job of the forensic scientist to translate the legal inquest into an appropriate scientific question, and to advise the judiciary on the capabilities and limitations of current techniques.

Physical evidence is any evidence that can undergo physical analysis. All physical evidence is circumstantial. That is, it supplies clues, but indirectly. The forensic scientist, and ultimately, the court of law must use inference and deduction to interpret the physical facts (Inman, 1997:3).

Basic to any discussion of this topic is a concise definition of the term *forensic*. Derived from the Latin, *forensis* (forum), it means *of, pertaining to, or used in a court of law; now used in relation to detection of a crime.* The term also means *of, pertaining to, or employing forensic medicine; the application of medical knowledge to legal problems* (The New Shorter Oxford English Dictionary, 1993:1002). Because of the legal implications, and the fact that anything that occurs within the context of the medical exam is subject to scrutiny in a court of law, the examination of the sexual assault victim is usually referred to as a *medical–legal* examination, sometimes informally shortened to the *med–legal* exam. Since biological body fluids deteriorate rapidly and will dissipate after a prolonged amount of time, the collection of physical evidence from the person of the victim is, in many states, confined to a 72-hour period. This framework is valuable for collection of *biological* specimens only, and should in no way be construed to suggest that a complete medical evaluation is unwarranted after 72 hours has elapsed from the time of the assault. A thorough physical exam should still be carried out to look for injuries to the body as well as the genital area. In some cases after 72 hours, a modified evidentiary exam may still be done, either to collect vaginal or cervical samples, or simply for reference standards, which may be compared to physical evidence found at the crime scene.

Evidence Kits

Sexual assault evidence kits are various types of forensic packaging systems, or sets of containers in which to contain and package all the collected physical evidence from a particular case. Their design varies with different law enforcement agencies, regions, and manufacturers. As shown in Fig. 5–1, these kits are usually preassembled, with envelopes or containers to hold individual items separately and avoid contamination from other items. Some newer kits, such as the combined Los Angeles Sheriff's and LAPD kit (Fig. 5–1), include a urine specimen cup and a separate bag for the inclusion of a copy of the medical–legal exam form. It is important to remember that in a rape, the victim's body is the primary crime scene. Utmost care must be taken to collect, preserve, package, and retain evidence in a secure manner. Sexual assault evidence kits are *not* the same as *rape kits,* the latter are the tools of the trade of the offender, used in the commission of the rape, such as masks, gloves, duct tape, ligature, or binding material.

A sealed, unopened evidence kit should be used for each exam. The purpose herein is to preserve *chain of custody,* the forensic idiom that refers to the need for absolute accountability at every step in the evidence collection process. The chain of custody begins with the individual collecting the sexual assault evidence. Every individual along the way who assumes responsibility for any evidence must document the handling and transfer of custody of that evidence so that there are no breaks in the chain of possession, or chain of custody. Correct documentation will safeguard the case against allegations of alteration or loss of evidence. When evidence undergoes a transfer in the chain of custody, the following data should be logged:

- Name of person transferring the custody.
- Name of person receiving the custody.
- Date and time of the transfer of evidence.

Whenever possible, the chain of evidence should be kept to a minimum. The chain data can be printed onto the evidence containers or envelopes, or attached on a printed form, or

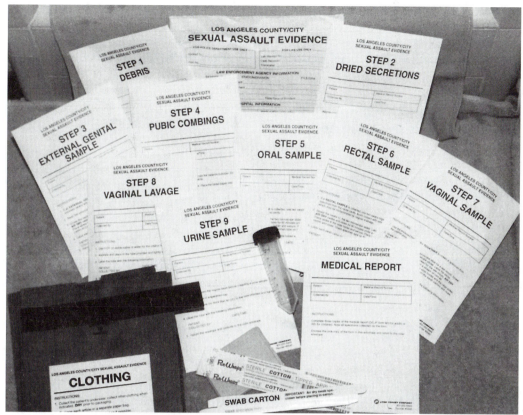

Figure 5–1. Sexual assault evidence kit. Custom kit for Los Angeles County/City Sexual Assault Evidence (includes urine specimen cup and envelope for medical–legal form). (*Courtesy of Los Angeles County Sheriff's Department Crime Laboratory.*)

labels. Individual envelopes should be sealed with tape, and the person should sign their name across the width of the tape to show that the envelope has not been opened.

The *time* of collection of the evidence is important for the interpretation of any findings by the criminalist. At the conclusion of collection and packaging of the kit, the evidence will be released to law enforcement.

Specimens for Evidence of Semen, Sperm, and Genetic Typing

Years ago, the discovery of spermatozoa (sperm) at the time of a rape exam was given much more significance as "proof" that pene-

tration took place. Semen may be lost more easily in the obstetrically traumatized patient. Without the mechanism of the human sexual response, the tenting effect of the vagina and cervix that results in the sperm reservoir will be lost. Additional reasons for lack of sperm recovery from the vaginal samples are ejaculation outside the vagina, either before or after intercourse, prolonged time between the assault and collection, vasectomy, condom use, activity of the victim such as douching, urinating, etc., conditions that cause azoospermia, and sexual dysfunction in the rapist. Bashinski et al (1985) found that in 25% of otherwise well-documented rape cases, no semen was found on vaginal swabs. Additionally, Groth and Burgess (1977) found that 34% of the serial rapists they studied experienced a sexual dysfunction of some kind, either retarded ejaculation, premature ejaculation, or impotence.

Oral Specimens

Oral samples are collected on cotton swabs and smeared onto two dry mount slides. Most protocols include collection of oral swabs if there is a history of oral copulation within the past 6 hours. According to Bashinski (1987), sperm recovery is unlikely after 2 hours in the living victim, although the literature has reported recovery from 6 to 13 hours. Devine (1997) reported finding only one positive oral specimen in a living victim in 12 years of examinations and over 350 cases. Oral samples are diminished almost immediately by normal activity such as salivating, talking, and swallowing. If the victim spits out the sample at the crime scene, the investigator should look elsewhere (clothing, bedding) for the sample. If this is the case, the item may have a higher yield, as there is not continued in vivo bacterial degradation. Sperm recovery in postmortem victims is greater than in living victims, but still rare (Devine, 1997).

Vaginal Specimens: Preparation of Slides and Swabs

Preservation and subsequent examination of the vaginal wet mount slide and the swab from which it was made are completed both for steps in evidence collection and to comply with legal requirements for retention of evidence (Bashinski, 1987). Sperm motility can only be observed on a wet mount slide at the time of the exam. As the slide dries, any living sperm dry out and become immobile. Sperm are more visible in a dried, stained smear than in an unstained wet mount. Therefore, a slide examined by the criminalist may yield positive findings, whereas the same slide was declared negative at the hospital. Another source of apparent discrepancy between findings at the medical exam and by

the crime lab lies in the examination of the slide at the hospital for *nonmotile* sperm. Sperm that have lost motility, or all or parts of their tails, are more difficult to discern and can be confused with other cellular elements on the slide. Except for fertility experts, most medical personnel do not examine the quantity of microscopic slides as does the criminalist, nor do they have the advantage of using phase contrast microscopes or cellular and nuclear stains to more easily identify sperm, either intact, or with heads only.

Slides are examined for the presence and quantitation of sperm, while swabs are examined for other semen constituents. If sperm are seen on slides, the orifice is considered positive; the criminalist will save the swabs for possible DNA analysis. Two slides per orifice are generally sufficient, although some protocols require *three* from the vaginal orifice (two dry mount and one wet mount slide).

The presence of motile sperm in the vaginal pool is one indicator of recent penetration and ejaculation. Normally, sperm will cease movement in the vagina within a short period of time, often within 30 minutes (Bashinski, 1987). In one controlled study, only 50% of the vaginal samples collected within 3 hours contained motile sperm (Soules et al, 1978). It is important to distinguish between vaginal and cervical samples, as sperm survival is greater in the cervix. The vaginal pool sample represents the most recent deposit of semen. Table 5–1 summarizes some of the studies reflecting sperm survival. An exhaustive review of the literature on sperm survival is beyond the scope of this text. While reviewing the literature for such studies, it is wise to pay special attention to the sample populations for factors that could affect sperm survival or sperm recovery.

If there was prior consenting sexual activity by the rape victim, it is vital to note this and collect appropriate samples to assist the criminalist's evaluation of analytical findings. There is mixing of the semen with the victim's own vaginal secretions. Interpretation of

► **TABLE 5–1.** MOVING RIGHT ALONG. . .A TALE OF TWO SPERM: MOTILE & NON-MOTILE

Study	Motile		Nonmotile	
	Vagina	*Cervix*	*Vagina*	*Cervix*
Bashinski (1987)	Sperm can cease moving in vagina within 30 min, review of literature: 50% positive within 3 hrs; n = 15 volunteers (Soules, 1978).		≈72 hrs *Oral:* unlikely after 72 hrs in *living victim;* *Rectal:* survival of sperm constituents variable; < vagina.	Considerably > vagina.
Hampton (1995) review of literature	8 hrs	2–3 days	24 hrs	2–3 days
Ramin et al (1992) rape victims	Up to 24 hrs in premenopausal group. Only within 6 hrs in postmenopausal group.			
Satin et al (1991) 114 pregnant rape victims; 114 nonpregnant victims	Pregnant group: 51% positive sperm total; 12% motile.		Pregnant group: 39%	
data collected on exams within 24 hrs	Nonpregnant: 46% positive total: 12% motile		Nonpregnant: 34%	
Silverman (1978) n = 675 of 980 volunteers			65% positive at 24 hrs; irregularly >10th day; rare after 10th day.	
Smally (1982); Bashinski (1987) review of literature	Average 3–4 hrs Occasionally 12–24 hrs (1) thus, postcoital interval: 3–8 hrs; rarely up to 24 hrs (1)Wallace Haagens (1975) Wecht (1969) Massey (1971)	Up to 7 days (2)Massey (1971) Austin (1975) Pollack (1943) Perloff (1964)	7–12 hrs; Occasionally 24 hrs Rare at 3 days Thus, postcoital interval is 12–18 hrs; rarely 24–48 hrs	7–17 days (3)Massey (1971)
Tintinalli & Hoelzer (1985) n = 372 rape victims	31% positive (on saline suspension); does not *specify* motility ≤12 hrs: 37%; 13–24 hrs: 14%; >24 hrs: 5%			

(*continued*)

▶ **TABLE 5–1.** (*Continued*)

Study	Motile		Nonmotile	
	Vagina	*Cervix*	*Vagina*	*Cervix*
Tucker et al (1990) review of literature	None after 12 hrs		Within 24 hrs: 100% recovery	Up to 17 days
Tucker et al (1990) SARS (Sexual Assault Resource Service) study: n = 1007	37% positive sperm up to 12 hrs; one at 39 hrs; n = 919 vaginal samples; motile, non-motile not speci-fied. *Oral:* n = 369; 1% positive (within 3 hrs) *Anal:* n = 210; 2% positive (within 4 hrs)			
Young et al (1992) literature review	24 hrs	>24 hrs		

results becomes more complex when there are multiple assailants and/or recent consensual sexual activity. Swab samples from the vagina, mouth, and rectum are analyzed by the criminalist for the presence of sperm and seminal constituents, such as acid phosphatase and P_{30} which is a male specific protein produced in the prostate gland. A P_{30} quantitation aids the criminalist in evaluating the amount of semen present in a sample. The presence of P_{30} can also confirm the presence of semen when no sperm cells are found. If semen is present, genetic typing tests may then be done. The criminalist may look at the phosphoglucomutase (PGM) enzyme system using conventional serology in an attempt to discriminate between possible donors and exclude individuals prior to utilizing DNA analysis.

Negative findings of seminal fluid on an orifice sample constitute four scenarios:

1. Lack of penile penetration in the orifice.
2. Penile penetration, without ejaculation.
3. Penile penetration, but with loss of semen between the time of the sexual contact, and the time of evidence collection.
4. No sexual contact at all.

Acid Phosphatase

Acid phosphate reagents are used to screen items such as swabs, clothing, and bedding to determine if there is seminal fluid present. Prostatic and vaginal acid phosphatase are enzymes that liberate inorganic phosphate from phosphoric esters. High levels of acid phosphatase are present in semen. Small amounts of vaginal acid phosphatase have been found in adult females. After ejaculation has occurred, there is mixing of the secretions from both the male and female. Shortly after coitus, the vaginal secretions will have high levels of acid phosphatase due to the male contribution. This level decreases rapidly over time as the post-coital interval increases. According to Bashinski (1987), extremely high levels are unlikely to be recovered from the vaginal fluids after 10 to 12 hours postcoitus. However, moderately high levels may be compatible with a longer range of time. Tucker et al (1990) found positive acid phosphatase in 62% of the vaginal samples up to 36 hours postassault. Of the positive specimens, 68% were collected within 5 hours; 88% of the positive samples were collected in 12 hours or less.

P_{30} (Seminal-specific Glycoprotein)

The discovery of P_{30} can confirm the presence of semen when no sperm cells can be found, such as in the case of the azoospermic rapist. This substance can be sloughed in seminal epithelial cells, which can be tested for DNA. The chief causes of azoospermia are vasectomy, congenital atrophy, undescended testicles, orchitis secondary to mumps, tuberculosis, gonorrhea, and coitus interruptus (Smally, 1982). Hampton (1995) reported that the presence of P_{30} indicates ejaculation within the past 48 hours. Due to the wide range of levels of P_{30} in males, negative P_{30} results should be evaluated cautiously.

Rectal Specimens

The rectal specimens are collected using cotton swabs, as described in Chapter 4. Two dry mount slides are made from the swabs; these are examined for the presence of sperm. Sperm survival is much more difficult in the rectum than in the vagina due to the quantity of foreign material and increased bacterial content. If care has not been taken by the examiner to wash the perianal area with water prior to the collection of the two rectal swabs, semen present on the skin may be introduced onto the rectal swab during the collection process. (An external genital swab should have been collected prior to this step.) If the collection is done properly, the quantity or density of sperm on the smear may assist the criminalist in determining if the semen was deposited directly into the rectum.

Penile Specimens

If a male victim has had oral copulation performed on him, and penile swabs are promptly collected, the saliva of the suspect may be recovered. Penile swabs of the glans and shaft are also collected during a suspect medical–legal exam, as noted in Appendix E.

Aspirates or Washings

In jurisdictions where the crime lab requests a vaginal aspirate or washing, *in addition* to vaginal swabs and slides, this specimen is now used almost exclusively for DNA analysis (Devine, 1997). Where STD tests are conducted as part of the clinical exam, a separate portion of the aspirate may be sent to the hospital lab for wet prep analysis.

OTHER EVIDENCE TO THE CRIME LABORATORY

Clothing

The clothing worn during the rape is usually collected as part of the physical evidence. If the victim has changed clothing, but has not showered, it may still be useful to collect the underpants worn to the exam, as they may contain stains from postassault drainage. According to Devine (1997), in cases where clothing is obtained, approximately 70% of victim's clothing is positive for semen in cases where the evidence kits are negative. With large items, such as bedding, sheets, etc., it is helpful to designate the position of the stain on the bed, eg, top, bottom, along with the initials of the collector. Because other stains may be present on the sheet or bedding item that originated from a *prior unrelated* consensual encounter(s) (possibly with more than one partner), the investigator can carefully encircle a wet or moist area to indicate its location so that when this item is dried, the criminalist can isolate the relevant stain for analysis.

Two sheets of paper (white exam table paper is excellent) should be placed on the floor, one on top of the other. The top sheet will collect any foreign debris that falls off the victim/clothing, while the bottom sheet will protect this sheet and the clothing from contamination by fibers or other particles on the exam room carpet. The bottom sheet will be discarded. The top sheet will be collected, folded into a bindle to capture any foreign debris, and placed in its own evidence bag. The patient removes shoes prior to standing on the paper. If law enforcement requests collection of the shoes for evidence, they can be packaged and sent separately. Prior to packaging each article of clothing, they should be observed for rips, tears, foreign matter, or stains. The clothing can be scanned with the Wood's lamp or alternate light source (ALS) to detect any areas of positive fluorescence. If the victim has sustained stab wounds or other severe injuries, these would obviously require emergency attention prior to the sexual assault response team (SART) exam. The SART examiner or other crime scene photographer should ensure that photographs be taken in the emergency room, prior to medical treatment. Later the examiner can use a technique called backlighting, or shining a bright light through the holes or tears in the clothing (Smerick, 1992). Upon illumination, the examiner notes whether the tears appear to be consistent with the location of the stab wounds on the body.

Articles of clothing with any significant findings should be photographed with a 35-mm camera, especially if the possibility exists that folding an item may alter a particularly striking effect that has been noted. For example, a shirt or blouse may have a particular pattern imprinted on it from grass or dirt stains, or some object upon which the victim was lying during the assault. Care should be exercised while folding clothing so as to avoid folding across a stain or allow the transfer of or loss of debris from one garment to another. Each article should be placed in a separate paper bag, sealed, and appropriately labeled for chain of custody. Plastic bags should never be used, as they retain moisture which allows the growth of bacteria and causes degradation of biological fluids. Not infrequently, the patient may report that a particular item of clothing is at home. The patient should then be instructed to save it and given a paper bag for collection. It should be submitted to law enforcement as soon as possible. Documentation on the medical form should indicate whether the victim changed clothing after the assault, the disposition of the clothing, significant findings, and a list of clothing items collected by the examiner.

Fingernail Scrapings

If the victim indicates that he or she may have scratched the assailant, fingernail scrapings, or cuttings, may yield bits of the assailant's blood or skin. DNA analysis can be performed on this tissue.

Foreign Materials

Foreign materials that may be present on the victim's body include blood, dried secretions, fibers, loose hairs, vegetation, dirt, gravel, and bits of glass. Loose head, pubic, facial, or body hairs belonging to the assailant(s) may adhere to the victim's own head hair or clothing. Some protocols include combing the head hair; others simply recommend close scrutiny for the presence of foreign hairs, debris, or dried secretions. All foreign materials collected from the victim must be packaged separately in paper bindles or envelopes supplied in the kit, and labeled with the location on the body or item of clothing.

Collection of Moist Secretions

These should be collected with a dry swab to avoid dilution. All secretion samples should be clearly labeled as to the site of collection and appearance.

Collection of Dried Stains

Stains or secretions that fluoresce with the Wood's lamp or ALS can be collected onto a swab that has been slightly moistened with *distilled water, never saline.* It is imperative to note the location of the stain. Ideally, a smear/slide should also be made of the stain. It is easier for a criminalist to assess sperm concentration on a slide. The entire swab sample can then be preserved for genetic typing (Devine, 1998).

Collection of Crusted Stains

Dried, crusted stains may be from semen or blood, and can be collected by gently scraping the area with the edge of a clean glass slide or the back of a sterile scalpel blade into an appropriate bindle or envelope. If the material is in the pubic hair, the matted hairs should be cut out and packaged separately. It must be remembered that samples collected by the above methods are not of *known* origin, but are rather of *suspicious* substances. Thus, whenever such samples are collected, it is important to also collect a *control swab,* from an unstained area of the body. Some criminalists prefer only one body control swab for Wood's lamp comparisons; others request a control for each dried stain sample. It is not necessary to make slides of control swabs.

Condoms

Not uncommonly, the assailant may leave a condom at the crime scene. Any liquid remaining in the condom is less stable than if the sample were dry. The condom is evidence *separate* from the victim's body, and is technically not in the jurisdiction of a medical–legal exam. Therefore, it is best to transport the condom to a criminalist for collection and documentation. *If* the sample *must* be collected during the medical exam in exigent circumstances collect one swab by swabbing the exterior of the condom. A second swab should be collected from the interior of the condom (both his and hers). The swabs should be air dried, as usual. The condom should be bindled and taken to the crime

lab as soon as possible. A small piece of sterile gauze is an acceptable substitute, but must be thoroughly air dried as well.

Matted Pubic Hair

Pubic hair may become matted with dried secretions, either from vaginal drainage after the assault, or if the suspect ejaculated outside the vagina. This may be obvious with gross visualization, or may be visible under ultraviolet (UV) or alternate light scanning. The matted hairs will be examined for the presence of semen.

Pubic Hair Combings

The examiner packages the paper towel or paper used to collect any hairs that may have fallen off during the combing or brushing of the pubic hairs. Hairs are best preserved by folding a bindle. The comb or brush should be included in the bindle. The hairs collected may be some of the victim's own, or may also contain hairs from the assailant. Hairs can be compared microscopically, and if hairs foreign to the victim are identified, they can be tested utilizing polymerase chain reaction (PCR) DNA.

Swabs of Bitemarks

Swabs collected from a bitemark may yield the saliva of the assailant, which can be analyzed for DNA (see "Procedures for Collection of Evidence from Bitemarks," Chap. 4 p. 92). A forensic odontologist should be consulted for review of the 35-mm photographs and any impressions of the bitemark taken by the forensic examiner. Sequential photographs of the victim over several days are advisable, as the wound pattern will change as time progresses. If a suspect is apprehended, the forensic odontologist can make or arrange for his dental impressions to compare to the three-dimensional impression of the wound and bruise pattern.

Reference Standards

Reference standards are specimens collected from the victim either at the time of the exam, or at a later time, depending on local policy. They are used to determine if the collected evidence specimens are foreign to the victim or the victim's own. They can also be used to identify or eliminate potential suspects. They may include the following specimens:

1. Liquid blood sample utilizing an EDTA tube for conventional and DNA analysis. Serology samples cannot be interchanged with toxicology samples.
2. Pulled head hairs: 15 to 20; representing different areas of the head.
3. Pulled pubic hairs: 15 to 20; representing different areas of genital area.
4. Saliva sample: liquid, or two swabs, or gauze/cotton pledget (depending on local crime lab protocol).
5. Male victim: facial or body hair samples.

If possible, it is best not to obtain a saliva reference sample at the time of the initial medical exam if there is a recent history of oral copulation (Devine, 1998).

Hair grows in three stages, with each stage having subtle differences in morphology. These stages include:

- Anagen—the actively growing stage; the roots of these hairs are best for DNA analysis.
- Catagen—the resting stage.
- Telogen—ready to be shed; hairs in this stage are most likely to be shed during an assault.

Forced hair removal may remove hairs in the anagen and catagen stages. Hair that is cut lacks the essential morphologic features that are found at or near the hair root. Samples collected only by combing removes telogen phase hairs. While these are less useful as a reference sample of the victim, they may contain foreign hairs from the assailant (Young, 1992).

Pulling is the best method of hair removal for forensic sampling and comparison. This collects both anagen and catagen hairs. Foreign hairs that may link the victim to the suspect during the crime are obviously only going to be present at the initial exam and should be collected at that time, by combing, or careful examination of the head for the presence of foreign matter. Many jurisdictions do not collect any of the reference samples at the time of the exam, but wait until a forensic comparison is deemed necessary by the crime lab. Since the victim's own reference standards are not going to change unless the individual colors or has a permanent, it is a matter of local protocol. The other viewpoint holds that it is more effective to collect all samples at one time, since the victim has to submit to so many other procedures. This avoids a return visit just for the collection of reference samples. One factor that may influence this decision is the size of the jurisdiction served as well as the caseload and storage capacities for biological evidence that a particular crime lab may possess. Except in exigent circumstances, adhere to the protocol of the jurisdiction; variation may cause problems, such as inconsistencies in procedures.

Blood Alcohol and Urine Toxicology

Depending on local protocol, blood for a blood alcohol level may be drawn, and urine collected, on both victims and suspects. Some jurisdictions do this for all cases within a specified time range in order to provide consistency of technique and uniformity of protocol. In this manner, certain patients do not seem to be *singled out* for these tests. Although it may seem to inject bias if the victim has ingested alcohol or drugs prior to the assault, there are strong arguments for testing:

- Drug and alcohol use is recognized as prevalent in society, especially in age groups most often associated with sexual assault.
- Drug and alcohol use is a recognized factor for increasing a victim's risk level; this is

not the same as a causation, nor is it an excuse for the assailant. Rather, the effects of the drug or alcohol impair judgment and may preclude informed consent for any activity, inclusive of sexual acts.

- In programs where all victims are routinely asked to submit a sample, it cannot be argued by the defense that the suspect was tested and yet the victim did not have to comply.
- If the case proceeds to trial, and the victim did indeed partake of either drugs or alcohol, it will almost certainly come out at some point in the investigation. The issue of a victim's use of drugs and/or alcohol can be effectively handled without compromising the case, if it does not seem that efforts were made to hide this knowledge.
- Because drug and alcohol abuse will eventually be revealed, it may well be more compassionate to have a supportive nurse explain the above rationale; the victim can actually participate in the process and discuss any fears or concerns as they arise.
- It is more pragmatic to have a consistent policy than to expect practitioners or individual police officers to "select" which cases seem suspicious and should therefore be tested.

Clearly, this is one area that must have the support of all the multidisciplinary team members. Regardless of the approach, a jurisdiction determines the needs of all parties, especially the victim, and these must be incorporated from the onset to facilitate the investigation. Further discussion of more recent drugs that have been employed in the arsenal of the rapist are discussed later in this chapter, under Rohypnol and gamma hydroxy butyrate (GHB).

Preservation of Evidence

To ensure proper preservation of evidence collected during the exam, all swabs and slides must be air dried prior to packaging. Biological evidence degrades rapidly as long as there is moisture in the sample. Wet swabs that are put in ventilated tubes require 10 to 20 hours to thoroughly dry. If these same swabs are placed in closed tubes immediately after collection, they take 150 to 250 hours to dry, if at all. Swabs and slides that are actively air dried in a stream of *cool air* for *60 minutes* become sufficiently dry to arrest biological degradation (Bashinski, 1987). Every swab and slide should be individually labeled and coded in such a manner that it is possible for the criminalist to know which slide was prepared from which swab.

Label individual items with these data:

- patient name
- medical record number or case I.D. number
- brief description/name of item
- location on body
- date/time/initials of collector

Small items should be packaged inside larger ones. Initial each bindle and preserve chain of custody. Proper air drying is as important as freezing. See *California v. Nation* (1980) below.

Storage

Tubes of liquid blood taken for reference should be refrigerated, not frozen. The remainder of the kit, swabs, slides, and samples of secretions or stains from clothing should all be routed to the crime lab to be *frozen* as soon as possible.

In *California v. Nation* (1980), the court held that the prosecution did not meet its burden of establishing that it had taken reasonable efforts to preserve a semen sample. Although the slide taken from the victim was retained, it was not preserved properly. This precluded subsequent analysis by the defense. The court held that later analysis might not only have impeached the witness for the prosecution, but might have enabled the defendant to be exonerated.

DNA IN SEXUAL ASSAULT CASES

Conventional Serology

Evidentiary samples collected from the victim may be submitted to genetic typing tests, based on the ABO blood group system (A, B, AB, and O), Lewis system, the phosphoglucomutase (PGM) system, and the peptidase A red cell enzyme systems. Eighty percent of the population are known to be "secretors," that is, their body fluids (semen, vaginal fluids, saliva, and perspiration) contain these same genetic markers. By obtaining reference samples from the victim (and suspect, if available), secretor status can be determined, and results compared to those present in the evidentiary samples. Each of these genetic types occurs with a particular frequency in the population. Evidentiary samples from the victim contain the victim's own vaginal secretions, plus the semen from the assailant. Other substances that might be present include saliva, blood, and feces. The criminalist analyzes specimens to determine which genetic markers originated from the victims; those foreign to the victim come from the semen donor.

DNA

With the advent of DNA (deoxyribonucleic acid) analysis, more information can be obtained from those samples yielding positive semen results. DNA is the blueprint of life and the genetic material that determines who and what we are. This blueprint information is coded in four base pairs that are the building blocks of DNA. These are *adenine (A), thymine (T), guanine (G),* and *cytosine (C).* These bases are strung in a linear fashion; the base sequence determines genetic attributes. The double helix structure of the DNA molecule is similar to two entwined ribbons, attached or held together at the "rungs," or crossbars by the four base pairs; these pair in an obligatory fashion, known as *complementary base pairing.* Thus, A always pairs with T and G always pairs with C. This complementary base pairing pattern allows DNA to replicate itself, passing on genetic information to the next generation. When the double DNA helix is intact, the structure is double-stranded. Special enzymes undo the double strand, making it a single strand. Nucleotides (unit of nucleic acid) are then brought in. Depending on the order of the existing strand (template), a new base attaches to a complementary base, creating a second half. Thus, using half of the original helix, two new molecules are created, identical to the original. This process is the basis of PCR analysis (Inman, 1997:33).

Genetic information resides inside a chromosome, an organelle within the nucleus of a cell body. Chromosomes are transmitted from parent to child, and become the vehicle by which inherited traits are passed from one generation to the next. Each human cell has 23 pairs of chromosomes. We have two copies of each chromosome, one provided by each parent. Thus our full genetic complement consists of an inherited half from our father's genetic blueprint, and likewise from our mother. Slight variations in our DNA provide for differentiation between us. *Alleles* are different forms of the same gene, or marker. A *locus* (plural: *loci*) is a specific physical location of a gene on a chromosome. A *genome* is the total genetic make-up of an organism (Inman, 1997).

The objective of both DNA analysis and conventional serology is to reduce the number of possible donors of a given sample. With DNA, it is possible to determine a genetic type by the occurrence of several loci in combination. The frequencies of these types in the population are much lower than for conventional serology (Inman, 1997). Additionally, DNA has greater stability than the protein and enzyme markers used in conventional serology.

DNA was described in 1944 by Oswald Avery as the cellular constituent that transfers heritable traits from one generation to the next. James Watson and Francis Crick, in 1953, defined the double helix structure of the

DNA molecule. In 1980, a human gene map was constructed by Botstein, using restriction fragment length polymorphism (RFLP). The first forensic use of DNA was by Alec Jeffreys, in 1984, when he applied RFLP technology to personal identification, in the cases of two child murders in the English Midlands. He called his method *DNA fingerprinting*. It was also the first time where an accused suspect was exonerated and proved innocent, based on DNA findings. Scientists no longer refer to DNA fingerprinting, but rather *DNA typing* or *DNA profiling*. In 1986, Kary Mullis invented PCR (polymerase chain reaction) and changed the face of molecular biology forever (Inman, 1997).

There are many noncrime scene uses of DNA analysis. Some of these are:

- identification of genes involved in diseases
- immigration and paternity disputes
- the identification of missing persons, eg, child abduction
- identification of the remains of Vietnam veterans (after two decades)
- identification of victims of mass disasters
- trace evidence in bombings
- anthropology and ancient history (mitochondrial DNA tests on a mummified, 1100-year-old Indian matched the tuberculosis bacterium; this exonerated Columbus from importing TB to the New World)
- animal genetics: endangered species, migration, and breeding patterns. (Inman, 1997: 19–20)

Forensic DNA was first introduced into the United States in 1986. It incorporates molecular biology, genetics, and statistical analysis. The basis of using DNA testing is that, with the exception of identical twins, each person's DNA is unique. While DNA is more stable than the proteins used in conventional serology, degradation can still occur, rendering the sample less useful. Factors producing degradation include exposure to sunlight and UV light, time, temperature, humidity, chemi-

cals, and biological contamination. Outside the living body, body cells are exposed and vulnerable to degradation. Biological processes can be slowed by removing moisture and decreasing the temperature (drying and freezing) of the samples. A *mixed sample* is one that contains DNA from more than one source individual. This is expected in a rape, where the mixing occurs after ejaculation when the seminal fluid may mix with the victim's biological fluids. A *contaminated sample,* on the other hand, can be caused by nonbiological means, eg, the addition of soaps and chemicals, or biological contamination by bacteria or fungi. Medical–legal specimens, such as blood and semen, must be protected from this type of contamination, which causes degradation. Contamination can also be from a human source, eg, by the addition of the collector's DNA into the sample either during or after collection. Latex gloves and personal protective equipment prevent introduction of this type of contamination (Devine, 1997).

Results: Significance of a Match

In the determination of a possible association between an evidence sample related to the crime and a reference sample from a particular individual, there are three possible conclusions:

- *Exclusion:* The two DNA types are different and originated from different sources. Any exclusion is absolute.
- *Inconclusive:* It is not possible to be sure if the samples have similar DNA types based on results of the test. No more is known after the analysis than before. This may be due to degradation, contamination, or similarity in the types of the donors.
- *Match:* The types are similar, and could have originated from the same source. Scientists give a very narrow meaning when they use the word "match". The term is limited to mean that no significant differences were observed between the two samples in

the particular test(s) conducted. The possibility exists that two samples may be different, but the test used has failed to reveal those differences. The strength of DNA lies in its immense powers of discrimination (Inman, 1997:87).

The two types of DNA testing currently being performed on sexual assault evidence are PCR and RFLP. Table 5–2 compares both techniques.

Restriction Fragment Length Polymorphism (RFLP)

This analysis provides the highest degree of discrimination. Many loci have been established for this type of analysis. The more places (loci) examined, the greater the chances of finding a difference. In forensic work, RFLP loci have been chosen that may have hundreds of variations at each locus. This increases the chance that samples from different people will be differentiated (Inman, 1997:37).

▶ **TABLE 5–2.** DNA IN SEXUAL ASSAULT CASES

RFLP	PCR
HOW MUCH SEMEN IS PRESENT? Is there enough for RFLP?	If not enough semen present for RFLP, then conduct PCR.
Technique uses probes to detect variations in DNA fragments which are separated according to differences in length of fragment created by cutting DNA with restriction enzymes.	Process mediated by DNA polymerase; yields millions of copies of desired DNA fragment
Two segments or bars maximum per person. If more than 2 bars, there is more than 1 person.	Molecular Xerox (DNA amplification). Only small segment of DNA of interest is copied; makes enough copies until sufficient quantity to look at.
Requires more sample and better quality DNA than PCR analysis.	Works with very tiny, even degraded samples, eg, a few hundred sperm or a blood drop the size of a pinhead. Sensitivity: requires 100× less sample than that required for RFLP.
Taken individually, excludes greater number of people as potential sample donors.	Gives smaller numbers than RFLP for statistics.
Contamination not an issue with RFLP	Due to sensitivity, contamination *is* an issue; with PCR *must* wear latex gloves and personal protective equipment. Any DNA will be copied, eg, collector's perspiration on hot day.
Analytic time: 6–8 weeks; uses radioactive labels (time-consuming process); looks at exposed parts of film radioactivity. Probes exposed to radioactivity 1–2 weeks per probe (1 week if strong, 2 if weak). Now with chemiluminescence, analytic time is shortened to 2–4 weeks.	Time: 2–4 weeks, start to finish.
Can tell number of donors; Can distinguish between multiple semen donors (eg, in a gang rape).	Think PCR for cigarettes, hair, saliva, bills, envelopes, T-shirts, hats, bandannas, etc.
Is accepted in the scientific community.	Is accepted in the scientific community.
Type of analysis used in Combined DNA Index System (CODIS); 290 (sex offender) registrants have to give a Blood sample at time of parole.	

Information compiled with assistance of Devine, 1997 and Devine, 1998.

A comparison is made of the pattern of bars on the autoradiograph to determine if two samples originated from the same source. RFLP is a desirable technique of analysis after sexual assault because a differential extraction is done to separate the male DNA from the female fraction, and may distinguish the number of donors. This is ideal in the analysis of samples from the victim of a gang rape (Devine, 1996).

Polymerase Chain Reaction (PCR)

This type of analysis is often called molecular "Xeroxing". This technique is DNA amplification, wherein a specific section of DNA in the sample is copied, or amplified. Only a small segment is copied, and with extremely high fidelity to the original. This technique allows information to be gained from even limited or degraded samples (Inman, 1997:41).

COMBINED DNA INDEX SYSTEM (CODIS)

Utilizing DNA analysis, a bloodstain from the crime scene of a 4-year-old mass murder in Oklahoma was matched to a suspect in California. DNA from a blood stain at the 1992 crime scene was matched to a reference sample taken in 1991, from the suspect in a California prison. The suspect had been convicted in California in 1988 for rape, kidnapping, and assault. On release for parole, he was required by California law to submit a blood and saliva sample. At a national crime conference in 1995, the Director of the Oklahoma DNA Crime Laboratory asked other criminalists to check their state DNA databanks against the DNA profile of a bloodstain from the Oklahoma murder. A crime bill passed in 1994 authorized the FBI to establish CODIS, and allowed states to exchange DNA records in criminal investigations. To date, all states have now passed laws that require convicted felons, sex offenders, and other violent offenders to submit to blood samples for DNA typing (Zachary, 1997).

CODIS is a nationwide computer index system. The DNA profiles stored in CODIS comprise a database for comparison with criminal cases that involve biological evidence, eg, sexual assault and murder. The process can focus ongoing investigations by linking and combining fragmented information from unsolved crimes. It helps develop a suspect profile by combining fragmentary investigative information from unsolved crimes, when the police know which cases are indeed related. Finally, CODIS can match the DNA profile from a rape case without a suspect to the state's DNA database. This entire process is similar to the automated fingerprint identification system (Miller, 1996). Due to the high recidivism of these crimes, specifically sexual assaults, offenders on parole are required to submit a reference blood sample. This increases the likelihood of solving serial sexual assaults.

FLUNITRAZEPAM (ROHYPNOL) AND GAMMA HYDROXY BUTYRATE (GHB)

The 1990s have ushered in a new arsenal of drugs found on the streets and used in the realm of sexual assault. Confronting the problems of illegal drug use is nothing new for law enforcement, but the manner in which two of these relatively recent arrivals are used has had dire consequences at large, and poses serious complications for the sexual assault victim. The media have given these drugs widespread attention and refer to them as "date rape drugs." They should more aptly be deemed "rape drugs," since victims may be given the drug by someone they are unaware of, but who has targeted them. These drugs can be slipped into a drink and the suspect may wait to approach the victim until after she is already under the influence. The assailant may be sensitive to the victim's confused state and offer to walk her outside or give her a ride home. While appearing to leave with the suspect of her own volition, she is not really in control of her faculties. These drugs bring the nightmare of rape to a new level of horror; quite often the victim delays seeking help or medical attention because she cannot remember sufficient details to *know* that she was raped much less convince others of the fact. If victims have to convince themselves because of inadequate memory, how will they convince others to believe them? Add to this difficult scenario the fact that confusion and fogginess may linger for a few days after ingestion of one of these substances, well after identifiable evidence has dissipated.

The two most familiar drugs of this type are flunitrazepam (Rohypnol) and gamma hydroxy butyrate (GHB). A great deal of information on these two drugs is now coming to the forefront. The majority of the information contained herein comes from both personal interviews and written information provided by Detective Trinka Porrata of the Los Angeles Police Department's Narcotics Division. Detective Porrata's expertise is based not only on years of law enforcement experience in narcotics, but extensive recent research and study, coupled with exposure and experience with victims, suspects, and actual crimes involving the use of these drugs.

Rohypnol (flunitrazepam) belongs to the same family of drugs as Valium, Librium, and Xanax (benzodiazepines). Rohypnol is colorless, tasteless, and odorless. The manufacturer plans to change the pill so that it will fizz and color any drink to which it is added. This, however, must first be approved by all countries in which the substance is sold, so it may still be quite some time before these reported changes are realized in the US. Additionally, the color change will not be apparent in dim light and can take 20 minutes to activate (Porrata, 1998). In the United States, Rohypnol was first discovered in South Florida in 1992, originating in Mexico and Colombia. It is nei-

ther manufactured nor sold in the United States, and thus does not legally exist in this country. However, it is marketed in 64 countries of the world, mostly in Europe and Latin America, as a hypnotic sedative to decrease anxiety, for musculoskeletal relaxation, and to treat sleep deprivation. It is also used as a pre-anesthesic and during conscious surgery, where the patient's cooperation is needed. Due to the amnesia this drug produces, the patient will not recall the surgery. Therapeutic dosage is generally 0.5 to 2 mg.

GHB use has been increasingly prevalent in young people between the ages of 15 and 35, especially at rave parties and clubs. The individual may be talked into trying a new drink. While GHB is considered a behavioral depressant, Dr. Wallace Winters, in his studies 30 years ago, found GHB to cause central nervous system excitation patterns similar to epileptic seizures (Porrata, 1997). GHB was formerly embraced by some body builders in their efforts to stimulate the production of growth hormone. As of November 1997, at least 21 deaths were listed as GHB-related. Although it is off the shelves of health food stores, recipes abound on the Internet, and the majority of circulating GHB is "home brew." This easily made, deadly concoction consists of ingredients available from chemical supply houses. The pH *should* be lowered by adding vinegar or another acid, but this is often not the case. Instead of being in the pH range of 8 to 9, it is often as high as 11 to 14. Acetone, which is sometimes added in an effort to make GHB into a powder form, can cause an explosion. This has occurred where a batch of GHB was being made in between runs of methamphetamine.

Both Rohypnol and GHB obviously pose great danger to sexual assault victims and voluntary users alike. They also pose a safety hazard for officers responding to the scene, due to the extreme unpredictability of behavior that ensues. The victim reporting for a medical exam may well seem disoriented, confused, and have difficulty with recollection of events. Their credibility should not be discounted; from the rapist's perspective, the amnesia and confusion are the keys to carrying out the crime.

The possibility that a victim may have ingested one of these substances can heighten the already charged situation of a sexual assault. The clinician, however, must exercise prudence and utilize a calm approach, both for the victim's sake and the accurate, reliable collection of historical facts and physical evidence. The urine specimen can be collected in any event, as is routinely done in some jurisdictions. It is imperative, however, not to *suggest* to the victim that they may have had something "slipped" to them. The victim should not be led into believing that this has occurred. Rather, the examiner should be alert to this possibility if the facts, sequence, and timing of events that are recalled by the victim are consistent with known patterns of behaviors and sequelae from these drugs. In other words, if it seems the victim's behaviors, physical manifestations, or gaps in their history match the effects of these drugs, then it may be a plausible explanation for what either the clinician or victim believes has happened. It is not the role of the forensic examiner to make this deduction without confirmation. This can be accomplished by drug testing, or should that prove negative, other variables.

It is not unusual for drug testing for either of these substances to be negative, because victims of Rohypnol- or GHB-ingestion may not report for an exam until after the drugs have been cleared from their system. In these cases, other salient features of the investigation can support your hypothesis. There are now numerous experts (criminalists, law enforcement, and a few medical experts who have extensive experience in community-based clinics), who can be consulted for input, advice, and opinions. To prematurely give the victim the suggestion that they may have been assaulted in this manner, without sufficient information is a disservice to the victim, even when done with the best of intentions. Rather, wide-scale education and information efforts within the community and targeted to vulnerable populations for the purpose of preventing this tragedy should be supported and encouraged. If it seems likely that the sexual assault victim has indeed been given one of these drugs, this individual deserves our utmost consideration, medical care, and the availability of support services. Table 5–3 summarizes the properties and effects of both Rohypnol and GHB.

SUMMARY

This chapter has discussed the myriad forms of physical evidence that is sought and gathered during the medical–legal examination of the sexual assault victim. The use of new technology and the adaptation of older techniques, coupled with scientific breakthroughs such as DNA profiling, have greatly impacted the evidentiary yield and forensic utility of physical specimens obtained by the forensic examiner. Much of the evaluation of physical evidence is based on traditional models, eg, collection of biological evidence and reference samples from the victim and suspect. Newer trends include the standardization of evidence collection kits and uniform protocols for the collection, preservation, and storage of this evidence.

Newer trends exist from the perspective of the assailant as well, such as wearing condoms, and further rendering victims powerless by the administration of potent, dangerous drugs in the commission of the crime. Forensic science has made significant efforts to keep up with these trends through research and development of protocols and testing for these agents. Technology and research will no doubt continue to advance in these areas, thus equipping not only the criminalist, but the clinical forensic examiner, with new ideas and innovative methods to match the crime.

Despite all of the scientific breakthroughs that will arrive, the quality of the subsequent

▶ TABLE 5–3. PROPERTIES AND EFFECTS OF ROHYPNOL AND GAMMA HYDROXY BUTYRATE (GHB)

	ROHYPNOL	GHB
Drug classification	Benzodiazepine; CNS depressant	Behavioral depressant and hypnotic; anesthetic, but *not* analgesic.
Street names	Roofies, roches, ropies, R-2, Mexican valium, poor man's Quaalude, forget-me pill	Liquid X, liquid ecstasy, Grievous Bodily Harm, Georgia Home Boy, scoop, Great Hormones at Bedtime, water, everclear
Control classification	Schedule IV controlled (CA) and Schedule IV federally	Schedule II (CA); federal legislation pending
Method of ingestion	Small white tablet in a blister pack; can be slipped unnoticed into victim's drink. Often used in conjunction with alcohol and/or other drugs.	Primarily distributed as a liquid; typically used in conjunction with alcohol and other drugs which potentiate effects. *Unpleasant, salty taste* often disguised by mixing in herbal or other strong tasting/alcoholic beverages: Oatmeal cookie drink: Goldschlager, Long Island iced teas, margaritas. Victims of GHB-related rapes often convinced to try "unusual concoction" or "energy drink"; thus *do not sense danger* behind the salty taste.
Onset of action	Within 30 min; may be seen to leave of own volition, but *not* in mental control.	Rapid, after absorbed.
Peak	1–2 hrs	20–60 minutes
Duration	≥8–12 hrs; falls to half of peak after 16–36 hrs; may awake in 10–12 hrs with fatigue, confusion, inability to focus attention, for as long as 2 days after ingestion.	4–5 hours
Half-life	23–33 hrs	20–60 min, for dose of 12.5 mg/kg body weight. Almost completely oxidized to CO_2.
Manifestations/symptoms	Drowsiness, confusion, inability to focus, memory impairment, visual problems, dizziness, confusion, urinary retention, GI problems. Occasional brief periods of lucidity during blackout (similar to alcoholic blackout); may see rapist in cameo appearances ("sees" parts of the rape), but unable to resist, escape. Anterograde amnesia: limits recall of the crime. May occasionally cause excitability or aggressive behavior.	Makes most people *vomit* (do not recall), nausea, visual disturbances. Intense intoxication: may act like "happy" drunk or "mean" drunk; amnesia, coma, enhancement of sexual interest, reduces inhibitions. Eyes: nystagmus in higher doses.

▶ **TABLE 5–3.** (*Continued*)

	ROHYPNOL	**GHB**
	May be photographed during sexual acts, while under the influence.	May be photographed during sexual acts, while under the influence.
Life-threatening potential	Hypotension, hallucinations, delirium, cardiovascular collapse	Uncontrolled seizures, respiratory depression
Chronic use	Dependence; lessening of amnesic effect; may use ≥3 (2 mg) tabs without unconsciousness.	
Method of testing	Urine collected *ASAP,* and frozen; screen for benzodiazepine; if positive, get confirmation of Rohypnol via gas chromatography and mass spectrometry.	Urine collected *ASAP* and frozen (only about 5% is excreted in urine). Refrigerate until freezing is possible.
Testing: *Realistic* window of opportunity	If within 5–7 hrs of ingestion, blood *may* be significant.* Urine: up to 36 hrs (collect up to 72 hrs)	Blood: 4–6 hrs Urine: 12 hrs (collect up to 72 hrs)

*Very rare; blood usually has no more drug left by the time the victim is being examined.
Compiled, with permission, from information provided by Detective Trinka Porrata, LAPD, 1998.

biochemical analysis will continue to ultimately depend on the quality of the evidentiary exam and the expertise of the examiner. Medical experts must achieve and maintain a close liaison with the criminalist to ensure that the process becomes as good as it can get.

REFERENCES

Bashinski, J. (1987). Sexual assault evidence and the criminalistics laboratory. In: *California Medical Protocol for Examination of Sexual Assault and Child Sexual Abuse Victims.* Sacramento, CA: Office of Criminal Justice Planning.

Bashinski, J., Blake, E.T. & Cook, C. (1985, May). Detection of Spermatozoa on the Vaginal Swabs from Victims of Sexual Assault: The ER versus the Crime Lab. Presented at the California Association of Criminalists. Oakland, CA.

Brown, L. (Ed.). (1993). *The New Shorter Oxford English Dictionary.* Vol. 1. Oxford: Clarendon Press.

California v. Nation, v 26 Cal 3d 169, 161 Cal Rptr 299, 604 P2d 1051 (1980).

Devine, E. (1996). Supervising Criminalist, Los Angeles Co. Sheriff's Dept., Scientific Services Bureau. Evidence Issues: Sexual Assault Investigations Course. Robert Presley Institute of Criminal Investigation. Los Angeles, CA.

Devine, E. (1997). Supervising Criminalist, Los Angeles Co. Sheriff's Dept., Scientific Services Bureau. Evidence Issues: Sexual Assault Investigations Course. Robert Presley Institute of Criminal Investigation. Los Angeles, CA.

Devine, E. (1998). Supervising Criminalist, Los Angeles County Sheriff's Dept. Personal communication.

Groth, N. & Burgess, A.W. (1977). Sexual dysfunction during rape. *N Engl J Med, 297:*764.

Hampton, H. (1995). Care of the woman who has been raped. *N Engl J Med, 332*(4):234–237.

Inman, K. & Rudin, N. (1997). *An Introduction to Forensic DNA Analysis.* Boca Raton, FL: CRC Press.

Miller, J. (1996). What is CODIS? [Sidebar]. Washington DC Forensic Science Systems Unit, FBI Laboratory.

Porrata, T. (1997, November). Flunitrazepam (trade name: Rohypnol) and gamma hydroxy butyrate (aka GHB). Training information, Los Angeles

Police Department. Narcotics Group, Field Enforcement Section, Central Bureau Unit. Los Angeles, CA.

Porrata, T., Los Angeles Police Dept. (1998). Personal communication.

Ramin, S., Satin, A., Stone, I. & Wendel, G. (1992). Sexual assault in postmenopausal women. *Obstet & Gynecol, 80*(5):860–864.

Satin, A., Hemsell, D., Stone, I., Theriot, S. & Wendel, G. (1991). Sexual assault in pregnancy. *Obstet & Gynecol, 77*(5):710–714.

Silverman, E. (1978). Persistence of spermatozoa in the lower genital tracts of women. *JAMA, 240*(17):1875–1877.

Smally, A. (1982). Sperm and acid phosphatase examination of the rape patient: Medicolegal aspects. *J Fam Pract, 15*(1):170–171.

Smerick, P. (1992). Crime scene photography. In: Douglas, J., Burgess, A.W., Burgess, A.G. & Ressler, R. (Eds.). *Crime Classification Manual.* New York: Lexington Books.

Soules, M, Pollard, A, Brown, K. & Verma, M. (1978). The forensic evaluation of evidence in alleged rape. *Am J Obstet Gynecol, 130:*142–147.

Tintinalli, J. & Hoelzer, M. (1985). Clinical findings and legal resolution in sexual assault. *Ann Emerg Med, 14*(5).

Tucker, S., Ledray, L. & Werner, S. (1990, July). Sexual assault evidence collection. *Wisconsin Medic J,* 407–411.

Young, W., Bracken, A., Goddard, M. & Matheson, S. (1992). Sexual assault: Review of a national model protocol for forensic and medical evaluation. New Hampshire sexual assault medical examination protocol project committee. *Obstet & Gynecol, 80*(5):878–883.

Zachary, N. (1997, July). New forensic technologies: DNA databanks. The Institute of Criminal Investigation (ICI) Follow-Up. Sacramento, CA.

SUGGESTED READINGS[1]

Annas, G. (1992, June). Setting standards for the use of DNA-typing results in the courtroom—the state of the art. *N Engl J Med, 326*(24):1641–1644.

Austin, C. (1975). Sperm fertility, viability and persistence in the female tract. *J Reprod Fertil, 22*[Suppl.]:75.

Brauner, P. (1992). The evidence notwithstanding—a case report on a rape. *J Foren Sci, 37*(1):345–348.

Chakraborty, R. & Kidd, K. (1991, December). The utility of DNA typing in forensic work. *Science, 254:*1735–1739.

DNA analysis on unsolved rape cases. (1998). [Bulletin.] Los Angeles Co. Sheriff's Dept., Scientific Services Bureau, DNA Laboratory. Los Angeles, CA.

Eubanks, W. (1988, October). FBI laboratory DNA evidence examination policy. *Crime Laboratory Digest, 15*(4):114.

Greydanus, D., Shaw, R. & Kennedy, E. (1987). Examination of sexually abused adolescents. *Seminar Adol Med, 3:*59–65.

Ledray, L. & Netzel, L. (1997). DNA evidence collection. *Journal of Emergency Nursing, 23*(2):156–158.

Massey, J., Garcia, C. & Emich, J. (1971). Management of sexually assaulted females. *Obstet & Gynecol, 38:*29.

Perloff, W. & Steinberger, E. (1964). In vivo survival of spermatozoa in cervical mucus. *Am J Obstet Gynecol, 88:*439.

Pollack, O. (1943). Semen and seminal stains: Review of methods used in medicolegal investigations. *Arch Pathol, 35:*140.

Rambow, B., Adkinson, C., Frost, T. & Peterson, G. (1992). Female sexual assault: Medical and legal implications. *Ann Emerg Med, 21*(6):78–82.

Sutherland, G. & Richards, R. (Eds.). (1994). DNA repeats—a treasury of human variation. *N Engl J Med, 331*(3):191–193.

Wallace-Haasen, M., Duffy, B. & Holtrop, H. (1975). Recovery of spermatozoa from human vaginal washings. *Fertil Steril, 26:*175.

Wecht, C. & Collom, W. (1969). Medical evidence in alleged rape. *Leg Med Ann,* p. 269.

Weiss, R. (1989). DNA takes the stand. *Science News, 136:*74–76.

---

[1] Some of these readings are included primarily for historical reference, as they have been cited by many previous authors.

6

The Rapist: Aspects of Deviant and Criminal Sexuality

This chapter focuses on the rapist. Statistics and incidence data give us important information as to the prevalence and trends of these crimes. Studies of offender dynamics and behavior help us to understand what the victim has endured. Clinical research and the application of the forensic sciences help us to perform better medical examinations and incorporate technology to study and correlate physical injuries to the crime. The crime of rape is a dynamic event involving at least two individuals. The interaction between the victim and rapist, albeit distasteful, is still a relationship, like a lock and key. Understanding the motives of the rapist by analyzing his behavior during the span of this relationship with the victim can yield valuable insight into the criminal mind and help to identify, apprehend, and prosecute the assailant. In addition to crime scene indicators, the victim is the ultimate source of information about the rapist.

The purpose of this chapter is neither to supplant nor presume final expertise on offender dynamics in these highly specialized areas of clinical research and the application of the law enforcement perspective. Rather, it is to provide an overview and describe for the forensic examiner the salient features of the subject, with the hope that an improved understanding of this subject will prove efficacious in establishing a thorough knowledge base and framework within which to conduct the examinations of both victims and suspects. To more fully grasp what the victim has had to endure, it behooves us to delve into the one responsible for their role as victim.

CRIMINAL INVESTIGATIVE ANALYSIS

The National Center for the Analysis of Violent Crime (NCAVC) was begun as a pilot project in 1984, and is now completely funded by the FBI. The three basic units of NCAVC are:

- Behavioral Science Services Unit
- Special Operations and Research Unit
- Investigative Support Unit

The NCAVC is staffed by crime analysts, psychologists, sociologists, criminologists, political scientists, and police specialists, all of whom provide investigative support, teach, and conduct research on serial and violent crimes, including homicides, sexual sadism, child abduction, arson, threats, assassinations, computer crimes, and matters of counter-intelligence (Munn, 1992:309). The Criminal Investigative Analysis Program (CIAP) is a component of the Investigative Support Unit (ISU), along with the Violent Criminal Apprehension Program (VICAP) and Arson and Bombing Investigative Services. Criminal investigative analysis is defined by the FBI as "*an investigative process that identifies the major personality and behavior characteristics of the offender based on the crimes he or she has committed*" (Munn, 1992:310). The law enforcement perspective of this analysis is a behavioral approach, with emphasis on the identification and apprehension of the offender (Munn, 1992).

All aspects of the crime are reviewed by the Criminal Investigative Analyst (CIA), including indicators at the crime scene, all partial reports (includes medical–legal and autopsy reports), and victimology (lifestyle, risk factors, history, personality), to name but a few. The CIA uses these and other tools to develop an offender profile and support suggestions for ongoing investigation.

INTERVIEW OF THE VICTIM

The profile of an offender can be constructed through careful victim interviewing, focusing on the analysis of behavior, and compilation of a profile. The CIA examines all components of the offender's behavior during the assault (physical, sexual, and verbal). Much of the following discussion of the importance of the victim interview is based on Hazelwood's 1983 article on the behavior-oriented interview of rape victims, which has provided a sound methodology and conceptual framework, and is still incorporated into law enforcement training today.

In addition to obtaining a physical description of the suspect, information on the offender's sexual, physical, and verbal behavior provides the investigator with insight as to possible motive. Additionally, classification into these three areas is more concise, consistent, and objective (Hazelwood, 1983).

PHYSICAL BEHAVIOR OF THE OFFENDER

Approach Used by the Offender

A key to the assailant's nature is his method of initial contact with the victim. The three basic methods used by serial rapists are the *con,* the *blitz,* and the *surprise attack.* During a *con,* the victim is approached openly. The assailant who succeeds with this type of approach has adequate social skills, evidenced by the boldness of his advance. The offender may seek or offer assistance to the victim, even going as far as posing as a police officer. After he has gained the victim's confidence and the victim is under his control, he suddenly, and often drastically, changes his behavior. The offender who uses the *blitz* approach is highly selfish and has difficulty relating to individual women. The aggression of the blitz is an expression of the assailant's hostility to women. Physical force is used to overcome the victim. He may use gags, blindfolds, binding materials, chemicals, or gases. In short, there is use of immediate, direct physical force. In the *surprise* approach, the rapist usually surprises the victim by stepping out from behind something, or in some other way waits to trap the victim. He may also approach the victim while she is asleep. Although the victim may be targeted or selected, the assailant using a surprise approach has insufficient confidence to make a direct approach.

Level of Force

In questioning the victim about the offender's physical behavior, the investigator determines the level of force that was used during the assault. This may be minimal, moderate, excessive, or brutal (Hazelwood, 1983). The report of force which does not leave physical marks is subjective, and the victim's rating will understandably be based on his or her own experiences with physical force. Thus, victims who have never before been struck, slapped, or spanked will relate differently than those who have experienced a great deal of physical violence in the past. Questions designed to elicit an objective determination are therefore employed. In general, levels of force can be classified as follows:

- Minimal force—little or no physical force used; there may be mild slapping in order to intimidate.
- Moderate force—repeated slapping, or hitting even without resistance by the victim. Use of profanity.
- Excessive force—the victim is beaten; nongenital trauma may be severe enough to require hospitalization. Use of profanity.
- Brutal force—sadistic torture; use of instruments and devices. There is intentional infliction of emotional and physical pain. Use of profanity.

Maintaining Control of the Victim

The *mere presence* of the offender may be sufficiently intimidating to the victim; the variables herein include the demeanor and bearing of the assailant and the victim's level of fear. *Verbal threats* by the assailant may adequately safeguard his control over the victim. If possible, the interviewer should try to obtain exact quotes of what the offender said. If the victim did not comply, were the threats actually carried out? The assailant may keep control over the victim by a *display of weapon(s)*. Critical questions are: at what point in the assault was the weapon displayed? did the victim actually see the weapon, or did the suspect say he had one (hidden)? was it a weapon of opportunity eg, kitchen knife, or was it one brought to the scene by the assailant? Finally, did the assailant inflict *injury with the weapon,* or primarily use it to intimidate? The final method of maintaining control over the victim is the actual use of *physical force*. The amount of force used (minimal, moderate, excessive, or brutal), provides a key to the assailant's motivation. The timing of the force is also significant. Interviews will ascertain if a particular behavior seemed to trigger the use of force, and the rapist's attitude toward the use of force.

Victim Resistance

From the perspective of the rapist, crying is not considered to be resistance. He may easily distort the crying to mean "tears of joy" (Prodan, 1998). Victim resistance may be verbal, passive, or physical. *Verbal resistance* consists of screaming, pleading, refusing, negotiating, or reasoning. The victim who employs *passive resistance* does not overtly resist, but does not comply either. *Physical resistance* consists of hitting, kicking, scratching, or other behaviors aimed at warding off or deflecting the assailant. If the victim attempted or used any of these methods, it is important to determine how the offender subsequently responded.

FBI research on sex offenders has implications for proponents of physical resistance and confrontation in situations with the likelihood of sexual assault. Research indicates that there is not one method to prescribe for the plight of a rape victim, and that to do so could place an individual in far greater danger. Because different rapists operate from different motives, it is impossible to predict how a particular rapist will respond unless the following is known beforehand: the location of the rape, the personality of the victim, and the type and motivation of the rapist (Hazelwood & Harpold, 1986). Much of this information has come directly or indirectly from rapists themselves. Hazelwood and Harpold (1986) believe that potential victims have an excellent chance for survival with proper advance preparation by training in the assessment of personal strengths and weaknesses, learning techniques of manipulating the environment to the disadvantage of the rapist, and understanding the types of rapists, motives, and patterns of assaultive behavior (Hazelwood & Harpold, 1986).

VERBAL BEHAVIOR OF THE OFFENDER

The verbal aspect of a sexual assault reflects some of the offender's interpersonal and social skills. Some of the indicators are subtle. Some are embarrassing and even revolting for the victim to recount. Here again, it is important to assure victims that anything they can remember about the encounter may be significant. Any threats the offender made should be recorded. The circumstance of the threat should be noted, eg, did the assailant threaten to harm the victim if he or she did not comply with a particular act, or was the threat more of a warning, in effect, if the victim complied, he or she would not be hurt? Determining the context of such a statement may clarify the assailant's attitude. Did the

offender make the victim say or repeat certain words, phrases, or sentences? These should be noted, and again, the context of the *scripting* should be ascertained. This verbiage may reflect some of the offender's fantasy, or be a way to humiliate the victim. Did the offender respond in a certain way to anything the victim said, eg, if the victim verbally resisted, how did the assailant react?

SEXUAL BEHAVIOR OF THE OFFENDER

A full account of the sexual behavior of the rapist includes a great deal more than simply recording which sexual acts were inflicted on the victim. Sexual and other behaviors that the offender exhibits during the assault can reflect the influence of fantasy, which in turn, may provide clues to the kind of person responsible. These behaviors may also be indicative of a sexual dysfunction, or paraphilia. While we routinely ask about oral, vaginal, anal, and foreign object penetration, it is also important to query as to the frequency of each act, and whether any acts were *attempted*. If an act was attempted, what happened to thwart completion? The victim may very well be unsure about specific acts, or whether a suspect ejaculated. This is understandable and likely due to shame, anxiety, and the extreme stress of the assault. In these instances, then, the performance of an act should be recorded as "unsure". In the study of rapist typology, the *sequence* of sexual acts is quite significant in providing clues to the motive of the offender, and may be linked to fantasy, experimentation, or the wish to degrade or humiliate the victim. The rapist who proceeds with the assault in a sequence of fondling, kissing, oral copulation, followed by vaginal penetration, is generally of a different genre than the one who sodomizes the victim and then forces her to perform fellatio (see "Rapist Typologies," p. 130). The offender may also exhibit various paraphilias during his encounter with the victim. Articles may be missing from the crime scene which have little or no monetary value, but which hold significance for the assailant as a memento or souvenir of a "special event." Some items, such as a driver's license, will soon be missed by the victim if taken. But a single pair of panties or other personal item may go unnoticed for some time. Photographs are also "collectibles." The experienced offender may take measures to protect his identity, such as wearing a condom, gloves, or having the victim launder clothing or bed linens. Some assailants have even had their victim bathe or douche after the assault. The rapist also learns from past mistakes; the clever assailant will not repeat those things that led to a prior arrest(s) or conviction(s).

Bondage

Bondage is the restriction of movements, or use of the senses to enhance the sexual arousal of the offender. Bondage differs from binding, which is done for the purpose of restraining or restriction of the victim. Four characteristics of bondage include:

* The binding has *symmetry, neatness,* and *balance.*
* The victim is bound in a *variety of positions;* he or she is often photographed in those positions.
* The binding is *more than necessary to control* or secure the victim's movement.
* The binding is *elaborate* and excessive.

According to Dietz et al (1990), 77% of sexual sadists engaged in bondage of one or more of their victims.

SEXUAL DYSFUNCTIONS

Rape victims should be sensitively questioned about a possible sexual dysfunction of the assailant. As with much of the interview content, this may not be volunteered, but appropriate questions can be asked to elicit the likelihood.

A sexual dysfunction is characterized by a disturbance in sexual desire and psychophysiologic changes that characterize the sexual response cycle and cause marked distress and interpersonal difficulties (DSM-IV: 493). Sexual dysfunctions are listed in the *Diagnostic and Statistical Manual of Mental Disorders,* 4th ed. (DSM-IV) under the heading "Sexual and Gender Identity Disorders," and include:

* sexual desire disorders
* sexual arousal disorders (includes *male erectile disorder*)[1]
* orgasmic disorders (includes *male orgasmic disorder and premature ejaculation*)[1]
* sexual pain disorders
* sexual dysfunctions due to general medical conditions
* substance-induced sexual dysfunction
* sexual dysfunction not otherwise specified

Only male erectile disorder (erectile insufficiency), male orgasmic disorder (retarded ejaculation), and premature ejaculation will be discussed within the context of the sexual behavior of the rapist.

In a noted study of 170 convicted sex offenders, Groth and Burgess (1977) found a high prevalence of sexual dysfunction. Thirty-four percent of the offenders reported either erectile inadequacy (16%), premature ejaculation (3%), or retarded ejaculation (15%). The

---

[1]*Male erectile disorder* is a persistent or recurrent inability to attain or maintain an adequate erection until completion of sexual activity (DSM-IV:502).

Male orgasmic disorder (retarded ejaculation) is the persistent or recurrent delay or absence of orgasm following a normal sexual excitement phase (DSM-IV:509).

Premature ejaculation is the persistent or recurrent onset of orgasm and ejaculation with minimal sexual stimulation before, on, or shortly after penetration and before the person wishes it (DSM-IV:509).

dysfunctions appeared to be associated with the rape; almost none of the men reported having a similar dysfunction in their consenting relationships. Erectile inadequacy (male erectile disorder) occurred in 16%, usually during the initial phase of the sexual assault. Groth and Burgess (1977) used the term *"conditional impotence"* (secondary insufficiency) to describe those offenders who had an initial erectile insufficiency during the rape, resolved only when the victim did certain sex acts, such as forced fellatio or manual stimulation, or the victim struggled or resisted. Hazelwood (1983) reported that in similar cases submitted to the Behavioral Science Unit of the FBI, additional acts required by the victim included anal sex, analingus, scripting, and the wearing of certain clothes to resolve the conditional impotence.

The victim may be unaware that an offender experienced premature ejaculation. This offender may ejaculate spontaneously, without intromission (Groth & Burgess, 1977). Evidence of semen may be found instead on the bedding or clothing. The 15% incidence of retarded ejaculation represents a marked disparity from the general population of men seeking treatment for sexual dysfunction. The duration of penetration prior to ejaculation may be as long as 30 to 60 minutes (Hazelwood, 1983). At the time of their study, the reported incidence in the literature was 1 in 700 men, yet it was the second most common dysfunction in the rapist group (Groth & Burgess, 1977). Study of Behavioral Science Unit cases elicited an additional type of dysfunction, not mentioned in the literature, called *conditional ejaculation*. These rapists had no problem obtaining or maintaining an erection, but they could only ejaculate if certain conditions were met. Those conditions mostly involved paraphilic sexual acts (Hazelwood, 1983).

Paraphilias

Paraphilias are compulsive sexual behaviors. The paraphiliac's repertoire of sexual activity is limited in that both sexual arousal and satisfaction are reliant on sexual fantasies and behaviors considered abnormal or even deviant by the general population (Masters et al, 1994). These include: exhibitionism, sadism, transvestism, voyeurism, necrophilia, telephone scatologia, partialism, fetishism, zoophilia, coprophilia, klismaphilia, urophilia, piquerism, infibulation, frotteurism, and masochism. These paraphilias are briefly defined in Table 6–1. Some are more fully described in the glossary, using the definitions provided by the *American Psychiatric Association Glossary* (1994).

Paraphilias are recurrent, intense sexual urges, fantasies, or behaviors. They involve unusual objects, activities, or situations and result in notable distress or detriment to the individual's functional abilities in social, occupational, or other areas of life (DSM-IV: 493). The essential features of paraphilias usually involve nonhuman objects, the suffering or humiliation of self or a partner, children, or other nonconsenting partner, and the condition occurs over at least a 6-month period of time.

The paraphiliac's behavior is not simply "strange" behavior that might elicit shock, nor does it apply to experimentation with unusual, deviant, or even perverse sex. The true paraphiliac prefers or requires this type of sex for sexual arousal and sexual satisfaction to occur. For some, aberrant sexual activity may be a lifestyle or recreational choice, and not a sexual deviation (Masters & Johnson, 1994:214).

Paraphilias are classified under the category of "Sexual and Gender Disorders," in the *Diagnostic and Statistical Manual of Mental Disorders,* 4th ed. (DSM-IV) (1994), along with sexual dysfunctions, gender identity disorders, and sexual disorders not otherwise specified.

Masters et al (1994) hold that more basic than the frequency of the paraphilic behavior is the compulsiveness or sense of urgency, and the rigid focus on it. This serves to fuse the

▶ **TABLE 6–1.** PARAPHILIAS

Coprophilia	Sexual urges related to feces.
Exhibitionism	Exposure of one's genitals to a stranger.
Fetishism	Sexual urges involving nonliving objects (eg, high heels). The individual may masturbate while holding, rubbing, smelling object; may ask partner to wear object.
Frotteurism	Touching, rubbing against nonconsenting or unknowing person.
Hypoxyphilia	Sexual excitement produced by mechanical (decreased oxygen) or chemical asphyxiation (nitrites).
Infibulation	The cutting, alteration, branding, or infusion of the genitals (one's own or those of another).
Klismaphilia	Sexual urges related to enemas.
Masochism	Sexual arousal by being humiliated, beaten, bound, or otherwise made to suffer.
Necrophilia	Sexual arousal to corpses.
Partialism	Exclusive focus on part of a body (of a living person).
Pedophilia	Sexual attraction to prepubescent minor (one who is legally a child).
Piquerism	Piercing of the body.
Sadism	Sexual arousal, gratification occurs as a response to the suffering of another (psychological or physical).
Telephone scatologia	Lewd talking on telephone; usually done to strangers.
Transvestism	Cross-dressing; wearing clothing of the opposite sex.
Urophilia	Sexual urges related to urine.
Voyeurism	Observation of unsuspecting people who are naked or engaging in sexual activity.
Zoophilia	Sexual urges related to animals.

From Diagnostic and Statistical Manual of Mental Disorders, *4th ed (DSM-IV). (1994). Washington, DC: American Psychiatric Press; and Prodan, M. (1997).* Offender Issues: Sexual Assault Investigations Course. *Robert Presley Institute of Criminal Investigations, California Peace Officer Standards and Training. Presented at Los Angeles County Sheriff's Department, Los Angeles, CA.*

behavior with the person's identity. The paraphiliac assumes compulsive, ritualistic actions to decrease these driving forces. Fantasy-assisted masturbation may become extremely frequent for some paraphiliacs. For those with less severe cases, the paraphilic urge(s) may manifest only when the individual is experiencing acute stressors. Some sexual sadists reported far less intense gratification during sex with a consenting (even a masochistic) partner than during a nonconsensual encounter (Masters & Johnson, 1994:213–214).

According to Masters and Johnson (1994), the orgasmic satisfaction that the paraphiliac derives does not inevitably parallel that of the nonparaphiliac. Satisfaction comes more from the temporary reduction of negative feelings, anxiety, or depression. Following the sex act, these individuals feel less out of control. Paraphilic behavior is more prevalent in males. Paraphilic males reported more arousal diffi-

culties in nonparaphilic sexual encounters. The result was a greater frequency of sexual dysfunctions during nonparaphilic sex (Masters & Johnson, 1994).

Abel et al (1988) studied 561 nonincarcerated paraphiliacs, who had been assured confidentiality. They found that most of these individuals had experience with different types of sexually deviant behavior (as many as ten types were reported by some), in many situations without regard to age, gender, or familial relationship of the victim. The majority of the paraphiliacs could also become involved with adult partners without incorporating paraphilic fantasies and behaviors, showing that both paraphilic and nonparaphilic behaviors could coexist. With the exception of transsexuals, there is a significant incidence of crossing of deviant sexual behaviors. Most paraphiliacs participate in a variety of these behaviors; the paraphiliac with only one of these behaviors is rare (Abel, 1988). For some, paraphilic fantasies are obligatory for arousal and are always included. In other individuals, the paraphilic behavior(s) may be episodic, such as during times of stress (DSM-IV, 1994:522–523).

In the past, some paraphilic behaviors, such as exhibitionism, were considered to be nuisance offenses; it was believed that a practitioner of this paraphilia would not also engage in violent, aggressive sex crimes. The study by Abel et al (1988) suggested that this is not the case, and that these crimes should not be ignored or minimized.

RAPIST TYPOLOGIES

In 1977, Groth et al published results of a study which provided a conceptual framework for the typology of rape. They studied a population of 92 female victims and a sample of 133 convicted sex offenders. The rapes in the two groups were unrelated, but were congruent in time frame of occurrence (none of the female victims were raped by males in the offender sample). The study found that the salient features common to all of the forcible rapes were power, anger, and sexuality. These characteristics were all present in varying intensities, but did promote a distinct clustering of behavior patterns. This classification scheme was further modified in 1987 by Hazelwood and Burgess, and serves as a foundation for investigative analysis of rapists by the National Center for the Analysis of Violent Crime (NCAVC) of the FBI (Warren et al, 1991). Review and analysis of the rapist's behavior helps us understand the motive of a particular offender, and provides insight for focusing the investigation. The four research-based categories, or typologies of rapist, are power-reassurance, power-assertive, anger-retaliatory, and anger-excitation.

Throughout the typologies, rape is viewed as the use of sexuality to express power and anger. In their study, Groth and Burgess (1977) found power rapes (65%) to be more prevalent than anger rapes (35%). In the offender sample, anger-retaliatory rapes were the most frequent type of offense, but ranked third in the victim sample. The authors theorized that because anger rapists cause more physical trauma to their victims, this might result in higher conviction rates, thus overrepresenting the anger rapists in the study sample. The anger-excitation rapist was the least prevalent for both groups.

The following summaries are by no means all-inclusive. Rather, they are a brief, basic description of the four typologies. The information herein is combined from the previously listed extensive research by Groth, Burgess, and Holmstrom (1977), Hazelwood and Burgess (1987) Warren et al (1991), and others listed in the reference section at the end of this chapter. In addition, these summaries are representative of numerous presentations and courses attended by the author, and taught by Special Agent Supervisor Michael Prodan of the California Department of Justice.

Power—Reassurance Rapist

The goal of the power-reassurance rapist is to assuage his low self-esteem and doubts regarding his masculinity and sexual adequacy. The power-reassurance rapist usually selects victims in his own age range, as he may fantasize his victims will fall in love with him. Victims may be pre-selected. The assailant may even recontact the victim after the assault. His intent is not to punish or degrade the victim. This rapist builds his own ego by putting the female victim in a position where she cannot refuse him. He tends to use the surprise approach and minimal force. He maintains control over the victim by threats of a weapon. The geographic area of his choice is usually one close to his home, or one where he is comfortable with his surroundings. Premature ejaculation and erectile insufficiency are the most common sexual dysfunctions among this category.

Power—Assertive Rapist

The power-assertive rapist uses the rape as an expression of his masculinity, virility, mastery, and dominance. The date rapist is more likely to be a power-assertive rapist. He tends to use the con approach, and applies a moderate amount of force. The victim is generally one of opportunity (not pre-selected), and usually within the assailant's own age range. The geographic area of the assault is not likely to be that of the rapist's home or work. The victim will probably suffer repeated assaults. Retarded ejaculation is the most common sexual dysfunction.

Anger—Retaliatory Rapist

For the anger retaliatory rapist, the rape is an expression of rage and hostility. This assailant desires to get even with real or imagined wrongdoing, and to punish or degrade the victim. This rapist uses the blitz approach, and much more force than necessary to control the victim. He has an explosive temper, and assaults can be triggered by a stressful event involving a woman. He usually selects victims his own age, or slightly older, but may select elderly victims. The chosen victim may symbolize an individual known to the rapist. His encounters with the victim are brief, but sufficient to vent his rage. Weapons employed are those of opportunity, ie, kitchen knife, etc. If this assailant experiences a sexual dysfunction, it is most likely to be retarded ejaculation.

Anger—Excitation Rapist

The anger-excitation rapist derives pleasure and excitement from the suffering of his victim. His goal is to inflict physical or emotional suffering as well as have power and control over the victim. The sexual sadist exemplifies the anger-excitation rapist. This rapist is usually a white male of average to above average intelligence; some sexual sadists have been brilliant. His crimes have been fantasized for years and are premeditated. He use the con approach with a brutal level of force. The victims are strangers; age makes no difference, as long as the victims are not too young. They are taken to preselected locations, and may be kept for hours to days. Most of these rapists employ bondage, use instruments and devices to inflict torture, and tend to record their offenses, ie, videos, photographs. The knife is the weapon of choice. Anal sex is the preferred sex act. Retarded ejaculation is the most common dysfunction. If the victim survives, he or she may require extensive hospitalization.

The Serial Rapist

Landmark research was jointly done by the FBI's NCAVC and Ann Burgess of the University of Pennsylvania School of Nursing into the nature and characteristics of the serial rapist and his crimes. Extensive interviews were conducted by special agents with 41 incarcerated serial rapists. These men had committed 837 rapes and more than 400 attempted rapes. The 41 rapists selected had each committed 10 or more rapes. Some of the areas explored during the lengthy interviews were family background and demographics, education, sexual development, military life, employment history, sexual activity in marriage, criminal history, use of pornography and detective magazines, first offense, rape resistance and prevention, interrogation techniques, and the possibility of a sex offender hotline (suggested during one of the initial interviews of a rapist) (Hazelwood & Burgess, 1987).

The behavior of the serial rapists was described during and after the sexual assaults. Aspects of behavior were studied for the first, middle, and last rapes committed, and included premeditation, methods of approach, control of the victim, use of force, victim resistance, sexual dynamics of the rape, verbal activity, sexual dysfunction, evading detection, alcohol and drug use, and post offense behavior (Hazelwood & Warren, 1990).

The vast majority of victims were adult females, although 19% of the victims were children, and 2% were same-sex victims (male) (Hazelwood, R. & Warren, J. 1989).

The majority of the serial rapes studied were premeditated. The most common approach was the "con." Verbal threats and a threatening presence were sufficient to control the victim most of the time. In the majority of the rapes, minimal or no force was utilized by the rapist. In a little over 50% of the cases, there was resistance by the victim, either physical, verbal, or passive in nature. If the victim resisted the offender, he most commonly responded with verbal threats. A sexual dysfunction was evident in slightly more than one-third of the rapists. Preferred sexual acts were vaginal rape and fellatio. The rapists reported low levels of pleasure from the actual sexual acts. Use of precautionary measures did not cause great concern. Alcohol and drugs were used by the rapists one-third and slightly less than one-third of the time, respectively. The most often reported postassault behaviors were guilt and remorse, media watching of the case, and increase in substance abuse (Hazelwood & Warren, 1990).

Data from the first, middle, and last rapes of each offender were analyzed for the frequency of increased force over time, as their career progressed. Although the level of force used by the serial rapists did not increase overall, it did for ten of the sample, subsequently labeled "increasers" (Hazelwood et al, 1989). For this subgroup of rapists, there was a significant escalation of force from the first to the last rape. This may relate to a sadistic sexual preference. The "increasers" assaulted more victims (mean number of 40 vs. 22 victims). The interval between assaults averaged 19 days for the increasers, whereas it was 55 days for the nonincreasers. Moderate to fatal injuries were inflicted by 90% of the increasers during their last assaults. Anal intercourse occurred at a rate three times greater in the increasers than in the nonincreasers and ten times greater than the incidence reported by Holmstrom and Burgess in their 1980 study (Hazelwood et al, 1989). The sexual reaction of the offender was not deemed to be deviant because their arousal was induced by force and non-consent; rather their sexual response was deviant because these elements failed to inhibit arousal for them (Hazelwood et al, 1989).

The Criminal Sexual Sadist

Sexual sadism was named after the Marquis de Sade, by Richard von Krafft-Ebing. Writings by the Marquis depicted sexual acts coupled with domination, degradation, and violence. *Sexual sadism is the persistent pattern of becoming sexually excited in response to another's suffering* (Hazelwood et al, 1992:12). It is the suffering of the victim that the sexual sadist finds sexually arousing. While this section focuses on the sexually sadistic criminal, it is important to note that like other paraphiliacs, the sexual sadist does not necessarily engage in behaviors to fulfill the paraphilic need. These individuals may only have sexually sadistic fantasies. Other sexual sadists may engage freely consenting or paid partners to play the submissive role in the duet. Some sexual sadists do cultivate compliant victims; these individuals initially enter into a consensual relationship. They are later manipulated into activities of a sado-masochistic nature, becoming progressively and more deeply caught in the web. Such compliant victims differ from consensual partners in that most of them are wives or girlfriends who initially started out in conventional romantic relationships. They experienced severe emotional, physical, and sexual abuse and social isolation, and were gradually coerced into participating in more progressive deviant behaviors. The sexually sadistic criminal crosses the line between fantasy and the real world, and enters into criminal actions without moral, social, or legal restrictions (Dietz et al, 1990). Although the prevalence of this type of sexual offender is infrequent, he is the most dangerous.

True sexually sadistic behavior must be differentiated from other forms of brutality and cruelty that may be manifested in a heinous crime. There may be evidence of severe torture, even mutilation, without true representation of sexual sadism (Dietz et al, 1990). It is the enduring pattern of sexual arousal to these acts that characterizes the sexual sadist. Pain cannot be inflicted on a dead or unconscious person; thus postmortem mutilation or necrophilia is not motivated by the same types of desires.

Dietz and colleagues (1990) studied 30 sexually sadistic criminals. Most of these cases had been submitted to the NCAVC. Every one of these criminals intentionally tortured and caused great psychological suffering to their victims. In this population of 30 men, 22 of them were responsible for 187 murders. The uncontrolled, descriptive study of these sexual sadists included characteristics of both the sexual sadist and his crime(s). Some of the salient features of this study are included in the description of the anger-excitation rapist (see "Rapist Typologies," p. 130). Of particular note is the greater incidence of forcible penetration of the anus and mouth than of the vagina. Anal rape was the most common sexual activity (22/30 offenders). This was followed, in descending order, by fellatio, vaginal rape, and foreign object penetration. Most of the victims (two-thirds) were subjected to at least three of these four acts (Hazelwood et al, 1992). Dietz et al (1990) did not attribute the greater incidence of anal rape to be a study artifact present with male victims, as this was also true for offenders who attacked only female victims. Many of

the offenders had a history of adult homosexual activity. Possibly this predisposed this sample of offenders to anal and oral sex; concomitantly, these acts could exemplify the desire to humiliate and degrade the victim. All but one assailant in this group were white, and 43% were married at the time of the offense. Some offenders repeatedly used the same torture methods, suggesting (although this was not conclusive), that it was a signature, or calling card of the rapist. This study confirmed the association of other sexual deviations in this group of paraphiliacs. Over half kept detailed documentation (written, photographic, video) of their exploits. The sexual sadist crimes were extremely well planned and executed (Dietz et al, 1990).

As a result, these crimes are devastating in the heinous nature of the acts performed and the effects on survivors, families, and friends of murdered victims. All professionals exposed to the tragic destruction wrought by these savage acts are cognizant of the terrible aftermath. Yet, we have learned much from the thorough studies and research done in an endeavor to understand the motives and behaviors of this most vicious and dangerous of rapists. Each facet of information learned about these terrible crimes can be used by law enforcement to identify, apprehend, and, it is hoped, prevent some of the horror. Forensic examiners can use this knowledge for medical–legal application to the medical exam, and to anticipate implications for possible psychosocial sequelae.

SUMMARY

The various aspects of criminal sexuality and deviant sexual behavior provide background information for the criminal investigative analysis of sexual assaults. The investigative interview of the rape victim has application and significance to the forensic examiner, as well as law enforcement. Review of the nature of the assault, as evidenced by the physical, verbal, and sexual behavior of the offender, including aspects of sexual dysfunction and paraphilias have been included in this chapter. The various typologies of rapists provide a conceptual classification of these crimes. Finally, studies on actual crimes committed by the serial rapist and the sexual sadist enlighten us as to the scope and importance of the problem.

This chapter has explored the dynamics of rape from the other perspective, that of the rapist, in an attempt to provide insight into the whole enigma of rape. The use of this information in the context of a theoretical framework can guide the examiner throughout interactions with the victim, and indeed with the criminal justice system. Although unsavory to consider, the view of the crime from the perspective of the rapist gives us valuable knowledge of often subtle issues. Ultimately, this knowledge can serve us well and potentiate our efforts to provide optimal care for the rape victim.

REFERENCES

Abel, G., Becker, J., Cunningham-Rathner, J., Mittelman, M. & Rouleau, J. (1988). Multiple paraphilic diagnoses among sex offenders. *Bull Am Acad Psychiatry Law, 16*(2):153–167.

Diagnostic and Statistical Manual of Mental Disorders, 4th ed. (DSM-IV). (1994). Washington, DC: American Psychiatric Association.

Dietz, P.E., Hazelwood, R. & Warren, J. (1990). The sexually sadistic criminal and his offenses. *Bull Am Acad Psychiatry Law, 18*(2):163–178.

Groth, A.N. & Burgess, A. (1977). Sexual dysfunction during rape. *N Engl J Med, 297*:764–766.

Groth, N., Burgess, A. & Holmstrom, L. (1977). Rape: Power, anger, and sexuality. *Am J Psychiatry, 134*(11):1239–1243.

Hazelwood, R. & Burgess, A. (Eds.). (1987). *Practical aspects of rape investigation: A multidisciplinary approach.* New York: Elsevier.

Hazelwood, R. & Harpold, J. (1986, June). Rape: The dangers of providing confrontational advice. *FBI Law Enforcement Bulletin.* US Department of Justice. Washington, DC.

Hazelwood, R. & Warren, J. (1990, February). The criminal behavior of the serial rapist. *FBI Law Enforcement Bulletin.* US Department of Justice. Washington, DC.

Hazelwood, R. & Warren, J. (1989, January/February). The serial rapist: His characteristics and victims, part 1. *FBI Law Enforcement Bulletin.* US Department of Justice. Washington, DC.

Hazelwood, R. & Burgess, A. (1990, September). An introduction to the serial rapist: Research by the FBI. *FBI Law Enforcement Bulletin.* US Department of Justice. Washington, DC.

Hazelwood, R., Dietz, P.E., & Warren, J. (1992, February). The criminal sexual sadist. *FBI Law Enforcement Bulletin.* US Department of Justice. Washington, DC.

Hazelwood, R., Reboussin, R., & Warren, J. (1989, March). Serial rape: Correlates of increased aggression and the relationship of offender pleasure and victim resistance. *Journal of Interpersonal Violence, 4*(1):65–78.

Holmstrom, L. & Burgess, A. (1980). Sexual behavior of assailants during reported rapes. *Arch Sex Behav, 9*:427–439.

Masters, W., Johnson, V. & Kolodny, R. (1994). *Heterosexuality.* New York: Harper Collins.

Munn, C. (1992). The investigative support unit's role in assisting law enforcement. Chap. 8, In Douglas, J., Burgess, A.W., Burgess, A.G. & Ressler, R. (Eds.). *Crime Classification Manual.* New York: Lexington Books, pp. 309–313.

Prodan, M. (1997). Offender Issues: Sexual Assault Investigations Course. Los Angeles County Sheriff's Department. Robert Presley Institute of Criminal Investigation. California Peace Officer Standards and Training (P.O.S.T.). Los Angeles, CA.

Prodan, M. (1998). Special Agent, South Carolina Law Enforcement Division. Behavioral Science Unit, Personal Communication.

Warren, J., Reboussin, R., Hazelwood, R. & Wright, J. (1991). Prediction of rapist type and violence from verbal, physical, and sexual scales. *Journal of Interpersonal Violence, 6*(1):55–67.

SUGGESTED READINGS

Crowley, S. & Prodan, M. (1996). Correlation of Genital Findings to Offender Typology: Collaboration Between Forensic Nurse Examiner and

Criminal Investigative Analyst. Paper presented at American Academy of Forensic Sciences. Nashville, TN.

Deming, J., Mittelman, R., & Wetli, C. (1983). Forensic science aspects of fatal sexual assaults on women. *J Foren Sci, 28*(3):572–576.

Deviant and Criminal Sexuality. (1991). National Center for the Analysis of Violent Crime (NCAVC). Quantico, VA: FBI Academy.

Douglas, J. & Munn, C. (1992). Modus operandi and the signature aspects of violent crime. Chap. 5. In: Douglas, J., Burgess, A.W., Burgess, A.G. & Ressler, R. (Eds.). *Crime Classification Manual.* New York: Lexington Books, pp. 259–268.

Douglas, J. & Munn, C. (1992). The detection of staging and personation at the crime scene. Chap. 4. In: Douglas, J., Burgess, A.W., Burgess, A.G. & Ressler, R. (Eds.). *Crime Classification Manual.* New York: Lexington Books, pp. 249–258.

Douglas J., Burgess, A.W., Burgess, A.G. & Ressler, R. (1992). *Crime Classification Manual.* New York: Lexington Books.

Douglas, J., Burgess, A., Burgess, A. & Ressler, R. (1992). *Pocket Guide to the Crime Classification Manual.* New York: Lexington Books.

Greenfeld, L. (1997, February). *An analysis of data on rape and sexual assault. Sex Offenses and Offenders.* NCJ-163392. Bureau of Justice Statistics. U.S. Department of Justice, Office of Justice Programs. Washington, DC.

Lowe, G. & Prodan, M. (1993, September). C.S.A.I.A. Training on Sexual Assault. California Sexual Assault Investigators Association Annual Training. Sacramento, CA.

Prodan, M. & Lowe, G. (1993, June). Criminal Sexuality: Serial Rapist Typologies. SART and Law Enforcement Spring Training, San Luis Obispo, CA.

Reese, J. (1979, August). Obsessive compulsive behavior, the nuisance offender. *FBI Law Enforcement Bulletin.* U.S. Department of Justice. Federal Bureau of Investigation. Washington, DC.

Ressler, R., Burgess, A. & Douglas, J. (1983, January). Rape and rape-murder: One offender and twelve victims. *Am J Psychiatry, 140*(1): 36–40.

Rosler, A. & Witzum, E. (1998). Treatment of men with paraphilia with a long-acting analogue of gonadotropin-releasing hormone. *N Engl J Med, 338*(7):416–422.

Training Key. No. 210. (1974). The Professional Standards Division of the International Association of Chiefs of Police. International Association of Chiefs of Police. Gaithersburg, MD.

APPENDIX

Physical Evidence for Submission to Criminalistic Laboratories

FORENSIC SAMPLES

Evidence	Collection	Packaging	Storage
Bloodstains	1. Collect entire stained item (or) 2. Cut out stained area and adjacent control area (or) 3. Scrape a crust (or) 4. Moisten sterile cloth swatch or cotton swab with distilled water and apply to stain. Note: Correctly collected samples should appear dark brown or black in color.	1. Paper bag or paper wrap 2. Paper envelope or bindle (control packaged separately) 3. Bindle 4. Glass tubes, glass in envelopes, bindles (each sample separate from the other)	*Must be air-dried when frozen*
Vaginal samples	Using cotton swabs, forensic examiner makes collection from the vaginal vault (and cervix); the sample is then smeared over labeled glass slides.	*Air dry* or use swab dryer (if available). Swabs and slides are retained. Package in paper or uncapped plastic tubes and slide mailers, respectively.	*Frozen*
Rectal and oral samples	Using cotton swabs, forensic examiner makes collection from the appropriate orifice; the sample is then smeared onto labeled glass slides.	Same as with vaginal samples.	Same as with vaginal samples.
External stain samples	Stains are located by forensic examiner utilizing a Wood's lamp or ultraviolet (UV) light source. A body surface control sample should also be taken from an unstained area. Note: It is imperative that the location of the external stain be documented on the medical–legal examination form, as well as labeled on the slide and the swab container.	Same as with vaginal samples.	Same as with vaginal samples.

(continued)

FORENSIC SAMPLES (*Continued*)

Evidence	Collection	Packaging	Storage
Urine sample (victim)	Have victim urinate in a sterile container.	The container should have a lid that provides an airtight seal.	*Frozen* (must be maintained frozen to test for gamma hydroxy butyrate [GHB]).
	Note: It is imperative to get a urine sample for Rohypnol as soon as possible from the victim.		
Clothing/bedding	Entire item *Note:* With bedding, it can be helpful to designate the position (of a stain) on the bed.	Paper bags, butcher paper wrap *Note:* Each item packaged separately.	*Air dry; frozen*
Pubic combings	Forensic examiner to conduct.	Hair and comb/brush are placed in a bindle and then placed in the appropriate evidence envelope.	*Frozen* (can be subsequently placed in room temperature storage if there are no biological concerns).
Condoms	Collect entire item. *Note:* Criminalist will collect a separate sample from the outside and the inside, so minimal handling is essential.	Paper bag/envelope. *Note:* If there is visible liquid in the condom and it cannot be sampled right away, it should be packaged in an airtight container and frozen.	*Frozen*
Conceptus (product of an abortion) *Note:* This evidence requires prior arrangements with both the physician performing the procedure and the criminalist examining the conceptus.	Obtain all tissue from the procedure.	*No formalin*	*Take directly to the criminalist*
Cigarette butts/ envelopes	Collect entire item.	Paper envelope or bag.	*Frozen*
Trace evidence (glass, fibers, loose hairs, etc.)	Collect using forceps, gloved fingers, or tape lifts.	If collected with forceps, place in a paper bindle. Tape lifts should be packaged on a Mylar sheet or in a plastic petri dish.	Room temperature
Shoe prints/tire tracks	Photograph using L-shaped scale, tripod, and level with the plane of the camera film, parallel to the	Casts should be secured in boxes.	Room temperature

FORENSIC SAMPLES (*Continued*)

Evidence	Collection	Packaging	Storage
	subject, using oblique lighting at each of the four sides, minimum four photos per subject. *Note:* Black and white film is highly recommended for high contrast. Casts can be made, if appropriate.		
Firearms	Carefully retrieve without placing anything down the barrel. Unload prior to packaging. *Note:* If you are unfamiliar with a particular firearm, have a firearms expert unload it; *do not* attempt to unload it yourself.	Secure in a cardboard box.	Consider multiple evidence processing prior to storage (blood collection, prints); if additional processing is to be done, it should be done prior to submission to the firearms examiner.
Projectiles/cartridge casings	Carefully collect items separately. NOTE: Do not mark the evidence item directly; label and seal the packaging.	Paper envelopes or small zip-lock bags.	Room temperature
Document evidence	Carefully collect items with forceps (consideration should be given to fingerprints).	Place in a prelabeled envelope. *Note:* Do not mark the item or label the envelope before placing the item inside; if you label it after the item is inside, this will obscure or add to any indented writing.	Room temperature
Ligatures	Do not untie any knots. If you must cut the ligature, cut it away from any knots and mark your cut.	Paper bag or envelope.	*Frozen* (can be subsequently placed in room temperature storage, if there are no biological concerns).
Bitemarks	Consult a forensic odontologist; photodocument with and without a dental L-shaped (American Board of Forensic Odontologists [ABFO]) scale. *Note:* Photos should be taken over a few days, as the bruises will change appearance. Swabbings should be taken of the area prior to casting.	Swabs should be air-*dried* and packaged in paper.	Swabs should be *frozen*.
Other evidence	Consult a criminalist prior to collection if you are not familiar with a particular item of evidence.	Consult a criminalist.	Consult a criminalist.

(*continued*)

FORENSIC SAMPLES *(Continued)*

Evidence	Collection	Packaging	Storage
Reference Standards			
Blood (from the victim, suspect, and any consensual partner, if applicable)	Medical personnel draws into EDTA (purple top) vial.	Label the tube, label the evidence envelope.	Transfer sample to lab *as soon as possible; refrigerate* if there is a delay; *do not freeze.*
Saliva or buccal swab	1. Gauze pad, cotton swatch placed in the mouth of donor and saturated (or) 2. Cotton swab; sweep the mouth between the cheek and gum.	*Air dry;* package in paper.	*Frozen*
Hairs (pubic, head, facial, body)	Pull 20 or more hairs from different areas. *Note:* Make sure the head hair is pulled from the front, top, sides, and back.	Paper bindle or envelope. *Note:* Each body surface sample should be packaged separately and labeled.	Room temperature
Tissue from a decomposed victim	Forensic pathologist makes collection. No formalin; deep muscle, organ, or bone tissue should be collected, depending on the state of decomposition.	Specimen container	*Frozen*

Note: All evidence submissions should be sealed with tamper-resistant seals. Staples alone are an insufficient seal. All seals should be initialed.

Reprinted with permission from Devine, E. (1997). Supervising Criminalist, Los Angeles Co. Sheriff's Dept., Scientific Services Bureau. California Commission on Peace Officer Standards and Training (P.O.S.T.). Sexual Assault Investigation Guidelines/ Course Curriculum.

B

APPENDIX

Sexual Assault Examination: Evidentiary Checklist

1. Notify rape crisis advocate.
2. Open a sealed sexual assault evidence kit.
   - Remove urine specimen cup and obtain urine sample, maintaining chain of custody. Refrigerate during exam.
   - Remove urine HCG pregnancy test from refrigerator (sensitivity <50 milli IU HCG).[1]
3. Obtain consents:
   - law enforcement, authorizing exam
   - patient
   - medical records release (per local protocol)
   - parent (<12 y.o.)
   - HIV
4. Obtain history (depending on local protocol, may range from cursory medical interview and account of assault, to a joint investigative history with law enforcement):
   - events in chronologic order
   - sequence of sexual acts
   - positions used during assault
   - alcohol/drug use by victim or suspect
   - sexual dysfunction of rapist
   - loss of consciousness: duration
   - LMP
   - last consenting intercourse
   - postcoital interval of assault
5. General PX: Note objective behavior; include affect, demeanor, emotional status, vital signs, height, weight, allergies, medications, last tetanus gait.
6. Clothing: Collect clothing worn during assault; examine and package each item separately in paper bags. Have patient take off shoes and undress on two sheets white paper; do not shake clothing.
7. Darken room; scan with Wood's lamp or alternate light source (ALS); note findings. If positive for stains, dried secretions, fluorescence, use small amount distilled water on swab(s) to collect sample(s). *Swab* each dried secretion with separate pair of swabs, eg, bitemark for saliva, dried blood, dried semen. *Smear* swabs on *two slides*. Make *control* from unstained area of body.
8. Photograph all nongenital trauma: For bitemarks, collect two swabs, photograph with and without L-shaped ABFO scale. Cast, per protocol. Refer to forensic odontologist.
9. Head: Collect foreign matter, debris, fibers
   Collect forensic swabs—two from *oral* cavity; make two slides from these (if history of oral copulation within 6 hours).
   Reference samples[2]
   head hairs (20 tugged)
   saliva sample (liquid, or two swabs, or gauze/cotton pledget)
   Gonorrhea cultures[3]

---

[1] Some programs prefer *serum* pregnancy tests either before or just after the physical exam.
[2] Where local protocol includes collection of STDs.
[3] Where local crime lab protocol includes collection of reference samples at time of initial exam.

10. Fingernail scrapings or cuttings, if indicated by history.
11. Genital/anal: Gross visualization before colposcopy and collection of specimens.
    Cut/collect any matted pubic hair.
    Comb pubic hair: collect any loose hairs and package the brush/comb.

Collect any dried and moist stains/secretions; use small amount distilled water. Collect control swab.
Reference: Pubic hair samples—20 tugged (different areas).[3]

Colposcopic Examination

Colposcope I.D. tag in camera
Examine and photograph anatomic sites:

clitoris	hymen	vagina	perineum
labia majora	fossa navicularis	cervix	rectum
labia minora	posterior fourchette	anus	

Swabs/Slides *Genital: Female*

External genital area (labia and external genital area): Two swabs and slides; moisten with distilled water; swab with two swabs together; smear on two slides.

Vaginal pool: Three to four swabs collected *simultaneously* from posterior fornix; make *wet mount* slide to check for motile sperm, from swab No. 3. Make two *dry mount* slides. Package wet mount slide in separate slide holder.

Cervix: One swab and one slide, if 48 hours postassault, or if history of consensual sexual intercourse within 72 hours. Send swabs and slides to crime lab in evidence kit.

Gonorrhea and chlamydia from cervix; wet prep. (Other herpes.)[2]

Swabs/Slides *Genital: Male*

Penile swabs: One from shaft; one from glans. If uncircumcised, swab under foreskin. Send to crime lab.

Urethral gonorrhea and chlamydia[2]

Swabs/Slides *Anal*

Known or suspected sodomy: To avoid contamination of rectal swabs, first clean perianal area with water.

After careful inspection and photo colposcopy of anal area, insert anoscope. Visualize and photograph. Through anoscope, collect two rectal swabs and make two dry mount slides for evidence kit.

Rectal gonorrhea[2]
Rectal chlamydia: must be *culture,* not screening test.

12. Laboratory

Crime Lab

Blood alcohol (nonalcohol prep swab)
Urine toxicology, classic drug screen for
  Rohypnol, gamma hydroxy butyrate
  (GHB), as appropriate.

Hospital (per local protocol)

Syphilis (RPR, VDRL)
HIV (separate consent)
Pregnancy: Serum qualitative or urine HCG
  less than 50 milli IU HCG
Hepatitis panel
STDs: Wet prep, chlamydia, gonorrhea,
  herpes

13. Emergency contraceptive pills (ECPs):
  (within 72 hours of intercourse)
  - Must first obtain a negative preg-
    nancy test.
  - Patient reads and signs consent for
    ECPs.
  - Observe patient 20–30 minutes after
    taking. Can administer with mecli-
    zine (Bonine), 25 mg to reduce nau-
    sea and likelihood of vomiting.
  - Ovral, 50 mg: Two stat, and two in
    12 hours.
  - Lo-Ovral or other low-dose hor-
    mone: Four stat and four in 12 hours.
14. Specimens to crime lab:
  - Swabs and slides individually la-
    beled, coded to show which slides
    prepared from which swab and time
    collected.
  - All swabs and slides should be *air-
    dried for 60 minutes* in a stream of
    cool air.
  - Containers (tubes, bindles, enve-
    lopes, bags) for individual items

labeled: patient name, contents, body
location, hospital, time, initials of
collector.
  - Copy of medical–legal form included
    in the sexual assault evidence kit.
Kit is sealed with tamper-resistant seal;
includes date/time, initials.
15. Documentation: Entire medical–legal
  form completed. (May be separate hospital medical record for documentation
  of medical, gynecologic history, medications, etc.) Include *summary of findings:*
  - time frame compatible with history
  - evidence of injury (genital/nongenital
    physical findings)
  - findings consistent with history pro-
    vided
Dictated narrative summary also recommended.

*Maintain chain of custody of all evidentiary
items.*

Tanner Stages

Girls	**Pubic Hair**	**Breasts**
Stage 1	No pubic hair, except vellus (fine body hair similar to abdominal hair).	Preadolescent: elevation of nipple only.
Stage 2	Sparse growth of long, slightly pigmented downy hairs (straight or curly), mostly along the labia.	Breast buds: elevation of breast and nipple as small mounds; areolar diameter increases.
Stage 3	Hair is darker, curlier, and coarser; spreads sparsely over the symphysis pubis.	Breast and areola continue to enlarge and elevate; no separation of contours of the breast, areola.
Stage 4	Hair is coarse, curly, and adult-like; covers more area than in Stage 3, but not as great as adult; no lateral spread to thighs.	Areola and nipple project to form secondary mound above level of breast.
Stage 5	Hair adult-like in quality, quantity; spreads laterally to medial thighs, but not up over abdomen.	Mature adult female stage; only the nipple projects. Areola recedes to the general contour of the breast (in some, areola continues to form secondary mound).

Boys	**Pubic Hair**	**Penis**	**Testes and Scrotum**
Stage 1	No pubic hair, except vellus (fine body hair similar to abdominal hair).	Preadolescent size: same size and proportions as in childhood.	Preadolescent: same as in childhood.
Stage 2	Sparse growth: long, slightly pigmented, downy hair; straight or curly; mostly along base of penis.	Slight or no increase in size.	Testes increase in size; scrotum increases and becomes somewhat reddened and altered in texture.
Stage 3	Hair is darker, curlier, coarser; spreads sparsely over symphysis pubis.	Larger, especially in length	Further enlarged.
Stage 4	Hair is coarse, curly, and adult-like; hair covers more area than in Stage 3, but not as great as adult; no lateral spread to thighs.	Further increases in length and width; glans development.	Further enlarged; darkening of scrotal skin.
Stage 5	Hair adult-like in quality, quantity; lateral spreading to medial thighs, but not abdomen.	Adult size and shape.	Adult size and shape.

(From: Hay, W.W. Jr., Groothuis, J.R., Hayward, A.R., & Levin, M.J. [1999]. Current pediatric diagnosis & treatment. Stamford, CT: Appleton & Lange.)

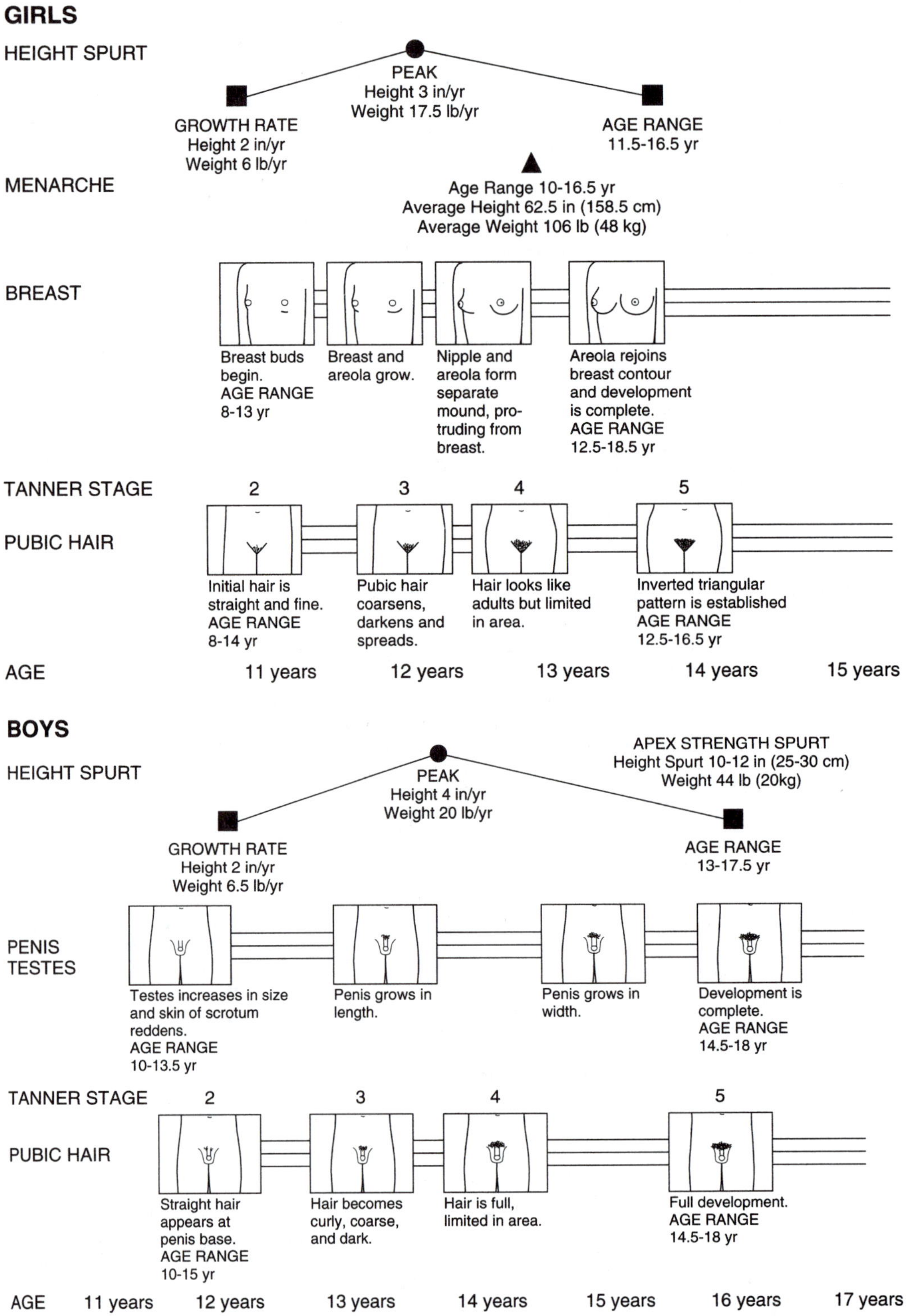

GIRLS

HEIGHT SPURT

PEAK
Height 3 in/yr
Weight 17.5 lb/yr

GROWTH RATE
Height 2 in/yr
Weight 6 lb/yr

AGE RANGE
11.5-16.5 yr

MENARCHE

Age Range 10-16.5 yr
Average Height 62.5 in (158.5 cm)
Average Weight 106 lb (48 kg)

BREAST

| Breast buds begin. AGE RANGE 8-13 yr | Breast and areola grow. | Nipple and areola form separate mound, protruding from breast. | Areola rejoins breast contour and development is complete. AGE RANGE 12.5-18.5 yr |

TANNER STAGE   2   3   4   5

PUBIC HAIR

| Initial hair is straight and fine. AGE RANGE 8-14 yr | Pubic hair coarsens, darkens and spreads. | Hair looks like adults but limited in area. | Inverted triangular pattern is established AGE RANGE 12.5-16.5 yr |

AGE   11 years   12 years   13 years   14 years   15 years

BOYS

HEIGHT SPURT

APEX STRENGTH SPURT
Height Spurt 10-12 in (25-30 cm)
Weight 44 lb (20kg)

PEAK
Height 4 in/yr
Weight 20 lb/yr

GROWTH RATE
Height 2 in/yr
Weight 6.5 lb/yr

AGE RANGE
13-17.5 yr

PENIS TESTES

| Testes increases in size and skin of scrotum reddens. AGE RANGE 10-13.5 yr | Penis grows in length. | Penis grows in width. | Development is complete. AGE RANGE 14.5-18 yr |

TANNER STAGE   2   3   4   5

PUBIC HAIR

| Straight hair appears at penis base. AGE RANGE 10-15 yr | Hair becomes curly, coarse, and dark. | Hair is full, limited in area. | Full development. AGE RANGE 14.5-18 yr |

AGE   11 years   12 years   13 years   14 years   15 years   16 years   17 years

Figure C-1. The Tanner stages. *(From Hay, W.W. Jr., Hayward, A.R., & Lenn, M.J. [1999]. Current pediatric diagnosis & treatment. Stamford, CT: Appleton & Lange.)*

D

APPENDIX

Dictation Format for Adult and Adolescent Sexual Assault Examinations

Medical–Legal examination: Narrative summary

Name (legal, as on their birth certificate); Last, First, Middle

AKA: Name they prefer, or have used in the past

D.O.B.

Date of Sexual Assault Response Team (SART) examination: month/date/year

Place of examination: SART or hospital site

   Time of SART examination: military times, or indicate A.M. or P.M.

Report requested by: Name of authorizing agency and individual

Reason for evaluation: "To evaluate . . . (patient) for concerns related to possible sexual assault."

Report based on: "Discussion with . . . [investigative personnel: name(s), agency, relationship to patient, if any], and a clinical evaluation and medical examination of . . . ."

Historical information: Narrative summary of the alleged sexual assault. Place the events and sexual acts in chronologic order, as much as possible. *Use objective* data and observations; avoid subjective impressions. Use direct quotes, if appropriate, and indicate as such, eg, if suspect forced victim to say certain things.

Physical examination: Describe physical exam *positions* used during exam (eg, supine, left-lateral, knee–chest, supine, with knees flexed onto abdomen). Describe *equipment* used (eg, 35-mm photography, colposcopy, anoscopy, alternate light source). Describe *techniques* used to enhance visualization (eg, use of xylocaine gel, balloon swabs, water, nuclear-staining dye, swab to probe hymenal borders).

Head, Ears, Eyes, Nose, and Throat (HEENT)

"Head is normocephalic. Pupils are equal, round, reactive to light and accommodation. Extraocular movements are full, normal. Right tympanic membranes appear dull and pink. Unable to visualize left, secondary to cerumen. Nose within normal limits (WNL); mucosa normal. Teeth are in good repair. Trachea is midline; thyroid not palpably enlarged. Buccal mucosa is clear. Frenulum normal."

Heart: "Rate is regular. Apical pulse: _____. No murmurs or extra systoles noted. BP: _____."

Chest: "Normal configuration. Lungs are clear to auscultation and percussion. RR: _____. Breasts are Tanner stage 4." (Describe any nongenital trauma.)

Abdomen: "Soft and nonprotruberant; scaphoid; normal bowel sounds."

Extremities: "Unremarkable" (or describe all nongenital trauma).

Genital exam: Describe following anatomic sites:

Genitals are Tanner stage: _____(if patient is adolescent).

clitoris	hymen	vagina	penis
labia majora	fossa navicularis	cervix	foreskin
labia minora	posterior fourchette	anus	scrotum
periurethra	perineum	rectum	testes

Note any pelvic, lower abdominal tenderness, discomfort.

Summary: "Based on the foregoing information . . ." (summarize exam findings):

1. presence of physical findings (eg, genital/nongenital trauma: presence of sperm)
2. exam consistent/inconsistent with history and time frame provided

Recommendations:

1. counseling and follow-up by trained and experienced therapist
2. colposcopic reexamination in 10–14 days to document resolution of genital trauma
3. referral for follow-up STD/pregnancy testing in 4–6 weeks
4. suspect medical–legal exam, if apprehended

Note: If victim is a minor, the examiner may recommend that any other children who may have come in contact with suspect also be evaluated for possibility of abuse.

APPENDIX

Suspect Examination Protocol

The examination of an alleged suspect(s) of a sexual assault may provide useful corroborative information to the investigation. If performed before the degradation of biological material, the exam may help link the suspect to the crime. If the victim is on her menses during the assault, and the suspect has not yet bathed, it may be possible to obtain a sample of her menstrual blood from a penile swab. In some jurisdictions, suspects of child sexual assault are tested for STDs, rather than routinely testing child victims. Also, changing laws regarding HIV allows for the victim to request that an alleged suspect be tested for his (or her) HIV status. Results are still highly confidential and usually only released to the ordering judge, who then provides for victim notification. During the interchange of the rape, a victim may inflict defense, or other wounds onto the body of the assailant. A physical exam of the suspect may help corroborate the victim's history. If the victim bites the suspect, swabbings, photographs, and castings can be made of the bite. The use of alternate light imaging of the suspect has helped to corroborate that a particular tool or weapon was consistent with the weapon used in the commission of a crime.

The suspect and victim should never encounter each other in the medical facility. Security and safety for the forensic examiner are vital, and should never be taken lightly. Law enforcement should be present for the entire exam process and collection of evidence.

The goal of the medical–legal exam of the suspect is to perform a forensic examination in accordance with state and local protocol, and to ensure adequate documentation on appropriate forms. The forensic examiner who conducts these exams on alleged suspects of sexual assault should be aware of relevant legal implications for their particular jurisdiction. If the suspect voluntarily consents to the forensic medical exam and any testing for STDs or HIV, the appropriate consents must be signed. If the suspect does not voluntarily consent, the examiner should know exactly what is covered under the search warrant/court order. A copy of the suspect protocol for medical–legal exams may be useful to law enforcement at the time of the request of a court order, especially if they desire to request STD testing.

EVIDENTIARY EXAMINATION

1. Open the sealed sexual assault evidence kit (for suspect, if separate kit available).
2. Obtain historical information and necessary data from law enforcement officer. Include:
   - date/time/location of assault
   - alleged sexual acts
   - salient information from victim exam, if known, eg, victim's report of identifying marks (scars, tattoos, defense inflicted wounds, bites by victim.)

- is victim on her menses? (if yes, has suspect showered?)

3. Obtain consent or review search warrant for:
   - medical exam
   - collection of specimens
   - STDs
   - HIV

4. Cursory medical interview (if suspect willing):
   - medications
   - allergies
   - major medical/surgical conditions
   - recent (60 days) history of urinary tract infections or anal/genital conditions
   - history of vasectomy

5. Clothing (if not already collected at time of custody):
   - Take off shoes and undress on two sheets white paper.
   - Examine and package each item separately in paper bag. Do not shake clothing.

6. General physical examination:
   - height, weight, vital signs, pupils (check for vertical or horizontal nystagmus), eye, hair, and facial hair color
   - note objective behavior and demeanor, affect, speech, coordination, right or left handedness
   - breath, body odor
   - tattoos, scars, birthmarks
   - needle marks
   - other identifying marks or lesions

7. Scan entire body with Wood's lamp or alternate light source (ALS), in darkened room. If positive for stains, dried secretions, or positive (+) fluorescence, use small amount distilled water on swab to collect. Swab each dried secretion with separate pair of swabs, eg, bitemark for saliva, dried blood, or dried semen stain (male victim). Smear swabs on two slides. Make control swab of unstained area.

8. Photograph all nongenital trauma. For bitemarks, collect two swabs, photograph with and without L-shaped ABFO scale. Cast, if per protocol. (Recommend referral to forensic odontologist as soon as possible.)
   - check for defense injuries caused by victim: abrasions, scratches, bleeding

9. Head/oral: *collect* foreign matter, debris, fibers
   - check oral cavity (buccal mucosa and frenulum); two oral swabs and slides, if indicated by history (≤6 hours postassault)
   - saliva reference sample (liquid, or two swabs, or cotton/gauze pledget)
   - collect reference hair samples:
     Head hair: 20 pulled, tugged
     Facial hair: 15–20 pulled, tugged
   - STDs: oral gonorrhea[1]

10. Collect body hair, if appropriate.

11. Fingernail cuttings/scrapings, if indicated.

12. Genital/anal:
    - collect any matted pubic hair
    - place paper under buttocks; comb pubic hair; package brush/comb; bindle and package paper
    - collect any dried/moist secretions, as in #7
    - collect pubic hair reference samples: 20–40 pulled hairs, from different regions
    - inspect anatomic sites: use photography, colposcopy, if indicated for:
      penis
      anus
      scrotum
      perineum
      (rectum)
    - check for signs of injury: abrasions, bites, lacerations; inspect mucocutaneous junction of meatus

---

[1] Collect STDs per local protocol and per consent or warrant.

- check for foreign materials, blood, feces, lubricant on penis
- *penile swabs:* collect at least one from shaft and one from glans; if uncircumcised, swab under foreskin

If indicated by history, collect rectal forensic samples: wash perianal area with water; insert anoscope. Inspect, photograph, and collect two rectal swabs. Make two dry mount slides. *Vinegar dip* can be used for screening suspicious lesions for condyloma. Dilute white vinegar with water. Dip or wrap penis and scrotum with saturated gauze. Wait few minutes and check for aceto-whitening. Or, can swab suspicious lesions with white vinegar.

13. Laboratory

Crime Lab	*Hospital Lab*
Blood alcohol	STDs: gonorrhea and chlamydia from penile urethra[1]
Urine toxicology	Gonorrhea and chlamydia *culture* from rectum
	Syphilis, HIV, hepatitis panel, herpes
	Gonorrhea culture from throat

14. Documentation: Document all *objective findings* on appropriate form(s). Include all specimens and time collected. Note procedures, such as photography and colposcopy. Keep copy of consents/warrants for sexual assault response team (SART) records. If using the same medical-legal form as for a victim, highlight the areas that are relevant to suspect exam, and complete only these. Refer to local protocol or your district attorney's office. For a suspect exam, the forensic examiner is primarily collecting physical evidence, and does not render an opinion as to whether a particular individual is indeed the assailant.

15. Specimens to crime lab:
- Specimens and slides individually labeled, coded to show which slides were prepared from which swab; date and time collected. All swabs, slides, air dried ×60 minutes in stream of cool air.
- Containers (tubes, bindles, envelopes, bags) for individual items labeled: patient name, medical record or case I.D. number, contents, body site, hospital, time, initials of collector.
- Copy of medical–legal form included in kit.
- Sexual assault evidence kit sealed with tamper-resistant seal; initials of collector, date/time of collection.
- Maintain chain of custody throughout.

F

Medical–Legal Form for Documentation of Sexual Assault Examination

PATIENT INFORMATION

Please print clearly and legibly

Name			Gender ☐ M ☐ F	Age	Time	Date
HMC#		DOB	Street Address			Apt.
Phone		City		State		Zip
Message Phone		Accompanied by				Relationship
Police Report Filed	☐ Yes ☐ No	Interpreter ☐ Yes ☐ No		Language		
If Yes, Police Department	Case #	Interpreter Name				
CPS Report	☐ Yes ☐ No	Photos ☐ 35 ☐ Polaroid ☐ None				
		Areas of Body				
If Yes, CPS Office and Intake Worker		Photos Placed ☐ In Evidence ☐ In Chart				
		Photographer				

TRANSFER OF EVIDENCE (To be completed when forensic evidence is transferred to police department)

I Hereby Certify That I Have Received From (Name)_____ at Harborview Medical Center the following items:

1.   2.   3.   4.

Officer's Name (Print)	Officer's Signature	Dept
Case #	Phone	Date/Time

DISCHARGE PLAN

Discharged To	Follow-up Appointment (Clinic Name /Date/Time Of Appointment)
Check Information Given ☐ Patient Education Materials	
If minor signs for own care, document reason, emancipation status, and maturity of minor.	**AUTHORIZATION FOR RELEASE OF INFORMATION** I hereby waive physician/patient relationship of confidentiality and authorize Harborview Medical Center to release copies of all information pertaining to this visit (including all information obtained from my examination and treatment) to: _____ Agency Patient or Legal Guardian Signature (below) _____

SW Name (Please print)	Signature	Discharge time	Date

PT.NO.

NAME

DOB

UNIVERSITY OF WASHINGTON MEDICAL CENTERS
HARBORVIEW MEDICAL CENTER - UW MEDICAL CENTER
SEATTLE, WASHINGTON

HSA Emergency Report

HMC 0586 REV APR 97   DRAFT   Page 1 of 7

HISTORY OF ASSAULT

Please print clearly and legibly

Date of Assault	Where Assault Occurred		Time of Assault	Hours Since Assault
#Assailants	#Sexual Assailants	Identity of Alleged Assailant/s	Age (if known)	Informant(s)

HISTORY OF ASSAULT (Narrative summary and patient's emotional state)

Use of Verbal Threats Describe ❏ Yes ❏ No ❏ Unk	Impaired Consciousness Describe ❏ Yes ❏ No ❏ Unk
Use of Physical Force Describe ❏ Yes ❏ No ❏ Unk	Use Of Foreign Object Describe ❏ Yes ❏ No ❏ Unk
Use of Weapon Describe ❏ Yes ❏ No ❏ Unk	Condom Used Describe ❏ Yes ❏ No ❏ Unk
Physical Injuries Describe ❏ Yes ❏ No ❏ Unk	Ejaculation Noted Describe ❏ Yes ❏ No ❏ Unk

Orifices Assaulted
- ❏ Oral   ❏ Unknown
- ❏ Vaginal   ❏ Other
- ❏ Anal   ❏ None

Did Patient
- ❏ Bathe/Shower   ❏ Change Clothes
- ❏ Douche   ❏ Bring Clothes
- ❏ Wear Tampon/Pad   ❏ Give Clothes to Police At Scene

Impression:

Plan:

SW Name (Please print)	Signature	Date

PT.NO.

NAME

DOB

UNIVERSITY OF WASHINGTON MEDICAL CENTERS
HARBORVIEW MEDICAL CENTER - UW MEDICAL CENTER
SEATTLE, WASHINGTON

HSA Emergency Report

TRAUMAGRAM

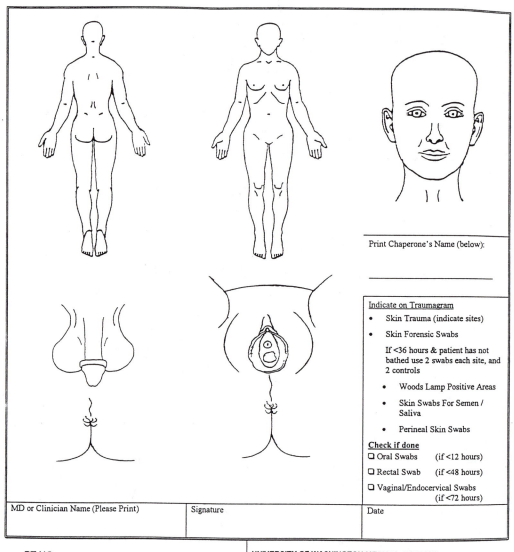

Print Chaperone's Name (below):

_____

<u>Indicate on Traumagram</u>
- Skin Trauma (indicate sites)
- Skin Forensic Swabs

  If <36 hours & patient has not bathed use 2 swabs each site, and 2 controls
  - Woods Lamp Positive Areas
  - Skin Swabs For Semen / Saliva
  - Perineal Skin Swabs

Check if done
☐ Oral Swabs   (if <12 hours)
☐ Rectal Swab   (if <48 hours)
☐ Vaginal/Endocervical Swabs
              (if <72 hours)

MD or Clinician Name (Please Print)	Signature	Date

PT.NO.

NAME

DOB

UNIVERSITY OF WASHINGTON MEDICAL CENTERS
HARBORVIEW MEDICAL CENTER - UW MEDICAL CENTER
SEATTLE, WASHINGTON

HSA Emergency Report

HMC 0586 REV APR 97   DRAFT   Page 3 of 7

MEDICAL EVALUATION

Please print clearly and legibly

MEDICAL HISTORY	
History of Assault (see SW note)	Ob-Gyn History
	Last Consensual Intercourse
	Last Menstrual Period
	Usual Contraception
	Previous Hepatitis Vaccine or Hx
Significant Past/Current Illnesses	Risk Factors of Assailant ❑ Multiple sexual assailants ❑ From viral endemic area ❑ Suspected IV drug user ❑ Known HIV or Hepatitis carrier
	<u>Contraindications to Emergency Contraception</u> ❑ Using effective contraception ❑ Depo ❑ Norplant ❑ IUD ❑ BTL ❑ Oral contraceptives
PMD	❑ Known or desired pregnancy, conception in past 5 days ❑ Patient declines emergency contraception
Current Medications	Allergies

Physical Examination			
General Appearance	COLPOSCOPY	❑ Yes	❑ No
	COLPOSCOPY PHOTOS	❑ Yes	❑ No
Demeanor	SPECULUM USED	❑ Yes	❑ No
	Vulva		
Skin			
HEENT	Hymen		
Chest	Vagina		
Abdomen	Cervix		
Extremities	Uterus		
Neuro	Adnexa		
	Anus		

OTHER		
MD or Clinician Name (Please print)	Signature	Date

PT.NO.

NAME

DOB

UNIVERSITY OF WASHINGTON MEDICAL CENTERS
HARBORVIEW MEDICAL CENTER - UW MEDICAL CENTER
SEATTLE, WASHINGTON

HSA Emergency Report

HMC 0586 REV APR 97   DRAFT   Page 4 of 7

MEDICAL PLAN

Please print clearly and legibly

Laboratory Tests

Wet Mount

Vaginal

pH _____

Clue cells _____

Trichomonas _____

Sperm/HPF _____

% motility _____

Other _____

Pregnancy Test
- ❑ Positive
- ❑ Negative
- ❑ Not done

Tox screen (s) (hospital)
- ❑ N/A
- ❑ Results: _____

ETOH level _____

❑ Gonorrhea   Site(s)_____

❑ Chlamydia   Site(s)_____

Other labs _____

Consults _____

Emergency Contraception and Vaccine Consent

The risks and benefits have been explained to me and I consent for:

❑ Emergency contraception

_____
Patient or guardian signature

❑ Hepatitis vaccine

_____
Patient or guardian signature

Notes:

Assessment:

1. _____
History

2. _____
Exam Findings

3. _____

4. _____

5. _____

6. _____

Plan:

1. ❑ See Medication Order Sheet   ❑ No medications

2. _____

3. _____

4. _____

5. _____

6. F/U_____

❑ Discharge Instructions Given

MD or Clinician Name (Please print)	Signature	Date

PT.NO.

NAME

DOB

UNIVERSITY OF WASHINGTON MEDICAL CENTERS
HARBORVIEW MEDICAL CENTER - UW MEDICAL CENTER
SEATTLE, WASHINGTON

HSA Emergency Report

HMC 0586 REV APR 97   DRAFT   Page 5 of 7

HSA STANDARD ORDERS

Please print clearly and legibly

Patient Name:	Patient HMC #	Date:

On Admission to ED:
- Vitals: Heart rate, blood pressure, respiratory rate,
- Triage to ER Doc: Head injury, lacerations, possible fractures, altered mental status

Routine Lab
- Urine Beta HCG (All females age 12 & above)
- Urine for forensic toxicology

MEDICATION ORDERS   ❏ No known drug allergies
❏ Medication allergies:_____

Medication	Dose	ER Stock	Pharmacy	Route	Time	Initials
❏ Azithromycin	1 gm PO x 1	❏	❏	_____	_____	_____
Alternatives for chlamydia prophylaxis ❏ Doxycycline 100 mg PO bid x 7 days		❏	❏	_____	_____	_____
For pregnant women: ❏ Amoxicillin 500 mg PO tid x 10 days		❏	❏	_____	_____	_____
❏ Cefixime	400 mg. PO x 1	❏	❏	_____	_____	_____
Alternatives for gonorrhea prophylaxis for significant penicillin allergy (anaphylaxis, hives,etc) ❏ Ofloxacin 400 mg PO x 1		❏	❏	_____	_____	_____
For pregant women: ❏ Ceftriaxone 250 mg IM x 1		❏	❏	_____	_____	_____
❏ Ovral tabs	2 tabs PO q 12h x 2	❏	❏			
❏ Promethazine	25 mg. 1 tab PO q 6h prn nausea x3	❏	❏			
❏ OTHER		❏	❏			
❏ OTHER		❏	❏			
❏ OTHER		❏	❏			

Injections	Dose	ER Stock	Pharmacy	Site Lot # Exp	Time	Initials
❏ Hepatitis B Immune Globulin	_____ ml IM buttock (0.06 ml/kg)	❏	❏			
❏ Hepatitis B Vaccine	1.0 ml. IM deltoid	❏	❏			
❏ Tetanus toxoid	0.5 ml IM	❏	❏			

❏ Arrange patient shower prior to discharge

MD or Clinician Name (Please print)	Signature	Date

PT.NO.

NAME

DOB

UNIVERSITY OF WASHINGTON MEDICAL CENTERS
HARBORVIEW MEDICAL CENTER - UW MEDICAL CENTER
SEATTLE, WASHINGTON

HSA Emergency Report

HMC 0586 REV APR 97   DRAFT   Page 6 of 7

ADULT

FORENSIC EVALUATION OF ALLEGED SEXUAL ASSAULT

Case # _____

2 copies to Police Officer
1 copy to Clinic

1. Identifying Information:
   Name _____
   DOB _____ Age _____ Sex _____ Race _____

   Alleged Assault:
   Date: _____
   Time: _____

   Forensic Exam:
   Date: _____
   Time: _____

2. General Forensic Exam: (Describe trauma) _____

3. Forensic Genital and Anal Exam: (Describe trauma) _____

4. Post Assault:

	Yes	No	
	☐	☐	Urination
	☐	☐	Douche
	☐	☐	Sponge bath
	☐	☐	Bath/Shower
	☐	☐	Defecation

5. Behavior type demonstrated during exam:

   ☐ Controlled   ☐ Expressed   ☐ Mixed

   ☐ quiet   ☐ tearful
   ☐ tense   ☐ sobbing
   ☐ fidgeting   ☐ yelling
   ☐ trembling   ☐ loud
   ☐ listless   ☐ agitated
   ☐ staring   ☐ other _____

   Responds to questions:

   ☐ briefly   ☐ reluctantly   ☐ readily

7. Summary of Evidence: Released to:

Yes	No		
☐	☐	Kit Collected	_____
☐	☐	Pubic hair	_____
☐	☐	Panties/Clothing	_____

   Condition _____

Yes	No	
☐	☐	Other _____

   Physical/Genital exam done with:

Yes	No		Yes	No	
☐	☐	Direct visualization	☐	☐	Colposcope exam
☐	☐	Bimanual exam	☐	☐	Pics taken # ___
☐	☐	Speculum exam			_____

6. Additional Observation or Remarks: _____

8. Testing: Sperm

	SEEN	MOTILE	NON-MOTILE	NOT SEEN	NOT DONE
Vaginal					
Oral					
Anal					

9. Instructions for Follow-up

		Yes	No
A.	ORAL	☐	☐
B.	WRITTEN		
	Agency brochures	☐	☐
	Medical follow-up inst.	☐	☐

I hereby authorize use of this report, collected evidence and any other report incidental thereto by the Memphis Police Services and/or other Shelby County cooperating law enforcement agencies.

Person
Examined _____

Parent or
Guardian _____

Date _____

MRCC _____ DHS _____

Examining
Clinician _____

Police
Officer _____

R&I # _____

CPT # _____

PHYSICAL EXAMINER'S CHECKLIST (FEMALE)

CASE # _____

VICTIM'S NAME (print) _____ AGE _____ RACE _____

DATE/TIME OF ASSAULT _____

DATE/TIME OF EXAM _____

1. Bloody external physical trauma excluding genitalia: Absent _____ Present _____

    Location(s) _____

2. Menstrual flow: Absent _____ Present _____ First day of last period _____

3. Bloody genital trauma: Absent _____ Internal _____ External _____ Vaginal _____ Anal _____

4. Sperm: Not Seen _____ Motile sperm seen _____ Non-motile sperm seen _____ Not Done _____

5. a. Douche after assault: Yes _____ No _____ Don't know _____

    b. Bath, shower after assault: Yes _____ No _____ Don't know _____

    c. Sponge bath after assault: Yes _____ No _____ Don't know _____

    d. Urinated after assault: Yes _____ No _____ Don't know _____

    e. Defecated after assault: Yes _____ No _____ Don't know _____

    f. Condom used during assault: Yes _____ No _____ Don't know _____

    g. Lubricant used during assault: Yes _____ No _____ Don't know _____

                                                                    Name of lubricant _____

    h. Foreign object used during assault: Yes _____ No _____ Don't know _____

                                                                    Name of object(s) _____

6. a. Vaginal assault: Yes _____ No _____ Don't know _____

    b. Last voluntary vaginal intercourse (within 4 days):   Yes _____ No _____ Don't know _____

        If less than 12 hours, time: _____ # of consensual partners in last 12 hours _____

7. a. Oral Assault: Yes _____ No _____ Don't know _____ Rinsed mouth before exam _____

    b. Last voluntary oral intercourse (within 4 days):   Yes _____ No _____ Don't know _____

        If less than 12 hours, time: _____ # of consensual partners in last 12 hours _____

8. a. Anal Assault: Yes _____ No _____ Don't know _____

    b. Last voluntary anal intercourse (within 4 days):   Yes _____ No _____ Don't know _____

        If less than 12 hours, time: _____ # of consensual partners in last 12 hours _____

9. Emission of semen (victim's impression):

    a. Vaginal: Yes _____ No _____ Don't know _____ Intravaginal _____ Extravaginal _____

    b. Oral: Yes _____ No _____ Don't know _____

    c. Anal: Yes _____ No _____ Don't know _____

    d. Other area: Yes _____ No _____ Don't know _____ Location(s) _____

10. Fingernails: Samples taken   Yes _____ No _____

11. Miscellaneous sample from (name site) _____ to be tested for (name body fluid) _____

12. Miscellaneous sample from (name site) _____ to be tested for (name body fluid) _____

_____
                        Forensic Nurse Examiner's Signature

CASE NO _____

NAME OF VICTIM _____

DATE OF COLLECTION _____   TIME _____ AM - PM

NURSE/CLINICIAN _____

adult, female (front view)

adult, female (back view)

PHYSICAL CONDITION OF VICTIM:

INDICATE ALL SIGNS OF PHYSICAL TRAUMA - E.G., BRUISES, SCRATCHES, MARKS, DIS-
COLORATIONS (SIZE AND COLOR), OR BITE MARKS ON ANY PART OF THE BODY. (NOTE ALL
SIGNS OF TRAUMA ON THE APPROPRIATE ANATOMICAL DRAWING).

PREPUBERTAL FEMALE GENITAL and ANAL FORENSIC EXAMINATION

CASE NO. _____

NAME OF VICTIM _____

DATE OF COLLECTION _____ **TIME** _____ **AM - PM**

NURSE/CLINICIAN _____

Comments: _____
_____
_____
_____
_____

☐ Refused   ☐ Full Cooperation   ☐ Partial Cooperation

PHYSICAL EXAMINER'S CHECKLIST (MALE)

CASE # _____

VICTIM'S NAME _____ AGE _____ RACE _____

DATE/TIME OF ASSAULT _____ MARITAL STATUS _____

DATE/TIME OF EXAM _____

1. Bloody external physical trauma excluding genitalia: Absent _____ Present _____

2. Bloody genital trauma: Absent _____ Internal _____ External _____ Penile _____ Anal _____

3. Sperm: Seen _____ Motile _____ Non-Motile _____ Not Seen _____ Not Done _____

4. Bath, Shower: Yes _____ No _____ Don't Know _____

    Sponge bath: Yes _____ No _____ Don't Know _____

    Condom Used: Yes _____ No _____ Don't Know _____

5. Last voluntary intercourse (within 4 days):   Yes _____ No _____ Don't Know _____
    If less than 12 hours, time: _____

6. Oral Act: Yes _____ No _____ Don't Know _____ Rinsed mouth before exam _____

7. Anal Act: Yes _____ No _____ Don't Know _____

8. Emission of semen (victim's impression):

    Oral: Yes _____ No _____ Don't Know _____

    Anal: Yes _____ No _____ Don't Know _____

9. Fingernails: Clean _____ Blood _____ Scrapings taken _____

_____
Examiner's Signature

CASE NO _____

NAME OF VICTIM _____

DATE OF COLLECTION _____   **TIME** _____ **AM - PM**

NURSE/CLINICIAN _____

adult, male (front view)

adult, male (back view)

PHYSICAL CONDITION OF VICTIM:

INDICATE ALL SIGNS OF PHYSICAL TRAUMA - E.G., BRUISES, SCRATCHES, MARKS, DIS-
COLORATIONS (SIZE AND COLOR), OR BITE MARKS ON ANY PART OF THE BODY. (NOTE ALL
SIGNS OF TRAUMA ON THE APPROPRIATE ANATOMICAL DRAWING).

MALE GENITAL and ANAL FORENSIC EXAMINATION

CASE NO. _____

NAME OF VICTIM _____

DATE OF COLLECTION _____ TIME _____ AM - PM

NURSE/CLINICIAN _____

Left   Right

Comments: _____
_____
_____
_____
_____

☐ Refused   ☐ Full Cooperation   ☐ Partial Cooperation

G

APPENDIX

Medical–Legal Documentation Form and Nursing Care Plan for Sexual Assault Victims

NURSING CARE PLAN KEY
PAGE 1

THE NURSING CARE PLAN KEY IS PROVIDED AS A GUIDE FOR THE COMPLETION OF THE NURSING CARE PLAN (MSARC FORENSIC NURSE FORM: CARE PLAN/SOAP: 5/97). THE CARE PLAN MEETS THE STRUCTURE AND OUTCOME OBJECTIVES TO THE FOLLOWING SANE STANDARDS OF PRACTICE: THEORY, DATA COLLECTION, DIAGNOSIS, PLANNING, INTERVENTION, EVALUATION, QUALITY ASSURANCE, INTERDISCIPLINARY COLLABORATION, AND RESEARCH. THE INSTRUCTIONS FOLLOW:

Write in the: CASE #_____ & DATE: _____

INTRODUCTION: **The SANE is instructed to check the line on the left of the completed items. When there is no check, the item is considered not completed.**

✓INTRODUCE FORENSIC NURSE BY NAME : **The SANE is expected to introduce herself to the client by providing her name and stating that she is the forensic nurse.**

✓ROLE EXPLANATION OF FORENSIC NURSE/SEXUAL ASSAULT NURSE EXAMINER: **In an appropriate location, the SANE is expected to provide an explanation of the SANE role, including but not limited to crisis intervention, physical evaluation, evidence collection, medical treatment, health teaching, follow up recommendations including medical referral, and testimony.**

✓INFORMED CONSENT/REFUSAL OBTAINED: **The SANE is expected to provide an opportunity for the client to consent or decline services offered by the SANE at any time during the initial evaluation of the victim following a sexual assault. This may include an initial consent from the client and later declination of any and/or all services, e.g., injection with Rocephin or forensic examination.**

✓GRIEVANCE PROCEDURE SIGNED: **The SANE will provide an explanation of the Grievance Procedure Form and request a signature from the client. This form was developed in response to grant requirements and our desire to create an outlet for victims who want to complain about our services.**

MEDICAL CRISIS INTERVENTION:

✓REFERRAL TO ED/HOSPITAL: **When the SANE refers to a local hospital for emergent medical treatment, the SANE will check this portion and write in the name of the hospital and the department if available, i.e., The MED ED.**

PSYCHOSOCIAL INTERVENTION:

✓DCS/APS REFERRAL/NOTIFICATION (NAME OF AGENCY AND INDIVIDUAL): **When the SANE determines that appropriate social agencies for child or adult protection have not been notified, the SANE will check this portion and write in the name of the agency notified, i.e., DCS or APS and the name of the individual taking the report, i.e. Jane Doe. If the report is made outside the acute evaluation time frame documented on the forensic report, the SANE will need to write in the date and time of notification and initial.**

✓PSYCHOLOGICAL EVALUATION REFERRAL (NAME OF AGENCY AND INDIVIDUAL): **When the SANE refers to a local hospital for emergent psychological treatment, the SANE will check this portion and write in the name of the hospital and the department if available, i.e., MMHI.**

NURSING CARE PLAN KEY
PAGE 2

✔ EMERGENCY HOUSING (NAME OF AGENCY/INDIVIDUAL): When the SANE determines that appropriate housing is an acute need of the client, social agencies providing emergency housing may be notified. The SANE will check this portion and write in the name of the agency notified, i.e., Salvation Army and the name of the individual taking the report, i.e. Jane Doe.

ANTICIPATORY GUIDANCE:

HEALTH TEACHING

✔ PRE-EXAM PREPARATION: In an effort to provide for the client's control and comfort over the forensic examination process, the SANE will provide an explanation of activities which will be expected to occur during the examination. The SANE will provide an opportunity for questions and work with the client to prioritize their concerns.

✔ STD RISKS FOLLOWING SEXUAL ASSAULT: The SANE may discuss the risks of STD transmission following a rape. Condom use will be recommended to the client with any/all partners until screening tests remain negative for 1 year. The SANE will provide an opportunity for questions and work with the client to prioritize their concerns.

✔ PRE STDs SCREENING COUNSELING: The SANE will explain that MSARC services include free health screening for STDs, that the tests are confidential and will be developed by the Memphis & Shelby County Health Department. These tests can be considered baseline tests recommended by the CDC. If any of the tests are positive, the client may be notified by the Health Department and since these tests (if positive) are reportable, the client may be asked to provide a summary of their risk factors and the name(s) of their partners. If the Health Department does not notify the client about positive tests, it does not mean that their tests were negative. The SANE will provide an opportunity for questions and work with the client to prioritize their concerns.

✔ PREGNANCY INTERCEPTION: The SANE will explain that MSARC services include the dispensing of birth control pills in doses that have been shown to prevent pregnancy. The SANE will determine from the health history if the patient is a candidate for the medication. The consent form will be reviewed with emphasis on the mechanism of action and the side effects of the medication. The SANE will provide an opportunity for questions and work with the client to prioritize their concerns.

✔ PERINEAL INJURIES: For the patient who has perineal injuries following the sexual assault, the SANE will teach the client proper care of the injured tissue, making appropriate treatment recommendations including but not limited to signs and symptoms of infection, infection prevention, partner treatment, sitz baths, topical treatments, antibiotics, etc. The SANE will provide an opportunity for questions and work with the client to prioritize their concerns.

✔ INJURIES ELSEWHERE: For the patient who has a non-urgent injury following the sexual assault, the SANE will teach the client proper care of the injured tissue, making appropriate treatment recommendations including but not limited to signs and symptoms of infection, infection prevention, topical treatments, etc. The SANE will provide an opportunity for questions and work with the client to prioritize their concerns.

✔ HYGIENE: For the patient who has non-urgent injury due to hygiene, the SANE will teach the

client proper care of the injured tissue, making appropriate treatment recommendations including but not limited to appropriate perineal hygiene, signs and symptoms of infection, infection prevention, topical treatments, etc. The SANE will provide an opportunity for questions and work with the client to prioritize their concerns.

✓ GROWTH & DEVELOPMENT: When problems are detected with the growth and development in children, adolescents, adults, or families, utilizing current research the SANE will teach and/or recommend common therapies to individuals and/or families, i.e., toileting behavior in toddlers or adolescent impulsive behavior. The SANE will provide an opportunity for questions and work with the client to prioritize their concerns.

✓ OTHER HEALTH TEACHING: Include but are not limited to instructions covering safer sexual practices, Birth Control, etc.

HANDOUTS

✓ NURSING HANDOUTS DISTRIBUTED: Include but are not limited to copies of the Consent Form, Follow Up Recommendations Form, and the Pregnancy Interception Form.

✓ COUNSELING HANDOUTS DISTRIBUTED: Include but are not limited to the Counseling Card identifying the basics of the program.

✓ ADVOCACY HANDOUTS DISTRIBUTED: Include but are not limited to the Advocacy Card identifying the basics of the program.

✓ OTHER HANDOUTS (names): Include but are not limited to health pamphlets, i.e., STDs, Yeast, Self Breast Exam, etc.

DESCRIPTION OF SERVICES TO CLIENT

✓ DCS/APS: Protective Services are designated investigators for the state, compiling information to determine safety issues for children or dependent adults.

✓ LAW ENFORCEMENT: City, county, state, and federal officers are designated investigators, compiling information to determine if laws have been breached in their respective jurisdictions. The investigators present case files to the prosecuting attorneys within their jurisdictions.

✓ MSARC ADVOCACY: Provides intervention services during investigation, DA case reviews, and court escort services.

✓ MSARC COUNSELING: Provides short term or long term counseling services for individuals or groups.

✓ MSARC NURSING: Provides crisis intervention, physical evaluation, evidence collection, medical treatment and referral, and court testimony.

NURSING CARE PLAN KEY
PAGE 4

✓ OTHER SERVICES (names): **May include but are not limited to other services offered in the community, i.e., CCC, CAC, Midtown MHC, etc.**

FOLLOW UP RECOMMENDATIONS:

✓ **FOR STD SCREENING: The SANE will explain that MSARC SANEs follow the CDC recommendations for follow up testing at 2 weeks, 6 weeks, 3 months, 6 months, and 12 months for STDs. The tests are available from their PMD, MCO, or the MSCHD. The SANE will provide an opportunity for questions and work with the client to prioritize their concerns.**

✓ **FOR POST TEST COUNSELING FOR STDs: The SANE will explain that MSARC will receive the results of the STD screening completed on the first acute visit within one month. The patient will receive a letter from MSARC to schedule an appointment for Post-Test STD Screening Counseling at their convenience. To protect the privacy of the client, test results will not be given out over the telephone. Appointments for Post Test Counseling will be scheduled during office hours 9:00 AM - 3:00 PM and on Tuesday evenings 4:00 PM to 6:00 PM. During Post Test Counseling ,the SANE will provide the client with their test results, the meaning of their test results, and review of follow up recommendations. The SANE will provide an opportunity for questions and work with the client to prioritize their concerns.**

✓ **FOR HEALTH PROBLEM TO PMD/CLINIC: When detected, the SANE will provide specific follow up recommendations regarding other health problems detected during the acute evaluation following the sexual assault. The SANE will SOAP these problems for clarity. The SANE will provide an opportunity for questions and work with the client to prioritize their concerns.**

✓ **FOR MENTAL HEALTH COUNSELING: When detected, the SANE will provide specific follow up recommendations regarding mental health problems detected during the acute evaluation following the sexual assault. The SANE will SOAP these problems for clarity. The SANE will provide an opportunity for questions and work with the client to prioritize their concerns.**

✓ **OTHER (list): Other problems detected during the acute evaluation of sexual assault may be detected. The SANE will provide specific follow up recommendations regarding the identified problems detected during the acute evaluation following the sexual assault. The SANE will SOAP these problems for clarity. The SANE will provide an opportunity for questions and work with the client to prioritize their concerns.**

OTHER INSTRUCTIONS: **Other non-health problems detected during the acute evaluation of sexual assault may be detected. The SANE will provide specific follow up recommendations regarding these health problems detected during the acute evaluation followingthe sexual assault. The SANE will provide an opportunity for questions and work with the client to prioritize their concerns.**

City of Memphis
TENNESSEE

SEXUAL ASSAULT RESOURCE CENTER
901/272-2020 (Voice or TDD)

NURSING CARE PLAN (CHECK ALL COMPLETED ITEMS)

CASE #_____ DATE: _____

INTRODUCTION:
_____ INTRODUCE FORENSIC NURSE BY NAME
_____ ROLE EXPLANATION OF FORENSIC
           NURSE/SEXUAL ASSAULT NURSE EXAMINER
_____ INFORMED CONSENT/REFUSAL OBTAINED
_____ GRIEVANCE PROCEDURE SIGNED

MEDICAL CRISIS INTERVENTION:
_____ REFERRAL TO ED/HOSPITAL
           WHERE: _____

PSYCHOSOCIAL INTERVENTION:
_____ DCS/APS REFERRAL/NOTIFICATION (NAME OF AGENCY
AND INDIVIDUAL):
_____
_____ PSYCHOLOGICAL EVALUATION REFERRAL (NAME OF
AGENCY AND INDIVIDUAL):
_____
_____ EMERGENCY HOUSING (NAME OF AGENCY/INDIVIDUAL):
_____

ANTICIPATORY GUIDANCE:
HEALTH TEACHING
_____ PRE-EXAM PREPARATION
_____ STD RISKS FOLLOWING SEXUAL ASSAULT
_____ PRE STDs SCREENING COUNSELING
_____ PREGNANCY INTERCEPTION
_____ PERINEAL INJURIES
_____ INJURIES ELSEWHERE
_____ HYGIENE
_____ GROWTH & DEVELOPMENT
OTHER HEALTH TEACHING:
_____
_____
_____

HANDOUTS
_____ NURSING HANDOUTS DISTRIBUTED
_____ COUNSELING HANDOUTS DISTRIBUTED
_____ ADVOCACY HANDOUTS DISTRIBUTED
_____ OTHER HANDOUTS (names) _____

DESCRIPTION OF SERVICES TO CLIENT
_____ DCS
_____ LAW ENFORCEMENT
_____ MSARC ADVOCACY
_____ MSARC COUNSELING
_____ MSARC NURSING
_____ OTHER SERVICES (names) _____
_____

FOLLOW UP RECOMMENDATIONS:
_____ FOR STD SCREENING
_____ FOR POST TEST COUNSELING FOR STDs
_____ FOR HEALTH PROBLEM TO PMD/CLINIC
_____ FOR MENTAL HEALTH COUNSELING
_____ OTHER (list) _____
_____

OTHER INSTRUCTIONS:_____
_____
_____
_____

POST TEST COUNSELING
     LETTER SENT (circle one)   YES   NO
     APPOINTMENT SET FOR
(date/time):_____
     ATTEMPT TO CONTACT BY PHONE (if applicable)
(date/initials):_____ na   b   lm

TELEPHONE OR OFFICE ENCOUNTER NOTE

S:_____
_____
_____
O:_____
_____
A:_____
_____
_____
P:_____
_____
_____
_____

SANE:_____ DATE:_____

TELEPHONE OR OFFICE ENCOUNTER NOTE

S:_____
_____
_____
O:_____
_____
A:_____
_____
P:_____
_____
_____
_____

SANE:_____ DATE:_____

TELEPHONE OR OFFICE ENCOUNTER NOTE

S:_____
_____
_____
O:_____
_____
A:_____
_____
P:_____
_____
_____
_____

SANE:_____ DATE:_____

CHILDREN

Case # _____
Sibling Case # _____

FORENSIC EXAMINATION
OF
ALLEGED SEXUAL ASSAULT

2 copies to Police Officer
1 copy to Clinic

1. Identifying Information:
   Name _____
   Guardian ☐ Parent ☐ _____
   DOB _____ Age _____ Sex _____ Race _____
   Address _____
   City/State _____ Zip Code _____
   Phone (home) _____ (other) _____

Alleged Assault:	Forensic Exam:
Unknown: ☐	
Date: _____	Date: _____
Time: _____	Time: _____

2. Anal-genital chart

Female/Male General	WNL	ABN	Describe
Tanner stage			
Breast 1 2 3 4 5	☐	☐	_____
Genitals 1 2 3 4 5	☐	☐	_____
Medial aspect of thighs	☐	☐	_____
Perineum	☐	☐	_____

	Yes	No	
Vulvovaginal/urethral discharge (describe)	☐	☐	_____
Flat plaques/growths (describe)	☐	☐	_____

Female	WNL	ABN	Describe
Labia Majora	☐	☐	_____
Clitoris	☐	☐	_____
Labia minora	☐	☐	_____
Periurethral tissue/ urethral meatus	☐	☐	_____
Perihymenal tissue (vestibule)	☐	☐	_____
Hymen	☐	☐	_____
☐ Cresent			
☐ Annular			
☐ Other (describe)			
☐ Unable to determine (describe)			
Diameter of hymenal lumen			
☐ Horizontal _____ mm.			
☐ Vertical _____ mm.			
Posterior fourchette	☐	☐	_____
Vagina	☐	☐	_____
Other			_____

Exam position used for genital evaluation:
☐ Supine   ☐ Mother's lap
☐ Knee chest

Male	WNL	ABN	Describe
Penis	☐	☐	_____
☐ circumcised ☐ uncircumcised			
Urethral meatus	☐	☐	_____
Scrotum	☐	☐	_____
Testes	☐	☐	_____

Female/Male Anus	WNL	ABN	Describe
Buttocks	☐	☐	_____
Perianal skin	☐	☐	_____
☐ feces present			
Anal verge/folds	☐	☐	_____
Anal shape (describe)	☐	☐	_____
☐ linear			
☐ circular			
☐ irregular (describe)			
Anal tone	☐	☐	_____

Method of exam: ☐ Observation ☐ Digital exam
Anal dilation   ☐   ☐
☐ No dilation noted ☐ Funneling present
☐ External ☐ Internal Spincter relaxation
☐ Horizontal _____ mm. in _____ seconds
☐ Vertical _____ mm. in _____ seconds
☐ Feces in rectal ampulla
Anal tags   Location: _____
☐ Yes ☐ No
Anal fissures   Location: _____
☐ Yes ☐ No

Exam position used for anal evaluation:
☐ Supine ☐ Lateral recumbent ☐ Mother's lap
☐ Prone ☐ Knee chest

Summary of Evidence   Released to:
☐ Kit collected   _____
☐ No kit   _____
☐ Clothing   _____
☐ Other   _____

Genital exam done with:
Direct visualization   ☐
Colposcope   ☐
Pictures taken   ☐   # _____

Case # _____   **CHILDREN**

3.   PERTINENT PAST MEDICAL HISTORY

Menarche age .... ☐ N/A _____
Date of last menstrual period .... ☐ N/A _____
Note history of physical injuries   ☐ Yes ☐ No ☐ N/A _____

_____

Pertinent medical history of ☐ anal-genital injuries, ☐ surgeries
☐ diagnostic procedures, or ☐ medical treatment? If yes, describe:

_____
_____

Previous child abuse investigation? ☐ Yes ☐ No   ☐ Physical
(describe when and where)   ☐ Sexual
_____   ☐ Neglect

5.   Check behaviors observed during exam:

☐ tearful   ☐ fidgeting
☐ sobbing   ☐ trembling
☐ yelling   ☐ controlled
☐ loud   ☐ agitated
☐ quiet   ☐ listless
☐ tense   ☐ fearful
☐ cooperative   ☐ other _____

_____
_____

responds to questions:
☐ readily ☐ briefly ☐ reluctantly

4.   Symptoms described by patient: ☐ _____
                    by historian: ☐ _____
                    not evaluated: ☐ _____

Physical symptom/hx:
☐ Abdominal/pelvic pain   _____
☐ Vulvar discomfort or pain   _____
☐ Dysuria   _____
☐ Urinary tract infection   _____
☐ Enuresis (daytime or nighttime) _____
☐ Vaginal itching   _____
☐ Vaginal discharge   _____
   Describe color, odor, amount _____

☐ Vaginal bleeding   _____
☐ Rectal pain   _____
☐ Rectal bleeding   _____
☐ Rectal discharge   _____
☐ Constipation   _____
☐ Incontinent of stool (day/night) _____

Other: _____
_____
_____

6.   Additional Observation or Remarks: _____
_____
_____
_____
_____
_____
_____
_____
_____
_____
_____
_____
_____
_____
_____
_____
_____
_____
_____
_____
_____
_____
_____
_____

7.   Treatment:

Hospitalization:
   location _____
Prophylaxis:
   pregnancy _____
   gonorrhea _____

Testing:
   pregnancy _____ VDRL _____
   GC culture _____
   Referral _____

8.   Testing: Sperm

	SEEN	MOTILE	NON-MOTILE	NOT SEEN	NOT DONE
Vaginal					
Oral					
Anal					

9.   Instructions for Follow-up

                                          Yes No
A. ORAL   ☐ ☐
B. WRITTEN
    Agency brochures   ☐ ☐
    Medical follow-up inst.   ☐ ☐

This report of the examination is an investigative report used as evidence by Memphis Police Services, Shelby County law enforcement agencies, Tennessee Department of Human Services, and other cooperating agencies.

Investigating
Agency _____
DHS Social
Counselor _____
Date _____
MRCC Counselor _____

MRCC Forensic
Evaluator _____
Police
Officer _____
R&I # _____
CPT # _____

CASE NO _____

NAME OF VICTIM _____

DATE OF COLLECTION _____   **TIME** _____ **AM - PM**

NURSE/CLINICIAN _____

pre-school, female child (front view)

pre-school, female child (back view)

PHYSICAL CONDITION OF VICTIM:

INDICATE ALL SIGNS OF PHYSICAL TRAUMA - E.G., BRUISES, SCRATCHES, MARKS, DIS-
COLORATIONS (SIZE AND COLOR), OR BITE MARKS ON ANY PART OF THE BODY. (NOTE ALL
SIGNS OF TRAUMA ON THE APPROPRIATE ANATOMICAL DRAWING).

CASE NO _____

NAME OF VICTIM _____

DATE OF COLLECTION _____   TIME _____ AM - PM

NURSE/CLINICIAN _____

pre-school, male child (front view)

pre-school, male child (back view)

<u>PHYSICAL CONDITION OF VICTIM:</u>

INDICATE ALL SIGNS OF PHYSICAL TRAUMA - E.G., BRUISES, SCRATCHES, MARKS, DIS-
COLORATIONS (SIZE AND COLOR), OR BITE MARKS ON ANY PART OF THE BODY. (NOTE ALL
SIGNS OF TRAUMA ON THE APPROPRIATE ANATOMICAL DRAWING).

H
APPENDIX

Sexual Assault Response Team (SART) Continuous Quality Improvement (CQI)

Name or case I.D. number _____ Date of initial exam _____

Date reviewed _____

Reviewer _____ Years as examiner _____

Written Documentation

Medical–legal form complete?_____

Anatomic drawings (traumagrams) descriptive? _____

Appropriate forensic specimens collected? _____

Is evaluation consistent with findings and history? _____

Supplemental narrative summary done? _____

Photographs

Colposcopic photos are of good quality? _____

Sufficient photos to document findings? _____

Are photos consistent with evaluation? _____

Follow-up Examination

Interval since assault? _____

Follow-up exam consistent with prior exam? _____

Additional findings on follow-up? _____

Additional comments? _____

Yes/No/N/A/Comment

APPENDIX I

Sexually Transmitted Diseases (STDs)

INTRODUCTION

The vast majority of adult sexual assault response team (SART) programs administer prophylactic treatment to the adult and adolescent victim of acute sexual assault, based on current Centers for Disease Control (CDC) guidelines, included herein. It is imperative that the clinical forensic examiner be knowledgeable about the current recommendations for prophylaxis in the populations served. However, victims, partners, and families of sexual assault victims often have many concerns and myriad questions, both voiced and unspoken, regarding these issues. The rape victim has not voluntarily engaged in an unprotected act of sexual intimacy that places him or her at risk for acquiring a sexually transmitted infection. Yet, information abounds regarding the risks of unprotected sexual exposure. From junior and senior high school health classes, to the media, well-child exams, and public and private health care clinics, the message is clear: unprotected sex is dangerous. Worldwide, public health efforts have been employed to halt the progression of these contagious infections. Our youth are especially vulnerable, as sequelae from many of these infections have long-term implications. Despite educational efforts, STDs continue to carry a stigma that may hinder the seeking of health

care for treatment. This appendix, while being neither all-encompassing nor inclusive of all age groups, seeks to provide the clinical forensic examiner with a reference for the major infections. The examiner should be alert for both voiced and subtle concerns that may present at the initial exam. Appropriate referral for necessary follow-up should be provided. Follow-up care should address fears and concerns related to the possibility of exposure to a sexually transmitted infection during the assault.

The most frequently diagnosed infections in female sexual assault victims are trichomoniasis, bacterial vaginosis (BV), chlamydia, and gonorrhea. The finding of these STDs in victims does not necessarily imply acquisition from the assault, as the prevalence of each of these in sexually active women is substantial (CDC, 1998). Jenny et al (1990) estimated the following risks of acquiring a sexually transmitted disease from a sexual assault (postmenarcheal, ≥12 y.o.):

Neisseria gonorrhoeae	4.2%
Chlamydia trachomatis	1.5%
Trichomonas vaginalis	12.3%
Bacterial vaginosis	19.5%

Slaughter & Crowley (1993) studied an 8-year prevalence of STDs in 170 sexual assault suspects.

Disease	Samples Tested	% Positive (of Specimens)
N. gonorrhoeae	1/198	0.51
Syphilis (+ RPR)	3/121	3
(+ MHA-TP)[1]	0/3	0 (Biological False Positives)
Chlamydia	6/126	5
HIV	0/58	0
Hepatitis B	2/5	40
Herpes simplex virus	2/5	40

[1] See syphilis diagnosis

The prevalence of STDs was low (7%) in this population. There was no increase in the prevalence of STDs in those individuals with a previous history of incarceration or prior history of sexual assault. Of those tested for drugs and alcohol (50/170), 60% had positive results, but in this sample, there was also an infrequent history of narcotic use (3/170) (Slaughter & Crowley, 1993).

ADOLESCENTS AND STDs

The rates of some STDs are highest for adolescents. The greatest incidence of gonorrhea is for females between the ages of 15 and 19 years old. Clinic-based studies have demonstrated that this is true for chlamydia, and possibly human papillomavirus (HPV) as well. Nine percent of adolescents with acute hepatitis B have had sexual contact with a chronically infected person or multiple sex partners, or their sexual preference is homosexual (CDC, 1998).

Fifty percent of adults with HIV acquired the infection during adolescence, though manifestations of the disease often do not develop for 6 or more years. Sexually transmitted diseases are a major source of morbidity in both children and adolescents. These infections can have major sequelae in adolescents, including chronic hepatitis, pelvic inflammatory disease (PID), ectopic pregnancies, infertility, and cancer of the cervix (AAP, 1997).

The following salient factors put adolescents at an increased risk for acquiring an STD:

- younger age at initial sex
- multiple sex partners
- frequent unprotected sex/poor condom use
- current or past STD
- IV drug use
- patient or partner uses crack cocaine
- patient or partner has a history of exchanging sex for money or drugs
- homelessness, poverty
- male homosexuality
- sexually active heterosexuals <15 years old

The adolescent is biologically more susceptible to STDs. During adolescence, the cervix undergoes transition from the pubertal state to the mature adult cervix. At puberty, columnar cells cover the surface of the immature cervix. These columnar cells regress into the endocervical canal and are replaced with squamous epithelial cells as the adolescent matures. Infections such as chlamydia and gonorrhea have a predilection for columnar epithelium.

Oh and colleagues (1998) reported on the use of urine ligase chain reaction tests for chlamydia and gonorrhea to screen adolescents in a short-term juvenile detention center. Forty-six of the sample of 263 were females. Of these, 13% were positive for gonorrhea, and 28% for chlamydia. Three percent of the males were positive for gonorrhea; 9% were positive for chlamydia. Of note, the screenings were voluntary, and there was only a 1.5% refusal rate. Urine screening provided a less invasive method to discern those who required further medical evaluation, and enabled the evaluation and treatment of sexually transmitted infections and assessment for possible complications in *otherwise asymptomatic* cases in high-risk youths.

Health care providers that serve adolescent populations should be knowledgeable about confidential conduits of information and service related to STDs and AIDS. The American Academy of Pediatrics (AAP,1997) recommends that adolescents be advised:

- to abstain from sexual intercourse, *or*
- always use condoms (and discuss with them how to do so)
- that absolutely "safe sex" does not exist
- that monogamous relationships do not mean one sexual relationship at a time

SEXUAL ASSAULT AND STDS

1998 Centers for Disease Control Recommendations for Adults and Adolescents Post-Sex Assault

Initial Examination	Follow-Up
• Cultures: for gonorrhea and chlamydia from any sites of penetration or attempted penetration. • Wet mount and culture of vaginal swab for Trichomonas vaginalis infection. • If discharge or malodor, also examine for bacterial vaginosis and yeast infection (see Figs. I–1–I–4). • Serum: evaluation for HIV, hepatitis B, and syphilis.	Two weeks after assault: 1. To detect new infections. 2. To complete hepatitis B vaccine, if indicated. 3. Counseling and treatment for other STDs. Unless prophylactic treatment was provided at initial exam, repeat cultures, wet mount, and other tests. Serologic tests for syphilis and HIV infection should be conducted at 6, 12, and 24 weeks after assault, if initial tests were negative.

Recommended Regimen for Prophylaxis of Chlamydia, Gonorrhea, Trichomoniasis, and Bacterial Vaginosis

ceftriaxone 125 mg IM × 1
+
metronidazole 2 g PO × 1
+
azithromycin 1 g PO × 1 *or,* doxycycline 100 mg PO b.i.d. × 7 days

Patient Teaching	Tetanus Prophylaxis for Wound Management
• Symptoms of STDs; need for immediate exam if these occur. Need for abstinence from sexual intercourse until STD prophylactic treatment completed. • Postexposure hepatitis B vaccination (without HBIG) for those incompletely or never vaccinated. Follow-up vaccinations at 1 to 2 and 4 to 6 months after first dose (CDC, 1998).	Assess the nature of nongenital and genital trauma sustained by the victim and the victim's immunization history. Td = adult-use tetanus and diphtheria toxoid. TIG = tetanus immunoglobulin.

SEXUAL ASSAULT AND STDS (*continued*)

Vaccine History	Clean Minor Wounds		All Other Wounds	
	Td	*TIG*	*Td*	*TIG*
Unknown, or <3 previous doses *of Td*	Yes	No	Yes	Yes
≥3	No*	No	No†	No

* Yes, if >10 years since last dose.
† Yes, if >5 years since last dose.
(Atkinson, et al, 1997)

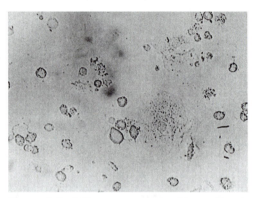

Figure I–1. Saline wet mount with motile trichomonads in the center. *(From DeCherney, A. & Pernol, M. [1994]. [Eds]. Current Obstetric and Gynecologic Diagnosis and Treatment. 8th ed. Norwalk, CT: Appleton & Lange, p. 692; reprinted with permission.)*

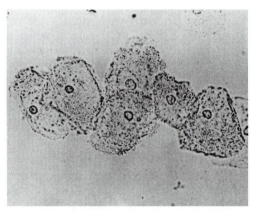

Figure I–2. Saline wet mount clue cells from *Gardnerella vaginalis* infection. Note the absence of inflammatory cells. *(From DeCherney, A. & Pernol, M. [1994]. [Eds]. Current Obstetric and Gynecologic Diagnosis and Treatment. 8th ed. Norwalk, CT: Appleton & Lange, p. 692; reprinted with permission.)*

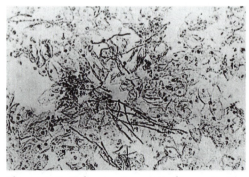

Figure I–3. Saline wet mount demonstrating *Candida albicans. (From DeCherney, A. & Pernol, M. [1994]. [Eds]. Current Obstetric and Gynecologic Diagnosis and Treatment. 8th ed. Norwalk, CT: Appleton & Lange, p. 692; reprinted with permission.)*

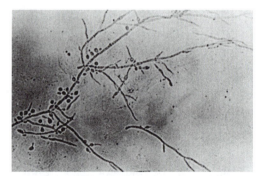

Figure I–4. KOH preparation showing branched and budding *Candida Albicans. (From DeCherney, A. & Pernol, M. [1994]. [Eds]. Current Obstetric and Gynecologic Diagnosis and Treatment. 8th ed. Norwalk, CT: Appleton & Lange, p. 692; reprinted with permission.)*

HIV INFECTION

The focus of HIV and AIDS in this appendix is on the possible risk to victims of sexual assault, recommendations for testing, and postexposure antiretroviral therapy, psychosocial issues related to HIV testing and reporting of results, and the need for adequate medical referral and follow-up. The risk of acquiring HIV during a sexual assault is low, but HIV-antibody seroconversion has been reported among persons where the only known risk factor was either sexual assault or sexual abuse. In considering the overall risk from an HIV-infected person during a single act of intercourse, the following factors should be considered:

- type of sex act (oral, vaginal, anal trauma)
- presence of physical trauma
- site of exposure to ejaculate
- presence of an STD
- exposure to blood, body fluids

According to Gostin et al (1994), there is insufficient evidence to determine if sex offenders have different rates of HIV infection that other offenders. The incidence of HIV/AIDS is 14 times greater in state and federal correction systems than in the general population. Thus:

Prevalence of AIDS in U.S. Population
14.65/100,00

Prevalence in Prisons
202/100,000

There has been a high variability in rates of infection of the same risk groups in different geographic locations. The per contact infectivity rate has been estimated to be <2/1000 contacts, (<0.2%) for male to female, with penile–vaginal intercourse. For anal receptive intercourse, the infectivity rate has been estimated to be 2/100 (2%). Lesions and blood in violent assaults may increase the probability of transmission (Gostin et al, 1994).

Many victims do fear the acquisition of STDs and specifically HIV/AIDS. When the exposure that induces this fear stems from a crime, the victim may feel even more powerless when confronted with this threat, regardless of the statistical probability of acquisition. The anxiety related to this particular fear is distinct from the other issues of rape trauma syndrome, and will not diminish immediately. If the assailant is unknown, there is no possibility of testing the accused; the victim must live with uncertainty for 6 months. This fear of AIDS is not purely egocentric on the part of the victim; it has been expressed by intimate partners of victims, who fear their own infection should the victim's results turn out to be positive (Baker et al, 1990).

To avoid compounding an already stressful event, it may not be appropriate to query every victim as to their concerns regarding HIV/AIDS. Rather, a gentle inquiry may allow the victim to bring up their own concerns. It may take 2 weeks for antibodies to be detectable in the blood; within 3 to 6 months the vast majority of infected individuals should seroconvert. Knowledge of test results enables the rape victim to make informed, educated choices regarding their health. Because of the highly charged emotional impact, concomitant with other features of rape trauma syndrome, it is prudent to ensure that adequate pre- and posttest HIV counseling is provided.

Postexposure Therapy with Zidovudine (AZT) for Victims of Sexual Assault

In a study of health care workers who had percutaneous exposures to HIV-infected blood, zidovudine has been associated with a reduced risk for HIV infection. As of this writing, the CDC does not make a recommendation regarding postexposure antiretroviral therapy after sexual exposure to HIV (CDC, 1998). Some providers do endorse postexposure therapy; the CDC recommends that if this course is chosen, the health care provider should consider potential benefits and risks of therapy, as well as the interval between the exposure and therapy. High-risk practices in the assailant (if known) and local epidemiology of HIV/AIDS should be assessed. Critical issues to be discussed with the patient regarding antiretroviral therapy are:

- Unknown efficacy and known toxicity of antiretrovirals
- Need for frequent medication dosing
- Need for close follow-up
- Need for strict compliance
- Need for immediate initiation of treatment for maximum effectiveness

Acute Retroviral Syndrome

This syndrome frequently occurs during the first few weeks after HIV infection, and before antibody test results become positive. It consists of an acute syndrome, characterized by fever, malaise, lymphadenopathy, and skin rash. The initiation of antiretroviral therapy during this period can delay the onset of HIV-related complications. If this condition is suspected, nucleic acid testing should be done to detect the presence of HIV. If the clinical forensic examiner becomes aware of these symptoms at the time of the patient follow-up exam, he or she should:

- Refer the patient to a medical provider; ensure appropriate consents for release of *necessary* medical information from the medical–legal exam. The traumatized state of many victims makes it difficult or uncomfortable to provide yet another medical provider with a clear and succinct history necessary for appropriate medical intervention.
- Ensure that the patient has appropriate emotional support. (The rape crisis advocate may be able to accompany the patient to other medical providers, to provide support and clarify information; clarify first with advocate.)
- If known assailant, contact the local district attorney. Inquire as to possibility of obtaining a court order for suspect's HIV status (if not already done). The jurisdiction should have an established protocol for the testing of accused and release of information of results (this is also an ideal time for an advocate to be present).

BACTERIAL VAGINOSIS

Condition	Organism	Lab Findings/ Diagnosis	Signs and Symptoms	Treatment
A clinical syndrome with replacement of normal vaginal flora by overgrowth of anaerobes, microorganisms, and *Gardnerella vaginalis*. H_2O_2-producing *Lactobacillus* species. Most prevalent cause of vaginal discharge.	Mixed bacterial infection; anaerobes, *Mobiluncus*. Various organisms responsible; *Gardnerella vaginalis* (Fig. I–2), *Prevotella* spp., *Mycoplasma hominis*, *Mobiluncus* spp., *Bacteroides*, non-H_2O_2-producing	1. Thin, homogenous white, noninflammatory discharge. 2. Clue cells on microscopic exam (Fig. I–2). 3. Vaginal pH >4.5 (only postpubertal; already alkaline in prepubertal). 4. Fishy odor of discharge before or after addition of 10% KOH ("whiff test").	One-half of females who meet clinical criteria are asymptomatic. Vaginitis: thin, malodorous vaginal discharge, clings to vaginal walls. Usually no dysuria or vulvar discomfort. Associated with adverse pregnancy outcomes	For nonpregnant females: Metronidazole 500 mg PO b.i.d. × 7 days *or,* Clindamycin cream 2%, one full applicator (5 g) intravaginally hs × 7 days. Do not use if patient is pregnant Metronidazole gel 0.75%, one

BACTERIAL VAGINOSIS (*Continued*)

Condition	Organism	Lab Findings/ Diagnosis	Signs and Symptoms	Treatment
	Lactobacillus strains.	Culture not recommended; not specific. Gram stain: determination of relative concentration of bacterial morphotypes.	(preterm delivery, premature membrane rupture).	full applicator (5 g) intravaginally b.i.d. × 5 days. Pregnancy (treat if symptoms present): Metronidazole 250 mg PO t.i.d. × 7 days. Recommended to screen and treat early in 2nd trimester.

CHLAMYDIA

Condition	Organism	Lab Findings/ Diagnosis	Signs and Symptoms	Treatment
Chlamydia trachomatis (CT) includes serotypes that cause trachoma, genital infections, chlamydial conjunctivitis, and infant pneumonia. Other serotypes (L1, L2, or L3), cause *Lymphogranuloma venereum* (LGV). LGV is rare in U.S. (CDC, 1998) and is an invasive, lymphatic infection. Initial local genital lesion, accompanied by regional lymphadenitis (Fig. I–5). Genital chlamydial infection is sexu-	*Chlamydia trachomatis.* Immunotypes D–K identified in 35–50% of cases of nongonococcal urethritis (NGU) in U.S. Obligate intracellular bacteria, survives by replicative cycle causing death of host cells; attaches and causes phagocytosis; remains inside cell; ruptures host cell; releases elementary bodies. Requires columnar epithelium or transitional epithelium.	Test for chlamydia from specimens from any site of penetration. *Culture:* In preadolescent child, need high specificity provided by isolation in cell culture. Cultures should be confirmed by microscopic identification of characteristic intracytoplasmic inclusions, preferably by fluorescein-conjugated monoclonal antibodies specific for *C. trachomatis* (CDC, 1998:59). Takes 3–7 days. If culture not available, nonculture	Frequently asymptomatic; may persist for months. Screening encouraged for 20–24 year olds (CDC, 1998). Easily induced endocervical bleeding from inflammation of columnar epithelium, but most endocervical and urethral infections are asymptomatic. May be urethral itching, burning on urination, mucopurulent discharge (either scanty or moderate), with hypertrophic cervical infiltrate.	Azithromycin 1 g PO × 1 dose, *or* Doxycycline 100 mg PO b.i.d. × 7 days. To increase compliance, CDC recommends dispense first dose on-site, using directly observed therapy (DOT). *Pregnancy:* Erythromycin base (not erythromycin estolate) 500 mg PO q.i.d. × 7 days or, Amoxicillin 500 mg PO t.i.d. × 7 days Preliminary data indicate that azithromycin may be safe and effective

(continued)

CHLAMYDIA (*Continued*)

Condition	Organism	Lab Findings/ Diagnosis	Signs and Symptoms	Treatment
ally transmitted and primarily manifested in males as a urethritis and in females as a mucopurulent cervicitis. Chlamydia in preadolescent children: *must consider sexual abuse.* Perinatally acquired CT of nesopharynx, urogenital tract, and rectum may persist >1 year. Rectal or genital infection with *C. trachomatis* among young children *may* persist as long as 3 years. Should consider possibility of abuse if no obvious risk factor for infection can be identified. Findings should be confirmed and implications carefully considered (CDC, 1998:111).	*Incubation Period:* Poorly defined: 7–14 days or longer.	tests, eg, nucleic acid amplification test, are acceptable substitutes. Good sensitivity, if confirmation available. Positive tests via nonculture test should be confirmed with 2nd test based on different diagnostic principle (CDC, 1998:109). Use culture for rectal specimen. Culture: use cotton, rayon, dacron, or plastic swab; aluminum: (batch tested Ca alginate acceptable). Storage: 4° C. (Loss of viability after 1 day). *Nonculture Tests:* Enzyme immunoassay (EIA) and direct fluorescent antibody (DFA) tests: false-negatives (–) and false-positives (+) may occur. *DFA:* 56–90% sensitivity; 94–99% specificity. *DNA probes:* 98.4% concordance with culture (STD intensive).	Salpingitis may be unassociated with symptoms. *Complications and Sequellae:* Pelvic inflammatory disease (PID), ectopic pregnancy, infertility *Males:* if receptive anal intercourse, may be infected with chlamydia proctitis.	in pregnancy, but insufficient data to recommend at this time (CDC, 1998).[1] Coinfection by chlamydia is common in cases of *N. gonorrhoeae;* therefore, provide presumptive Tx for chlamydia in patient with suspected GC (CDC, 1998). Abstain from intercourse until treatment complete (7 days after single dose regimen, or after completion of 7-day regimen). *Evaluate and treat partners:* those within 60 days prior to onset of symptoms/ positive diagnostic test. Treat sexual partners of a positive case presumptively. No need to do test of cure if Tx by azithromycin or doxycycline, unless symptoms persist or reinfection suspected. Azithromycin should be available for Tx if noncompliance is an issue. May be more cost-effective; can do single dose, directly observed therapy (DOT). For treatment of children refer to CDC 1998 guidelines.

[1] Some regional protocols do currently incorporate azithromycin during pregnancy.

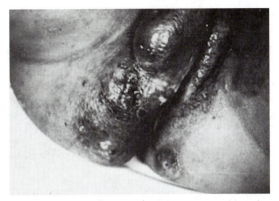

Figure I–5. Lymphogranuloma venereum. Note involvement of perineum and spread over buttocks. *(From DeCherney, A. & Pernol, M. (1994). (Eds). Current Obstetric and Gynecologic Diagnosis and Treatment. 8th ed. Norwalk, CT: Appleton & Lange, p. 761; reprinted with permission.)*

GONORRHEA

Condition	Organism	Lab Findings/ Diagnosis	Signs and Symptoms	Treatment
An acute bacterial infection which may cause infection, urethritis, cervicitis, pelvic inflammatory disease (PID), epididymitis, and disseminated infection. Most frequently reported communicable disease in the U.S.: 600,000 new cases each year (CDC, 1998); often coinfected with *Chlamydia trachomatis.* *Males:* most get symptoms that prompt treatment, but may not occur before	*Neisseria gonorrhoeae;* a Gram-negative intracellular diplococcus that primarily infects noncornified epithelial tissue. Organism primarily infects columnar or pseudostratified epithelium and requires intimate contact with epithelial or mucous-secreting cells. Dries/dies within 1 hr. Epithelial cells phagocytose and multiply Penicillinase-producing *N. gonorrhoeae* (PPNG) produce	Nonculture GC tests: Gram-stained smear; DNA probes; enzyme immunoassay (EIA) tests. None of these approved for specimens in children from mouth, rectum, or genital tract. Nonculture antigen detection tests used extensively, but do not provide definitive identification of *N. gonorrhoeae;* only presumptive. *Culture:* Streak onto selective media (eg, Thayer Mar-	Depends on site of infection. Uncomplicated gonococcal infection of cervix, urethra, and rectum: *Males:* anterior urethritis, causes purulent discharge and/or dysuria. *Females:* Only 60–80% have symptoms; urethritis, cervicitis (may be mild); uterine invasion in 20%. Pharyngeal and anorectal infection common. Rectal infection usually asymptomatic, but may	*Recommended:* Cefixime 400 mg PO × 1 *or,* Ceftriaxone 125 mg IM × 1 *or,* Ciprofloxacin[2] 500 mg PO × 1, *or,* Ofloxacin[2] 400 mg PO × 1 + Azithromycin 1 g PO × 1 *or,* Doxycycline 100 mg PO × 7 days *Alternative Regimen:* Spectinomycin, *or* Other single dose cephalosporin *or,* (*continued*)

GONORRHEA (*Continued*)

Condition	Organism	Lab Findings/ Diagnosis	Signs and Symptoms	Treatment
further transmission of infection. *Females:* may be asymptomatic until complications of PID, resulting in tubal scarring. Infection may be self-limited, or occasionally progress to chronic carrier state.	an enzyme that inactivates penicillin. Also TRNG and ORNG, but rare in U.S. (tetracycline-resistant and quinolone-resistant). *Incubation:* 2–7 days *Communicability:* Months, if untreated.	tin). Isolates are confirmed as *N. gonorrhoeae* by two different diagnostic methods. Use fresh medium; needs moist environment with 5% CO_2. Maintain temperature at 34–36° C. Gram stain of discharge, male urethra: gramnegative intracellular diplococci are diagnostic. Highly diagnostic in cervical smears. 1. Culture of exudates 2. Rapid stains 3. Antigen detection 4. Urine ligase chain reaction test *Rapid diagnosis:* 1. Stain: thin smear, air-dried, heat fixed; Gram stain. 2. DX: kidney bean-shaped diplococci within polymorphonucleocytes. 3. Antigen detection tests—DNA probe assay (also for chlamydia): 98.4% concordance with GC culture (STD Intensive, 1997).	be pruritis, tenesmus, discharge. Uncomplicated gonococcal infection of the pharynx: may produce exudative pharyngitis or adenitis. More difficult to eradicate; Unusual for coinfection with chlamydia at this site. *Sequelae:* Gonococcal meningitis and endocarditis. Gonococcal infections in infants and children. Conjunctivitis in the newborn.	Other single dose quinolone.[2] *Pregnancy:* No quinolones or tetracyclines. For treatment of children refer to CDC 1998 guidelines. *Specimen Collection:* *Urethra:* swab or expressed exudate; insert swab 2 cm; wait 10–20 seconds. *Cervix:* avoid lubricant; insert swab 2 cm; leave 20–30 seconds; rotate swab in os. *Rectum:* insert cotton swab 3 cm and rotate. *Pharynx:* rub two or three swabs over posterior pharynx or tonsils. Evaluation and Tx of sex partners within 60 days prior to onset of symptoms/ positive diagnostic test. Treat sexual partners of a positive case presumptively.

[2] Not if pregnant or under 18 years old.

HEPATITIS B VIRUS

Condition	Organism	Lab Findings/ Diagnosis	Signs and Symptoms	Treatment
A vaccine preventable viral infection; Hepatitis B surface antigen (HBsAg) is found in virtually all body secretions and excretions.	Hepatitis B virus (HBV); double-stranded DNA virus, surrounded by outer lipoprotein coat containing hepatitis B surface antigen (HBsAg).	*Three Antigen-Antibody Systems:* 1. HBsAg + anti-HBs 2. HB core antigen (HBcAg) + (anti-HBc) 3. HBeAg + anti-HBe	Only small % acute HBV is clinically recognized. Icteric disease: <10% children, 30–50% of adults.	*Post-Exposure Prophylaxis:* Childhood immunization schedule includes series of 3 Hep B vaccines. Vaccine is highly immunogenic: 50% of young adults after 1st dose; 85% after 2nd dose; 90% after 3rd dose, which provides longterm immunity. Give 1st and 2nd doses 1 month apart; 1st and 3rd dose 4 months apart.
Transmission: Percutaneous (IV, IM, SC, or intradermal) and permucosal exposure to infectious body fluids, eg, blood transfusions, needle sharing, hemodialysis, acupuncture, tattooing, needlesticks, sexual, and perinatal transmission.	Hepatitis B virus is stable on environmental surfaces ≥7 days; indirect inoculation possible (Benenson, 1995).	1. *HBsAg:* HBV surface antigen; several subtypes identified. *Anti-HBs:* Indicates past infection with positive immunity to HBV, passive immunity from hepatitis B immunoglobulin (HBIG), or immune response from hepatitis B vaccine.	Insidious onset: anorexia, vague abdominal discomfort, nausea + vomiting, arthragias, rash; may progress to jaundice. After acute HBV infection, risk of chronic infection varies inversely with age.	
Sexual transmission in 30–60% of the 240,000 new HBV infections in U.S. 1–6% become chronic (of those infected as adults).	*Incubation:* 45–180 days; average 60–90 days. *Factors affecting transmission:* Amount of virus in inoculum; mode of transmission; other host factors.	2. Antibody to core antigen develops in all HBV infections and persists indefinitely.		For victims of sexual assault at initial exam: If sexual assault victim not fully immunized (3 doses), administer vaccine at initial exam; schedule/refer for follow-up doses as needed.
Persons with chronic infection may or may not have a history of clinical hepatitis. Perinatal transmission: high likelihood of chronic antigenemia, which can lead to chronic hepatitis, cirrhosis, or hepatocellular cancer. 15–25% with	*Communicability:* All persons HBsAg-positive are potentially infectious.	3. HBeAg: presence in serum of HBsAg carrier indicates lower titer of HBV; correlates with viral replication and high infectivity. Anti-HBe: develops in most HBV infections; correlates with loss of replicating virus and lower infectivity. HBsAg may appear in blood within		If exposure to *known* Hepatitis B carrier or case of acute infection, and within 14 days, also give Hepatitis B immunoglobulin (HBIG) with vaccine. Pregnancy not a contraindication to Hepatitis B vaccine or HBIG.

(*continued*)

HEPATITIS B VIRUS (*Continued*)

Condition	Organism	Lab Findings/ Diagnosis	Signs and Symptoms	Treatment
chronic HBV die prematurely of cirrhosis or hepatocellular cancer. Second only to tobacco as a known carcinogen.		2 weeks; rarely, 6–9 months (average 30–60 days after exposure to HBV). Persists in chronic infection. IgM: antibody indicates recent infection; detectable for ≥4–6 months after infection. IgM anti-HBc present in high titer in acute infection; usually disappears within 6 months; indicates individual is potentially infectious.		Utilize universal blood and body fluid precautions.

HERPES SIMPLEX VIRUS

Condition	Organism	Lab Findings/ Diagnosis	Signs and Symptoms	Treatment
Herpes simplex virus (HSV) is an incurable, recurrent, inflammatory viral skin infection caused by the herpes virus. *Epidemiology:* HSV-1: Worldwide, orolabial transmission— spread of infected droplets from oral secretions. Causes most orolabial infections and ≈15% of genital herpes infections.	Virus belonging to *Herpesviridae* family. Double-stranded DNA virus; periodically reactivates. Virus persists during latent phase between recurrent infections, in sensory sacral ganglia. *Serotypes:* 1. HSV-1 2. HSV-2 3. varicella–zoster virus (VZV) 4. Epstein–Barr Virus (EBV) 5. Cytomegalovirus	*Virus culture:* "Gold" standard; both sensitive and specific; results within days. Allows virus typing, antiviral resistance testing. Intracellular specimen necessary. Must rub lesion with cotton or dacron swab for culture. Calcium alginate inactivates sample. Do not allow swab to dry; transport in appropriate medium. Deteri-	1. Gingivo- stomatitis 2. Pharyngitis 3. Genital infec- tion[3] (Fig. I–6) 4. Recurrent infection 5. Anorectal infection[4] 6. Neonatal infection 7. HSV infection in compromised host 8. Encephalitis 9. Esophagitis	Most HSV-2 cases have not been diagnosed; mild, unrecognized infections that intermittently shed virus in the genitourinary tract. Some first episode cases of genital herpes are manifested by severe disease. Systemic antiviral drugs partially control symptoms and signs for first clinical episode and re-

HERPES SIMPLEX VIRUS (*Continued*)

Condition	Organism	Lab Findings/ Diagnosis	Primary/ Recurrent	Treatment
HSV-2: Estimated 45 million persons in U.S. are infected (CDC, 1998). Most cases are of recurrent, genital herpes. Sexual transmission most common. Incidence > with multiple sex partners. Transmission to neonate during birth. Asymptomatic viral shedding common after genital HSV infection (important source of viral transmission).	(CMV) 6. human herpes virus-6 (HHV-6) 7. human herpes virus-7 (HHV-7) 8. human herpes virus-8 (HHV-8) HSV-2 has been recovered from cervices of asymptomatic females, and urethras and prostates of asymptomatic males. *Incubation:* 2–12 days *Communicability:* Secretions in saliva reported for as long as 7 weeks after recovery in cases of stomatitis. Many cases of genital herpes transmitted by individuals unaware they have the infection, or asymptomatic at time of transmission.	orates 48–96 hrs. Keep at 4°C. *Antigen Detection:* Sensitive and specific; results available in hours, but need special equipment. *Tzanck Prep, Pap:* Not very sensitive or specific, but widely available and inexpensive. *Serology:* Usually not indicated; limited. Western blot to differentiate HSV-1 vs. HSV-2.	*Primary Infection:* No prior infection with either HSV type. More severe than initial, nonprimary, or recurrent infections. *Local Symptoms:* Tender papules, vesicles, or ulcers; bilateral distribution common. Lesions heal by crusting and reepithelialization. Bilateral tender inguinal lymphadenopathy. Healing within 21 days–6 weeks. Cervical shedding: in 70–90% women. *Systemic Symptoms:* Fever, headache, myalgia, malaise; meningitis common, but mild. Can have subclinical primary infection. *Complications:* Extragenital spread, autoinnoculation, aseptic meningitis, transverse myelitis, autonomic nervous system dysfunction (neurogenic bladder, constipation, sacral anesthesia, impotence) (STD Intensive, 1997)	current episodes. Also used for daily suppressive therapy. They neither eradicate latent virus nor affect risk, frequency, or severity of recurrences after drug discontinued. Three antiviral medications with clinical benefit: acyclovir (nucleoside analog) valacyclovir famciclovir Acyclovir 400 mg PO TID × 7–10 days *or*, Acyclovir 200 mg PO t.i.d. × 7–10 days *or* Famciclovir 250 mg PO t.i.d. × 7–10 days, *or* Valacyclovir 1 g PO b.i.d. × 7–10 days. Other regimens for recurrent or daily suppressive Tx (refer to CDC, 1998). Daily suppressive therapy decreases frequency of genital herpes recurrences by ≥75% among patients with frequent recurrences (≥6 per year).

(*continued*)

HERPES SIMPLEX VIRUS (*Continued*)

Condition	Organism	Lab Findings/ Diagnosis	Signs and Symptoms	Treatment
			Recurrent Infections: Usually milder episode; prodrome common; healing is more rapid; Systemic complications uncommon. Cervical shedding infrequent. Recurrence rates vary widely.	Advise patients: No sexual activity until lesions or prodromal symptoms gone. Sexual transmission can occur during asymptomatic periods. Viral shedding > in patients with HSV-2 infection than HSV-1, and in patients who have had genital herpes <12 months.

[3] HSV-2: Eruption of deep-seated vesicles on base.
[4] Anorectal: usually HSV-2 (>85%); common cause of proctitis in anoreceptive homosexual men. May also occur in females with history of anal intercourse; Symptoms: Fever, dysuria, sacral paresthesias, pain, ulcers, inguinal adenopathy.

HUMAN PAPILLOMAVIRUS

Condition	Organism	Lab Findings/ Diagnosis	Signs and Symptoms	Treatment
Human papillomavirus (HPV); one of the most common STDs of the anogenital tract (Fig. I–7.) *Incubation:* 2–3 months; range 1–20 months (Craighill, 1993; Benenson, 1995). *Mode of Transmission:* Direct contact	Papovavirus group of DNA viruses (human wart viruses); >20 types of HPV can infect genital tract. At least 70 types of HPV isolated. Visible warts are usually HPV types 6 or 11; other anogenital region warts strongly associated with cervical dysplasia are 16,18,31,	Definitive diagnosis/detection of viral nucleic acid (DNA or RNA) or capsid protein. *Biopsy:* Subclinical infection often indirectly diagnosed via Pap smear, colposcopy, biopsy, and on penis, vulva, and other genital areas by the application of acetic acid solution.	Most cases are asymptomatic, subclinical, and unrecognized. Papillary growths, small at first; they tend to coalesce and form large cauliflower masses. Intraanal warts are usually due to receptive anal intercourse; are distinct from perianal warts, which can occur in females and	*Primary Goal:* removal of symptomatic warts. If left untreated, visible genital warts may resolve on their own, remain unchanged, or increase in number or size. No evidence indicates that Tx of visible warts affects development of cervical cancer (CDC, 1998).

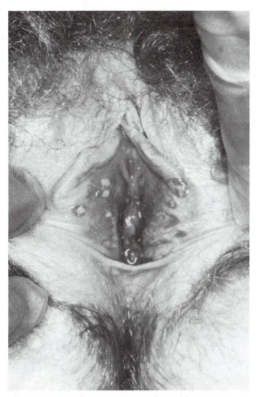

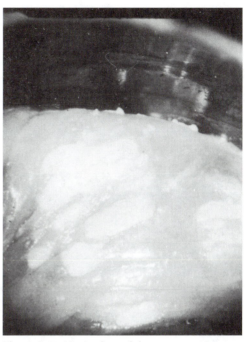

Figure I–7. Vaginal condylomata acuminata as seen with a colposcope (×13). *(From DeCherney, A. & Pernol, M. [1994]. [Eds]. Current Obstetric and Gynecologic Diagnosis and Treatment. 8th ed. Norwalk, CT: Appleton & Lange, p. 694; reprinted with permission.)*

Figure I–6. Ulcerating vesicles of herpes genitalis. *(From DeCherney, A. & Pernol, M. [1994]. [Eds]. Current Obstetric and Gynecologic Diagnosis and Treatment. 8th ed. Norwalk, CT: Appleton & Lange, p. 704; reprinted with permission.)*

HUMAN PAPILLOMAVIRUS (*Continued*)

Condition	Organism	Lab Findings/ Diagnosis	Signs and Symptoms	Treatment
	33, and 35 (Benenson, 1995). Visible warts on uterine cervix, vagina, urethra, and anus are sometimes symptomatic.	Acetowhitening is not a specific test for HPV; in low-risk population, may have false-positive, if this method is used for screening. Experienced clinicians find test useful for identification of	males with history of anal sex.	*Patient-Applied Treatment:* Podofilox 0.5%[5] solution or gel b.i.d. × 3 days, then 4 days with no Tx; repeat up to 4 cycles; *or,* Imiquimod 5%[5] cream at bedtime 3×/week, up to 16 weeks; *(continued)*

HUMAN PAPILLOMAVIRUS (Continued)

Condition	Organism	Lab Findings/ Diagnosis	Signs and Symptoms	Treatment
		flat genital warts. *Diagnosis:* Genital warts can be confirmed by biopsy, if necessary due to following reasons: 1. Diagnosis uncertain 2. Lesions do not respond to Tx 3. The disease worsens 4. Patient is immunocompromised 5. Warts are pigmented, indurated, fixed, and ulcerated		wash with soap and H_2O after 6–10 hrs. *Provider-Applied Treatment:* Cryotherapy with liquid nitrogen or cryoprobe; repeat every 1–2 weeks prn. Podophyllin resin 10–25%,[5] weekly as needed; *or,* Trichloroacetic acid (TCA) or Bichloroacetic acid (BCA) 80–90%; weekly, as needed; *or,* Surgical removal: tangential scissor excision, tangential shave excision, curettage, or electrosurgery.

[5] Safety not established during pregnancy.

PELVIC INFLAMMATORY DISEASE

Condition	Organism	Lab Findings/ Diagnosis	Signs and Symptoms	Treatment
Spectrum of pelvic inflammatory disorders (PID) of upper female genital tract. Includes combination of endometritis, salpingitis, tubo-ovarian abscess, and pelvic peritonitis. Acute PID difficult to diagnose: wide variation of	Usually based on clinical findings. Organism is *N. gonorrhoeae* in 25–50% of cases. These cases have greater frequency of fever and shorter duration of symptoms. 75% of women will have onset of symptoms within 1 week of menses.	No single historical, physical, or lab finding is both sensitive and specific for diagnosis of acute PID (CDC, 98). Laparoscopy; will not detect endometritis or subtle inflammation of fallopian tubes.	*Minimum criteria* to initiate empiric treatment: 1. Lower abdominal tenderness 2. Adnexal tenderness 3. Cervical motion tenderness *Additional criteria to support diagnosis of PID:* 1. Oral temp. >101° F (38°C)	*Parenteral Regimens:* Cefotetan IV, *or,* Cefoxitin IV, *and* doxycycline IV *or,* Clindamycin *and* gentamycin *Oral Treatment:* Ofloxacin 400 mg[6] PO b.i.d. × 14 days + metronidazole 500 mg PO b.i.d. × 14 days

PELVIC INFLAMMATORY DISEASE (*Continued*)

Condition	Organism	Lab Findings/ Diagnosis	Signs and Symptoms	Treatment
signs and symptoms; often mild, subtle symptoms. Dx usually based on clinical findings.	*Chlamydia trachomatis* is agent in 30–50% of cases: milder symptoms, duration 7–10 days. Mixed aerobic–anaerobic bacteria in 25–60% of cases. Anaerobes > aerobic bacteria, especially *Bacteroides* spp. Microorganisms of vaginal flora can also cause PID, eg, anaerobes, *G. vaginalis, H. influenzae,* enteric Gram-rods, *Streptococcus agalactiae, M. hominis, U. urealyticum*		2. Abnormal cervical or vaginal discharge 3. Elevated erythrocyte sedimentation rate 4. Elevated C-reactive protein 5. Lab documentation of cervical infection with *N. gonorrhoeae* or *C. trachomatis* *Definitive Criteria:* 1. Histopathologic evidence of endometritis on biopsy 2. Transvaginal sonography, other imaging techniques showing thickened fluid-filled tubes, with or without free pelvic fluid or tuboovarian complex 3. Laparoscopic abnormalities consistent with PID.	*Alternate Rx:* Ceftriaxone 250 mg IM ×1 *or,* Cefoxitin 2g IM + probenecid 1 g PO × 1 *or,* 3rd generation cephalosporin[6] + doxycycline 100 mg PO b.i.d. × 14 days If no response in 72 hrs, reevaluate to confirm diagnosis and consider parenteral treatment on outpatient or inpatient basis. Examine and treat sexual partners during 60 days preceding onset of symptoms. Male partners often asymptomatic. Treat sexual partners presumptively. If pregnant, high-risk for maternal morbidity, preterm delivery and fetal demise.

[6] No Quinolones if under 18 years old or pregnant.

SEXUALLY TRANSMITTED ENTERIC INFECTIONS

The following gastrointestinal syndromes can be sexually transmitted: proctitis, proctocolitis, and enteritis. Diagnosis and evaluation are usually by anoscopy, sigmoidoscopy, stool exams, and stool cultures. Organisms responsible for sexually transmitted enteric infections may be enteric bacterial pathogens, eg, *Shigella, Salmonella, Campylobacter* spp., or helminths, protozoa or viruses. Yield of cultures is greater if done through anoscope than via inserted swab (STD Intensive, 1997).

Proctitis	Proctocolitis	Enteritis
Inflammation of the rectal mucosa (distal 12–15 cm).	Inflammation of the rectal mucosa and colon (not limited to rectal mucosa; can extend up to or beyond 12–15 cm).	Inflammation of the small intestine (duodenum, jejunum, and or ileum)
Symptoms: anorectal pain/discomfort, pruritis, tenesmus, discharge (bloody or mucopurulent), blood in stool (hematochezia).	Symptoms as in proctitis, plus diarrhea and/or abdominal cramps. Symptoms overlap proctitis and enteritis.	Diarrhea and abdominal cramps, abdominal pain, bloating, cramps, nausea, flatulence, urgency, mucous discharge; without proctitis or proctocolitis.
Occurs predominantly in those who practice anal intercourse (CDC, 1998)	*Pathogens:* same as proctitis, plus: *Campylobacter* spp., *Shigella* spp., *Entamoeba histolytica, Chlamydia trachomatis* (LGV serovars, rarely), *Giardia lamblia, Salmonella* spp.	Most frequent pathogen: *Giardia lamblia* (usually need multiple stool specimens). *Also: Campylobacter jejuni, Shigella* (*sonnei, flexneri*), *Salmonella*
Clinical Diagnosis: acute/recent onset of proctitis in cases of anal receptive intercourse, most often sexually transmitted. Examine with anoscopy; if anorectal pus or polymorphonuclear leukocytes on rectal Gram stain smear, treat pending lab results:	In immunosuppressed HIV-infected patient, may be other opportunistic pathogens.	*Treatment: Giardia:* metronidazole; Quinacrine.
Ceftriaxone (or other agent effective for anal and genital gonorrhea) 125 mg IM × 1 + doxycycline 100 mg PO b.i.d. × 7 days (treat specific pathogen)	*Treatment* (Rx): based on specific diagnosis: *Campylobacter:* culture; Rx: erythromycin or ciprofloxacin.[6] *Shigella:* Culture; Rx: ciprofloxacin[6] or ampicillin *Entamoeba histolytica:* stool for ova and parasites (O&P); Rx: metronidazole	For other pathogens, treat, based on specific pathogen.
May be especially severe in patient with HIV infection.		In immunosuppressed HIV-infected patient, may be other opportunistic infections that are not usually sexually transmitted: Cytomegalovirus Mycobacterium avium-intracellulare *Salmonella* spp. *Cryptosporidium Microsporidium Isospora*
Check for other STDs: *N. gonorrhoeae, Chlamydia:* need rectal *culture* (also Lymphogranuloma venereum [LGV], syphilis, HSV. Coinfection with HSV may be very severe.		

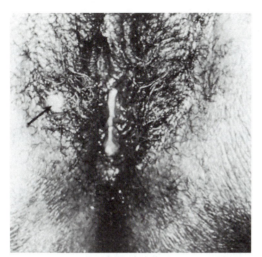

Figure I–8. Chancre of primary syphilis. *(From DeCherney, A. & Pernol, M. [1994]. [Eds]. Current Obstetric and Gynecologic Diagnosis and Treatment. 8th ed. Norwalk, CT: Appleton & Lange, p. 757; reprinted with permission.)*

A	B	C

Figure I–9. Trichomonas vaginalis as found in vaginal and prostatic secretions. **A.** Normal trophozoite. **B.** Round form after division. **C.** Common form seen in stained preparation. Cysts not found. *(From DeCherney, A. & Pernol, M. [1994]. [Eds]. Current Obstetric and Gynecologic Diagnosis and Treatment. 8th ed. Norwalk, CT: Appleton & Lange, p. 699; reprinted with permission.)*

SYPHILIS

Disease	Lab Findings/Diagnosis	Primary Syphilis
Syphilis is an acute and chronic treponemal disease, characterized clinically by primary lesions, secondary eruptions involving the skin and mucous membranes, long periods of latency, and late lesions of the skin, bone, viscera, central nervous system, and cardiovascular system.	Definitive methods to diagnose early syphilis are dark field examinations and direct fluorescent antibody tests of lesions, exudate, or tissue. Recovery period of treponemes is very brief; diagnosis is usually by history and serology.	Ulcer, chancre at site of infection. Chancre heals spontaneously. Serologic tests may be non-reactive at this stage, until 1–4 weeks.
Organism:	*Presumptive Diagnosis:*	*Chancre:* Indurated, firm, painless papule/ulcer with raised borders. May be increased, firm, painless, groin lymph nodes (Fig. I–8).
Treponema pallidum	With two types of serologic tests for syphilis:	
Mode of Transmission:	*Nontreponemal Tests:*	Unless in the external genital area, usually no genital lesions in females. May be lesions in cervix and vagina.
Transmitted by direct contact with infectious, moist lesions. Treponemes pass through intact mucous membrane or abraded skin.	*VDRL* (Venereal Disease Research Lab) and *RPR* (Rapid Plasma Reagin): Confirmatory (treponemal) tests, eg, FTA or MHA-TP should be performed at all times if the screening tests (RPR, VDRL) are positive.	Primary lesions may be many mm of skin area, in breast, nose, perineum.
Incubation:	*Treponemal Tests:*	Serologic tests positive in 70% at this stage.
The lesion (chancre) develops after 10–90 days (usually 3 weeks); heals spontaneously.	Fluorescent treponemal antibody absorption (FTA-ABS) or micro-hemagglutination assay for antibody to treponema pallidum (MHA-TP).	Most with reactive treponemal tests are reactive for life, regardless of disease activity. Treponemal antibody test titers correlate poorly with disease activity.
	False-positive nontreponemal test results in some medical conditions; Nontreponemal test antibody titers usually correlate with disease activity.	
	Results should be reported quantitatively. A four-fold change in titer necessary to demonstrate clinically significant difference between two nontreponemal test results.	
	Serofast Reaction: in some individuals, nontreponemal antibodies persist at low titers for a long time, even for life.	

Secondary Syphilis	Tertiary Syphilis	Latency	Treatment
Rash, mucocutaneous lesions, adenopathy; spirochetes spread hematogenously. General cutaneous eruption occurs in 2 weeks– 6 months (average, 6 weeks); heals spontaneously in 2–6 weeks.	*System Involvement:* Cardiac Neurologic Ophthalmic Auditory Gummatous lesions	Resolution of primary and secondary lesions or positive reactive serologic test. Individual is infectious in the first 2 years of latency. 25% have clinical relapses.	Parenteral penicillin G is the preferred drug for treatment of all stages of syphilis and is the only therapy with documented efficiency for neurosyphilis or syphilis during pregnancy.
Serologic tests positive at this stage.	These symptoms manifest 4–20 years after disappearance of primary chancre.	*Early Latent:* Latent syphilis acquired within previous year.	*Primary and Secondary:* (adults/recommended regimen): benzathine penicillin G, 2.4 million units IM, single dose.
Characteristic Dermatitis: diffuse, bilateral, symmetric, papulosquamous rash; involves palms, soles; may cover trunk, and be macular, papular, or pustular.	One-third of untreated cases, may have these symptoms: Gummatous (tertiary lesions of skin and bone) develop Cardiovascular: aortic aneurysm or aortic insufficiency.	*Late Latent:* Symptoms of unknown duration; all other cases of latent syphilis.	*Latent Syphilis:* Early latent: benzathine penicillin G, 2.4 million units IM, single dose. *Late/unknown syphilis:* benzathine penicillin G, 7.2 million units total (3 doses of 2.4 million units each) at 1-week intervals).
May have patchy alopecia, hepatitis, nephritis.	Neurologic: meningitis, tabes dorsalis paresis.	History of serologic evidence of previous infection.	*Tertiary Syphilis:* Benzathine penicillin G 7.2 million units total (3 doses of 2.4 million units each at 1-week intervals).
Perineal area: moist papules (condyloma lata); Darkfield tests of these lesions are positive.	25% fatal complications in tertiary syphilis. 25% never show ill effects.	Absence of lesions. Serologic tests usually reactive, titer may be low.	*Neurosyphilis:* Aqueous crystalline penicillin G, 18–24 million units/day, given as 3–4 million units IV q 4 hours × 10–14 days.
Serologic tests positive.			*Jarish Hexheimer Reaction:* Acute febrile reaction that may occur within first 24 hours of any treatment for syphilis (headache, myalgia).
			Communicability: Variable and indefinite; During primary and secondary stages, also in mucocutaneous recurrences during first 4 years of latency. Inapparent lesions during the latent period make it potentially infectious.
			Evaluation and Treatment of Sexual Partners:
			• *Primary syphilis:* From date of adequate Tx back to 90 days, prior to onset symptoms (chancre).
			• *Secondary syphilis:* From date of adequate Tx back to 6.5 months prior to onset of symptoms.
			• *Early latent:* 12 months prior to diagnosis.

TRICHOMONIASIS

Condition	Organism	Lab Findings/ Diagnosis	Signs and Symptoms	Treatment
Common, persistent protozoal disease of the genitourinary tract. Produces an inflammatory response; does not invade mucosa or tissue. *Mode of Transmission:* Contact with vaginal and urethral discharges of infected people during sexual intercourse. *Incubation:* 4–20 days; average 7 days; may be a symptom-free carrier for years.	Flagellate protozoan of genus *Trichomonas,* or related genera. *Three Species:* *Trichomonas* (T) *vaginalis* (Fig. I–9) *T. hominis* *T. tenax* Organism invades and persists in prostate, urethra, and seminal vesicles.	Clinical diagnosis confirmed by finding motile flagellates in *wet mount,* using normal saline solution (NSS) on slide with drop of discharge and coverslip (Fig. I–1) *Culture:* Need 1000 organisms Monoclonal antibody (DFA). 60% sensitivity; 75% specificity. May identify on culture or Pap.	Most men: no symptoms. Some have symptoms of nongonococcal urethritis (NGU). Many females are asymptomatic. Vaginal discharge: diffuse, malodorous, yellow-green, with vulvar irritation. Worse just after menstruation or pregnancy. Vulva: may only be visible in vestibule and labia minora, or may cause inflammation of labia majora, perineum, and surrounding skin. May be urinary symptoms (burning), but these are due to vulvitis. Speculum exam: may show generalized vaginal erythema, with multiple small petechiae ("strawberry spots"); these are not the same as epithelial punctatum.	Metronidazole 2 g PO × 1 *or,* 500 mg PO b.i.d. × 7 days Treat partners concurrently to avoid reinfection (present in 30–40% of male partners). Avoid sex until treatment completed and asymptomatic. Present in 85% of female partners of infected men. May have adverse pregnancy outcomes: premature membrane rupture, preterm delivery. If treatment failure, retreat with metronidazole 500 mg PO b.i.d. × 7 days.

REFERENCES FOR APPENDIX I

American Academy of Pediatrics (AAP). (1997). Section 2. In: Perer, G. (Ed.). *Red Book: Report of the Committee on Infectious Diseases,* 24th ed. Elk Grove Village, IL: American Academy of Pediatrics.

Atkinson, W., Furphy, L., Humiston, S., et al. (eds.). (1997). *Epidemiology and Prevention of Vaccine-Preventable Diseases. The Pink Book.* Atlanta: Department of Health and Human Services.

Baker, T., Burgess, A., Brickman, E. & Davis, R. (1990). Rape victims' concerns about possible exposure to HIV infection. *Journal of Interpersonal Violence, 5*(1):49–60.

Benenson, A. (1995). (Ed.). *Control of Communicable Diseases Manual,* 16th ed. Washington, DC: American Public Health Association.

Centers for Disease Control and Prevention (CDC). (1998). 1998 guidelines for treatment of sexually transmitted diseases. *MMWR, 47* No. RR-1.

Craighill, M. (1993). Human papillomavirus infection in children and adolescents. *Sem Pediatr Infect Dis, 4*(2):85–93.

Gillies, D. Health Services Agency Laboratory Director. County of Santa Cruz. (1998) Personal communication.

Gostin, L., Lazzarini, Z., Alexander, D., et al. (1994). HIV testing, counseling, and prophylaxis after sexual assault. *JAMA, 271*(18): 1436–1444.

Jenny, C., Hooton, T., Bowers, A., et al. (1990). Sexually transmitted diseases in victims of rape. *New Engl J Med, 322*(11):713–716.

Oh, M., Smith, K., O'Cain, M., et al. (1998). Urine-based screening of adolescents in detention to guide treatment for gonococcal and chlamydial infections. *Arch Pediatr Adolesc Med, 152*:52–56.

STD Intensive: STD Clinical Course Manual, Part II. (1997). San Francisco STD/HIV Prevention Training Center, San Francisco, CA.

Slaughter, L. & Crowley, S. (1993). Prevalence of Sexually Transmitted Diseases in Sex Offenders. Paper presented at the North American Society of Pediatric and Adolescent Gynecology (NASPAG). Colorado Springs, CO.

SUGGESTED READINGS FOR APPENDIX I

American Academy of Pediatrics (AAP). Committee on Child Abuse and Neglect (1998). Gonorrhea in prepubertal children. *Pediatrics, 101*(1): 134–135.

Augenbraun, M., Feldman, J., Chirgwin, K., et al. (1995). Increased genital shedding of herpes simplex virus type-2 in HIV-seropositive women. *Ann Int Med, 123*(11):845–847.

Brown, S., Becher, J. & Brady, W. (1995). Treatment of ectoparasitic infections: Review of the English-language literature, 1982–1992. *Clin Infect Dis, 20*(Suppl. 1):S104–S109.

Burgess, A., Jacobsen, B., Thompson, J., Baker, T. & Grant, C. (1990). HIV testing of sexual assault populations: Ethical and legal issues. *Journal of Emergency Nursing, 16*(5):331–338.

Curry, S. & Barclay, D. (1994). Benign disorders of the vulva and vagina. In: DeCherney, A. & Pernoll, M. (Eds.). *Obstetric and Gynecologic Diagnosis and Treatment,* 8th ed. Norwalk, CT: Appleton & Lange.

Embree, J., Lindsay, D., Williams, T., et al. (1996). Acceptability and usefulness of vaginal washes in premenarcheal girls as a diagnostic procedure for sexually transmitted diseases. *Pediatr Infect Dis J, 15*(8):662–666.

Gutman, L. (1995). Human papillomavirus infections of the genital tract in adolescents. *Adolesc Med: State of the Art Reviews, 6*(1):115–127.

Hammerschlag, M., Rettig, P. & Shields, M.E. (1988). False positive results with the use of chlamydial antigen detection tests in the evaluation of suspected sexual abuse in children. *Pediatr Infect Dis J, 7*(1):11–14.

Kellogg, N. & Parra, J. (1995). The progression of human papillomavirus lesions in sexual assault victims. *Pediatrics, 96*(6):1163–1165.

Ramin, S., Wendel, G. & Hemsell, D. (1994). Sexually transmitted diseases and pelvic infections. In: DeCherney, A. & Pernoll, M. (Eds.). *Obstetric and Gynecologic Diagnosis and Treatment,* 8th ed. Norwalk, CT: Appleton & Lange, pp. 754–784.

STD Intensive: STD Clinical Course Manual. (1993). San Francisco STD Prevention/Training Center. San Francisco, CA

Schwarcz, S., & Whittington, W. (1990 July/August). Sexual assault and sexually transmitted diseases: Detection and management in adults and children. *Rev Infect Dis, 12*(Suppl. 6), S682–S690.

Shafer, M. (1994). Sexually transmitted diseases in adolescents: Prevention, diagnosis, and treatment in pediatric practice. *Adolesc Health Update, 6*(2):1–7.

Siegel, R., Schubert, C., Myers, P. & Shapiro, R. (1995). The prevalence of sexually transmitted diseases in children and adolescents evaluated for sexual abuse in Cincinnati: Rationale for limited STD testing in prepubertal girls. *Pediatrics, 96*(6):1090–1094.

Siegfried, E., Rasnick-Conley, J., Cook, S., Leonardi, C. & Monteleone, J. (1998). Human papillomavirus screening in pediatric victims of sexual abuse. *Pediatrics, 101*(1):43–47.

Stedman's Medical Dictionary, 26th ed. (1995). Baltimore: William & Wilkins.

Stewart, D. & Jones, C. (1993). Controversies in STDs in Prepubertal Children. Presented at the meeting of North American Society of Pediatric and Adolescent Gynecology (NASPAG). Colorado Springs, CO.

Wald, A., Zeh, J. Selke, S., et al. (1995). Virologic characteristics of subclinical and symptomatic genital herpes infections. *N Engl J Med, 333* (12):770–775.

Wald, A., Zeh, J., Barnum, G., et al. (1996). Suppression of subclinical shedding of herpes simplex virus type 2 with acyclovir (part 1). *Ann Intern Med, 124*(1):8–15.

Glossary

abrasion Excoriation or circumscribed removal of superficial layers of skin or mucous membrane; a scraping away of a portion of the surface.

adhesion Process of adhering or uniting of two surfaces or parts, especially the union of opposing surfaces of a wound (eg, labial adhesions).

[1]anniversary reaction An emotional response to a previous event occurring at the same time of year. Often the event involved a loss and the reaction a depressed state. The reaction can range from mild to severe and may occur at any time after the event.

[1]bestiality Zoophilia; sexual relations between a human being and an animal. See also *paraphilias.*

[1]beyond a reasonable doubt That measure or degree of proof that will produce in the mind of the trier of facts a near-certain belief or conviction as to the allegations sought to be established. Of the three legal standards of proof, this is the highest level and the one required to establish the guilt of someone accused of a crime. Sometimes thought to represent a 95 out of 100 chance of certainty.

bruise Injury producing hematoma or diffuse extravasation of blood without rupture of the skin.

causation The fact of being the cause of something produced or happening. The act by which an effect is produced. This is a relevant tenet in the areas of negligence and criminal law.

[1]clear and convincing evidence The second-highest level or standard applied to determining whether alleged facts have been proven. This is the standard applied to civil commitment matters and similar circumstances in which there is the chance that valued civil liberty interests and freedoms are at stake. Sometimes thought to represent a 75 out of 100 chance of certainty.

contusion Any mechanical injury (usually caused by a blow) resulting in hemorrhage beneath unbroken skin.

---

[1] Definition from Edgerton, J. (1994). *American Psychiatry Glossary,* 7th ed. Washington, DC: American Psychiatric Press; reprinted with permission.

[2] Definition from Douglas, J., Burgess, A.W., Burgess, A.G. & Ressler R. (1992) Crime Classification Manual. New York: Lexington Books; reprinted with permission.

[1]**competency to stand trial** Legal test applied to all criminal defendants regarding their cognitive ability at the time of trial to participate in the proceedings against them. As held in *Dusky v. United States* (1960), a defendant is competent to stand trial if: (1) he or she possesses a factual understanding of the proceedings against him or her, and (2) he or she has sufficient present ability to consult with his or her lawyer with a reasonable degree of rational understanding.

CT scan (computed tomography) Imaging anatomic information from a cross-sectional plane of the body; each image is generated by computer synthesis of data transmitted by x-ray. It is obtained in many different directions in a given plane. CT imaging reveals bone and soft tissues (organs, muscles, and tumors). Tissues of similar density can be highlighted, and data from multiple cross-sections incorporated into 3-D images. Useful in determining density, size, and location.

[1]**castration** Removal of the sex organs. In psychological terms, the fantasized loss of the genitals. Also used figuratively to denote state of impotence, powerlessness, helplessness, or defeat.

[1]**character disorder (character neurosis)** A personality disorder manifested by a chronic, habitual, maladaptive pattern of reaction that is relatively inflexible, limits the optimal use of potentialities, and often provokes the responses from the environment that the person wants to avoid. In contrast to symptoms of neurosis, character traits are typically ego-syntonic.

[1]**cognitive** Refers to the mental process of comprehension, judgment, memory, and reasoning, in contrast to emotional and volitional processes. Contrast with *conative*.

[1]**coping mechanisms** Ways of adjusting to environmental stress without altering one's goals or purposes; includes both conscious and unconscious mechanisms.

[1]**coprophagia** Eating of filth or feces.

[1]**coprophilia** One of the paraphilias, characterized by marked distress over, or acting on, sexual urges involving feces.

[1]**cult** A system of beliefs and rituals based on dogma or religious teachings that are usually contrary to the ones established within or accepted by the community.

[1]**defense mechanism** Unconscious intrapsychic processes serving to provide relief from emotional conflict and anxiety. Conscious efforts are frequently made for the same reasons, but true defense mechanisms are unconscious. Some of the common defense mechanisms defined in this glossary are *compensation, conversion, denial, displacement, dissociation, idealization, identification, incorporation, introjection, projection, rationalization, reaction formation, regression, sublimation, substitution, symbolization,* and *undoing*.

[1]***déjà vu*** A paramnesia consisting of the sensation or illusion that one is seeing what one has seen before.

[1]**depersonalization** Feelings of unreality or strangeness concerning either the environment, the self, or both. This is characteristic of *depersonalization disorder* and may also occur in *schizotypal personality disorder, schizophrenia,* and in those persons experiencing overwhelming *anxiety,* stress, or fatigue.

[1]**designer drugs** Addictive drugs that are synthesized or manufactured to give the same subjective effects as well-known illicit drugs. Because the process is a covert operation, there is difficulty in tracing the manufacturer to check the drugs for adverse effects. Com-

mon examples are "ecstasy" and "eve," both of which are similar to *amphetamines.*

¹*Diagnostic and Statistical Manual of Mental Disorders* (DSM) The American Psychiatric Association's official classification of mental disorders.

DSM-I	The first edition, published in 1952.
DSM-II	The second edition, published in 1968.
DSM-III	The third edition, published in 1980.
DSM-III-R	The revised *DSM-III,* published in 1987.
DSM-IV	The fourth edition, published in 1994.

diffuse Disseminated; spread about, not restricted.

disease Interruption, cessation or disorder of body functions, systems, or organs (illness, sickness)

¹**dissociation** The splitting off of clusters of mental contents from *conscious* awareness, a mechanism central to hysterical conversion and *dissociative disorders;* the separation of an idea from its emotional significance and affect as seen in the inappropriate *affect* of schizophrenic patients.

¹**dysthymic disorder** One of the *depressive disorders,* characterized by a chronic course (ie, seldom without *symptoms*) with lowered *mood* tone and a range of other symptoms that may include feelings of inadequacy, loss of self-esteem, or self-deprecation; feelings of hopelessness or despair; feelings of *guilt,* brooding about past events, or self-pity; low energy and chronic tiredness; being less active or talkative than usual; poor concentration and indecisiveness; and inability to enjoy pleasurable activities.

ecchymosis Purplish patch caused by extravasation (leakage, passage) of blood into the skin; different from petechiae only in size; ecchymoses are >3 mm in diameter.

¹**ejaculatory incompetence (impotence)** Inability to reach orgasm and ejaculate despite adequacy of erection. See *orgasmic disorders.*

¹**elimination disorders** Included in this group are functional *encopresis* and functional *enuresis.*

¹**emancipated minor** A person under 18 years of age who is considered totally self-supporting. Legal rights afforded at adulthood are typically extended to an emancipated minor.

¹**encopresis, functional** An elimination disorder in a child who is at least 4 years of age, consisting of repeated passage of feces into inappropriate places (clothing, floor, etc.), not due to a *general medical condition.*

¹**endorphin** One family of endogenous brain peptides with morphine-like action; the other brain opioids are *dynorphin* and the *enkephalins.* The endorphins modulate pain perception and possibly mood and response to stress.

¹**enuresis, functional** An elimination disorder in a child who is at least 5 years of age, consisting of repeated voiding of urine into bed or clothing, and not due to any *general medical condition.*

epithelialization Formation of epithelium over a denuded surface; purely cellular, avascular layer covering all free surfaces, cutaneous, mucous, and serous, including glands and other structures derived from them.

columnar Formed of a single layer of cells, more tall than wide.

stratified squamous Epithelium consisting of several layers of keratin-containing cells; surface cells are scale-like; deeper cells are polyhedral.

simple squamous Single layer of scale-like cells.

[1]**erotic** Consciously or unconsciously invested with sexual feeling; sensually related.

erythema Redness of the skin due to capillary dilation.

excoriation Scratch mark, linear break in skin surface, usually covered with blood or serous crusts.

[1]**expert witness** One who by reason of specialized education, experience, and/or training possesses superior knowledge about a subject that is beyond the understanding of an average or ordinary layperson. Expert witnesses are permitted to offer opinions about matters relevant to their expertise that will assist the trier of facts (eg, jury) in comprehending evidence that the trier would otherwise not understand or fully appreciate.

[1]**female orgasmic disorder** One of the *orgasm disorders.*

[1]**fetishism** One of the *paraphilias,* characterized by marked distress over, or acting on, sexual urges involving the use of nonliving objects (fetishes), such as underclothing, stockings, or boots.

[1]**fetishism, transvestic** One of the *paraphilias,* characterized by marked distress over, or acting on, sexual urges involving cross-dressing, most frequently in a heterosexual male. The condition may occur with gender *dysphoria* as part of a *gender identity disorder;* but more commonly the transvestite has no desire to change his sex but

wants only at a particular time to appear to be female.

fissure Deep furrow, cleft, or slit.

anal fissure Crack or slit in the mucous membrane of the anus, very painful and difficult to heal.

force That which tends to produce motion in a body ([Latin] *fortis:* strong).

[1]**forensic psychiatry** A branch of psychiatry dealing with legal issues related to mental disorders.

fossa (Plural: ae) Depression usually more or less longitudinal in shape, below the level of a surface of a part (trench or ditch).

[1]**frigidity** Female sexual arousal disorder or female sexual desire disorder; it may consist of deficient or absent sexual fantasies and desire for sexual activity, aversion to and avoidance of genital sexual contact with a sexual partner, inability to attain or maintain the lubrication–swelling response of sexual excitement during sexual activity, or lack of a feeling of sexual excitement and pleasure during sexual activity.

[1]**frotteurism** One of the *paraphilias,* consisting of recurrent, intense sexual urges involving touching and rubbing against a nonconsenting person; common sites in which such activities take place are crowded trains, buses, and elevators. Fondling the victim may be part of the condition and is called *toucherism.*

Frye standard An admissability standard for scientific evidence which relies on the federal decision of *Frye v. the United States* (1923). The main criterion is general acceptance in the scientific community. *People v. Kelly* (1976) is the corollary ruling to Frye, on admissability of scientific evidence in California. Reliability must be established by experts. Experts must be properly qualified and correct procedures must be used.

¹fugue A *dissociative disorder* marked by sudden, unexpected travel away from one's customary environment, with inability to recall one's past and assumption of a new identity, which may be partial or complete.

¹habeas corpus ([Latin]: "you have the body") An order to bring a party before a judge or court; specifically, in regard to a person who is being retained within a hospital, to give the court the opportunity to examine that person and decide on the appropriateness of such retention.

hematoma Localized mass of extravasated blood that is relatively or completely confined within an organ or tissue, space, or potential space; the blood is usually clotted, or partly so.

hemorrhage Escape of blood through ruptured or unruptured vessel walls.

¹high-risk behavior Actions that put one in danger or render one vulnerable to harmful consequences. Needle sharing by addicts, for example, is high-risk behavior because of the likelihood of transmission of HIV or other pathogens.

¹homosexuality A primary erotic attraction to others of the same sex that is increasingly viewed as a constitutional, probably largely inherited trait. Overt homosexual behavior may be inhibited, delayed, or otherwise modified because of family or peer pressure, social bias, or internal conflict caused by the internalization of social prejudice.

hypervascularity Abnormally vascular; containing an excessive number of blood vessels.

¹impotence The inability to achieve or maintain a penile erection of sufficient quality to engage in successful sexual intercourse; male erectile disorder. Two types are described by Masters and Johnson: in primary impotence, there has never been a successful sexual coupling; in secondary impotence, failure occurs following at least one successful union. Compare with *orgasmic dysfunction*. See *sexual arousal disorders*.

¹inappropriate affect A display of *emotion* that is out of harmony with reality or with the verbal or intellectual content that it accompanies.

¹informed consent Permission by the patient for a medical procedure based on understanding the nature of the procedure, the risks involved, the consequences of withholding permission, and alternative procedures.

¹insanity defense A legal concept that holds that a person cannot be held criminally responsible for his or her actions because, due to a mental illness, the person was unable to form the requisite intent for the crime he or she is charged with at the time the crime was committed. Historically, a number of standards or tests have been devised to define criminal insanity. Some of these include the following:

- *American Law Institute/Model Penal Code test* A defendant would not be responsible for his or her criminal conduct if, as a result of mental disease or defect, he or she "lacked substantial capacity either to appreciate the criminality of his or her conduct or to conform his or her conduct to the requirements of law."
- *Crime Control Act (CCA)* of 1984 standard. In 1984, as part of sweeping federal legislation, the CCA altered the test for insanity in federal courts by holding that it was an affirmative defense to all federal

crimes that at the time of the offense, "the defendant, as a result of a severe mental disease or defect, was unable to appreciate the nature and quality or the wrongfulness of his [or her] acts. Mental disease or defect does not otherwise constitute a defense."

- **Durham rule** A ruling by the U.S. Court of Appeals for the District of Columbia Circuit in 1954 that held that an accused person is not criminally responsible if his or her "unlawful act was the product of mental disease or mental defect." This decision was quite controversial, and within several years it was modified and then replaced altogether by the same court that originally formulated it.

- **irresistible impulse test** Acquittal of criminal responsibility is allowed if a defendant's mental disorder caused him or her to experience an "irresistible and uncontrollable impulse to commit the offense, even if he [or she] remained able to understand the nature of the offense and its wrongfulness."

- **McNaughten rule** In 1843, the English House of Lords ruled that a person was not responsible for a crime if the accused "was laboring under such a defect of reason from a disease of mind as not to know the nature and quality of the act; or, if he knew it, that he did not know he was doing what was wrong." This rule, or some derivation of it, is still applied in many states today.

¹**klismaphilia** One of the *paraphilias,* characterized by marked distress over, or acting on, sexual urges involving enemas.

¹**labile** Rapidly shifting (as applied to emotions); unstable.

¹**libido** The psychic *drive* or energy usually associated with the sexual *instinct.* (Sexual is used here in the broad sense to include pleasure and love-object seeking.)

¹**male erectile disorder** One of the *sexual arousal disorders.*

¹**male orgasmic disorder** One of the *orgasmic disorders.*

¹**masochism** Pleasure derived from physical or psychological pain inflicted on oneself either by oneself or by others. It is called sexual masochism and classified as a *paraphilia* when it is consciously sought as a part of the sexual act or as a prerequisite to sexual gratification. It is the converse of *sadism,* although the two tend to coexist in the same person.

¹**masochism, sexual** One of the *paraphilias,* characterized by marked distress over, or acting on, sexual urges to be humiliated, beaten, bound, or otherwise made to suffer by the sexual partner. Among the frequently reported masochistic acts are restraint (physical bondage), blindfolding, whipping or flagellation, electrical shocks, or being treated as a helpless infant and clothed in diapers (infantilism).

²**modus operandi (MO)** The actions taken by an offender to successfully perpetrate the offense. MO is a learned behavior that evolves as the offender becomes more sophisticated and confident.

MRI (magnetic resonance imaging) Diagnostic radiologic modality that uses nuclear magnetic resonance technology, wherein magnetic nuclei (especially protons) of a patient are aligned in a strong, uniform magnetic field, absorb energy from tuned radiofrequency pulses, and emit radiofrequency signals as their excitation decays. These signals, which vary in intensity according to nuclear abundance and molecular chemical environment, are converted into sets of tomographic images. These images permit three-dimensional localization of point sources of the signals. The superior three-dimensional images of the body's interior delineates muscle, bone, blood vessels, nerves, organs and tumors, and the patient is not exposed to ionizing radiation.

[1]Munchausen syndrome (pathomimicry)
In *DSM-IV,* a chronic form of factitious disorder with physical symptoms that may be totally fabricated, self-inflicted, or exaggerations of preexisting physical conditions. The subject's entire life may consist of seeking admission to or staying in hospitals (often under different names). Multiple invasive procedures and operations are eagerly solicited. The need is to assume the sick role, rather than to reap any economic benefit or ensure better care or physical well being.

[1]necrophilia One of the *paraphilias,* characterized by marked distress over, or acting on, urges involving sexual activity with corpses.

[1]negligence In medical malpractice law, generally described as the failure to do something that a reasonable practitioner would have done (omission) or as doing something that a reasonable practitioner would not have done (commission) under particular circumstances.

[1]onanism (coitus interruptus) The term is sometimes used interchangeably with masturbation.

[1]orgasm Sexual climax; peak psychophysiological response to sexual stimulation.

orgasmic disorders One group of sexual dysfunctions; includes male orgasmic disorder (ejaculatory incompetence, retarded ejaculation), premature ejaculation, and female orgasmic disorder.

[1]paraphilias One of the major groups of *sexual disorders;* in *DSM-IV,* this group includes *exhibitionism, fetishism, frotteurism, pedophilia, sexual masochism, sexual sadism, voyeurism, transvestic fetishism,* and para-

philias not otherwise specified, which include *necrophilia* and *klismaphilia.* The paraphilias (also called *perversions* or sexual deviations) are recurrent, intense sexual urges and sexually arousing fantasies that involve nonhuman objects, children or other nonconsenting persons, or the suffering or humiliation of oneself or the sexual partner.

[1]pathognomonic A symptom or group of symptoms that are specifically diagnostic or typical of a disease.

[1]pederasty *Homosexual* anal intercourse between men and boys with the latter as the passive partners. The term is used less precisely to denote male homosexual anal intercourse.

[1]pedophilia One of the *paraphilias,* characterized by marked distress over, or acting on, urges involving sexual activity with a prepubescent child who, more often than not, is of the same sex.

[1]peeping See *voyeurism*

[2]personation Ritualistic actions by the offender at the crime scene that have significance only to the offender. The offender often invests intimate meaning into the scene in the form of body positioning, mutilation, items left, or other symbolic gestures involving the crime scene.

petechiae (Sing.: petechia); minute hemorrhagic spots, of pinpoint to pinhead size in the skin which are not blanched by diascopy.

petechial hemorrhage Capillary hemorrhage into the skin that forms petechiae (punctate lesions).

[1]posttraumatic stress disorder (PTSD) An anxiety disorder in which exposure to an exceptional mental or physical stressor is followed, sometimes immediately and sometimes not until 3 months or more after the stress, by persistent reexperiencing of the event, avoidance of stimuli associated with the trauma or numbing of general responsiveness, and manifestations of increased arousal. The trauma typically includes experiencing, witnessing, or confronting an event that involves actual or threatened death or injury, or a threat to the physical integrity of oneself or others, with an immediate reaction of intense fear, helplessness, or horror.

Reexperiencing the trauma may take several forms: recurrent, intrusive, and distressing recollections (images, thoughts, or perceptions) of the event; recurrent distressing dreams of the event; sudden feeling as if the event were recurring or being relived (including dissociative flashback episodes); or intense psychological distress or physiological activity if exposed to internal or external cues that symbolize or resemble some part of the event. The affected person tries to avoid thoughts or feelings associated with the event and anything that might arouse recollection of it. There may be amnesia for an important aspect of the trauma. The person may lose interest in significant activities, feel detached or estranged from others, or have a sense of a foreshortened future. The person may have difficulty falling or staying asleep, be irritable or have angry outbursts, experience problems concentrating, and have an exaggerated startle response.

¹premature ejaculation Undesired ejaculation occurring immediately before or very early in sexual intercourse. One of the *orgasmic disorders.*

pseudocyesis False belief that one is pregnant; accompanied by signs of pregnancy, eg, breast engorgement, abdominal enlargement. See *somatoform disorders.*

¹psychogenic pain disorder In *DSM-IV,* called pain disorder associated with psychological factors and classified as a *somatoform disorder,* pain for which adequate physical findings are absent and for which there is evidence that psychological factors play a causal role.

punctate Marked with points or dots differentiated from the surrounding surface by color, elevation, or texture.

¹rape Sexual assault; forced sexual intercourse without the partner's consent.

¹sadism, sexual One of the *paraphilias,* characterized by marked distress over, or acting on, desires to inflict physical or psychological suffering, including humiliation, on the victim.

¹sadomasochistic relationship Enjoyment of suffering by one person of an interacting couple with a complementary enjoyment in inflicting pain in the other.

¹satyriasis Pathologic or exaggerated sexual drive or excitement in the man. May be of psychological or organic *etiology.*

seminiferous Epithelium lining the convoluted tubules of the testis where spermatogenesis and spermiogenesis occur.

¹sexual arousal disorders One group of *sexual dysfunctions* that includes female sexual arousal disorder and male erectile disorder. Female arousal disorder refers to the inability to attain or maintain an adequate lubrication swelling response of sexual excitement until completion of sexual activity. Male erectile disorder (erectile *impotence*) refers to the inability to attain or maintain an erection until completion of sexual activity.

¹sexual dysfunctions One of the two major groups of *sexual and gender identity disorders;* includes *sexual desire disorders, sexual arousal disorders, orgasm disorders, sexual pain disorders,* sexual dysfunction due to a *general medical condition,* and substance-induced (intoxication/withdrawal) sexual dysfunction.

¹sexual pain disorders One group of *sexual dysfunctions* that includes dyspareunia and vaginismus. Dyspareunia refers to genital pain, in either a male or a female, before, during, or after sexual intercourse that is not due to a *general medical condition,* drugs, or medication. Vaginismus refers to recurrent or persistent involuntary spasm of the musculature of the outer third of the vagina severe enough to interfere with coitus.

¹shame An *emotion* resulting from the failure to live up to self-expectations.

shear Distortion of a body by two oppositely directed parallel forces. The distortion consists of sliding over one another of imaginary planes of the body parallel to the planes of the forces.

²signature Repetitive ritualistic behavior by the serial offender, usually displayed at every crime scene and having nothing to do with the perpetration of the crime. Repetitive personation.

smear A thin specimen, usually prepared by spreading material uniformly onto a glass slide. It may then be fixed and stained before microscopic examination.

sodomy Sexual conduct consisting of contact between the penis of one person and the anus of another. Any penetration, however slight, is sufficient to complete the act.

¹sodomy Anal intercourse. Legally, the term may include other types of perversion such as bestiality. See also *paraphilia.*

¹soma The body.

¹somatization disorder One of the *somatoform disorders,* characterized by multiple physical complaints not fully explained by any known medical condition, yet severe enough to result in medical treatment or alteration in lifestyle. *Symptoms* include pain in different sites and other symptoms referable to the gastrointestinal tract and the sexual/reproductive system, or those suggestive of neurologic involvement.

¹somatoform disorders A group of disorders with symptoms suggesting physical disorders but without demonstrable organic findings to explain the symptoms. There is positive evidence, or a strong presumption, that the symptoms are linked to psychological factors or *conflicts.* In *DSM-IV,* this category includes *somatization disorder, conversion disorder, hypochondriasis, body dysmorphic disorder,* and *pain disorder.* Included as a somatoform disorder not otherwise specified is *pseudocyesis.*

sphincter Formed by a muscle that encircles an orifice; contraction of the muscle constricts the lumen, or orifice.

    external anal sphincter Spindle-shaped (fusiform) ring of striated muscle fibers surrounding the anus, attached posteriorly to the coccyx and anteriorly to the central tendon of the perineum; this sphincter is subdivided into subcutaneous, superficial, and deep portions.

    internal anal sphincter Smooth muscular ring, formed by an increase of circular fibers of the rectum, located at the upper end of the anal canal, from the internal to the outer voluntary external anal sphincter. The sphincter is maximally contracted when the rectal ampulla is empty or at rest, or relaxed to accommodate a distending fecal mass.

²**staging** Alteration of the crime scene prior to the arrival of police either by the offender to redirect the investigation away from the most logical suspect or by family or friends of the victim to protect the victim or victim's family.

¹**standard of care** In the law of medical negligence, that degree of care that a reasonably prudent medical practitioner having ordinary skill, training, and learning would exercise under the same or similar circumstances. Unless the practitioner is considered an expert or specialist, the requisite degree of care is held to be only "ordinary" and "reasonable" care. If a physician's conduct falls below the standard of care, he or she may be liable in damages for any injuries resulting from such conduct.

¹**subpoena** A command, typically at the request of a litigating party, to appear at a certain time and place to give testimony on a certain matter. Unless signed by a judge, a subpoena is not a court order compelling testimony but merely a court-issued order to show up.

¹**subpoena duces tecum** A command to produce specified records or documents at a certain time and place at trial.

swelling Enlargement, eg, protruberance or tumor.

tear A discontinuity in a structure's substance (laceration).

telangiectasia Dilation of the previously existing small or terminal vessels of a part.

¹**tort** Civil wrongs subject to lawsuit by private individuals, as distinguished from criminal offenses, which are only brought or prosecuted by the state on behalf of its citizens.

¹**voyeurism** Peeping; one of the *paraphilias,* characterized by marked distress over, or acting on, urges to observe unsuspecting people, usually strangers, who are naked or in the process of disrobing, or who are engaging in sexual activity.

wound Trauma to any of the tissues of the body, especially trauma caused by physical means, and with interruption of continuity; can be a surgical incision.

gunshot Made with bullet, or other missile, projected by firearm.

gutter Tangential; makes a furrow without perforating skin.

incised Clean cut, as by sharp instrument.

laceration Torn or jagged wound, or an accidental, cut wound. The process or act of tearing the tissues.

nonpenetrating injury Especially within thorax or abdomen, progresses without disrupting the surface of the body.

open Wound in which tissues are exposed to air.

penetrating Wound with disruption of body surface that extends into underlying tissue or into the body cavity.

perforating A wound with an entrance and exit opening.

puncture A wound in which the opening is relatively small as compared to the depth, as produced by a narrow, pointed object.

scar The fibrous tissue replacing normal tissues destroyed by injury or disease.

stab wound Puncture wound produced by stabbing motion of a knife or similar object.

SUGGESTED READINGS

Anderson, K., Anderson, L. & Glanze, W. (Eds.). (1994). *Mosby's Medical, Nursing, and Allied Health Dictionary.* St. Louis: Mosby-Year Book.

American Professional Society on the Abuse of Children (APSAC). (1995). *Practice Guidelines: Descriptive Terminology in Child Sexual Abuse Medical Evaluations.*

Black's Law Dictionary, 6th ed. (1990). St. Paul, MN: West Publishing Co.

Douglas, J., Burgess, A.W., Burgess, A.G. & Ressler, R. (1992). *Crime Classification Manual.* New York: Lexington Books.

Edgerton, J. (1994). *American Psychiatric Glossary,* 7th ed. Washington, DC: American Psychiatric Press, Inc.

Stedman's Medical Dictionary, 26th ed. (1995). Baltimore: Williams & Wilkins.

Index